'This book should be highly recommended reading for scholars interested in foreign policy decision-making, economic assistance policies, and the integration of former communist states into the "new" Europe. It is unique in seeking a truly comparative mapping of the evolution of aid policy across five formerly communist states, states that have moved from the aid recipient to the aid donor category. It offers a rich theoretical approach for such comparison and through the use of face-to-face interviews and analyses of reports and reviews on the performance of these states, rich evidence with which to apply the framework. Particularly fascinating is the interplay between outside actors, bureaucracies, and domestic stakeholders in the development and execution of economic policy. The result is a richer understanding of both aid development policy and the complex politics of foreign policy decision-making, all done in an appropriate, comparative perspective.'

Professor Thomas J. Volgy, Professor,
School of Government and Public Policy, University of Arizona

'Szent-Iványi and Lightfoot have provided a well-argued and lucid assessment of the international development policies of new EU member states from Central and Eastern Europe. Their book sheds new light on divergent and problematic compliance with international development practices and norms in the CEE countries. It produces telling evaluations of the reasons why these countries still fall short of many elements of international development policy. This book is a 'must read' for all those studying the foreign policies of new EU member states.'

Dr. Dan Marek, Palacký University, Czech Republic,
co-editor The New Member States and the European Union.
Foreign Policy and Europeanization

New Europe's New Development Aid

This book examines the international development policies of five East Central European new EU member states, the Czech Republic, Hungary, Poland, Slovakia and Slovenia. These countries turned from being aid recipients to donors after the turn of the Millennium in the run-up to EU accession. The book explains the post-2004 evolution and current state of foreign aid policies in the region and the reasons why these deviate from many of the internationally agreed best practices in development cooperation. It argues that after the turn of the Millennium, a 'Global Consensus' has emerged on how to make foreign aid more effective for development. A comparison between the elements of the Global Consensus and the performance of the five countries reveals that while they have generally implemented little of these recommendations, there are also emerging differences between the countries, with the Czech Republic and Slovenia clearly aspiring to become globally responsible donors. Building on the literatures on foreign policy analysis, international socialization and interest group influence, the book develops a model of foreign aid policy-making in order to explain the general reluctance of the five countries in implementing international best practices, and also the differences in their relative performance.

Balázs Szent-Iványi is a lecturer in Politics and International Relations at Aston University, Birmingham, United Kingdom. He also holds an associate professor position at Corvinus University, Budapest, Hungary.

Simon Lightfoot is a senior lecturer in European Politics at the University of Leeds, United Kingdom.

BASEES/Routledge Series on Russian and East European Studies

Series editor: Richard Sakwa, Department of Politics and International Relations, University of Kent

Editorial Committee:
Roy Allison, St Antony's College, Oxford
Birgit Beumers, Department of Theatre, Film and Television Studies, University of Aberystwyth
Richard Connolly, Centre for Russian and East European Studies, University of Birmingham
Terry Cox, Department of Central and East European Studies, University of Glasgow
Peter Duncan, School of Slavonic and East European Studies, University College London
Zoe Knox, School of History, University of Leicester
Rosalind Marsh, Department of European Studies and Modern Languages, University of Bath
David Moon, Department of History, University of York
Hilary Pilkington, Department of Sociology, University of Manchester
Graham Timmins, Department of Politics, University of Birmingham
Stephen White, Department of Politics, University of Glasgow

Founding Editorial Committee Member:
George Blazyca, Centre for Contemporary European Studies, University of Paisley

This series is published on behalf of BASEES (the British Association for Slavonic and East European Studies). The series comprises original, high-quality, research-level work by both new and established scholars on all aspects of Russian, Soviet, post-Soviet and East European Studies in humanities and social science subjects.

New Europe's New Development Aid

Balázs Szent-Iványi and Simon Lightfoot

Routledge
Taylor & Francis Group

LONDON AND NEW YORK

First published 2015 by Routledge

2 Park Square, Milton Park, Abingdon, Oxon OX14 4RN
711 Third Avenue, New York, NY 10017, USA

Routledge is an imprint of the Taylor & Francis Group, an informa business

First issued in paperback 2017

British Library Cataloguing in Publication Data
A catalogue record for this book is available from the British Library

Library of Congress Cataloging in Publication Data
Lightfoot, Simon.
    New Europe's new development aid / Simon Lightfoot and Balázs Szent-
Iványi.
        pages cm. – (BASEES/Routledge series on Russian and East European
studies)
    1. Europe, Central–Foreign economic relations–Developing countries. 2.
Developing countries–Foreign economic relations–Europe, Central. 3.
Economic assistance, European–Developing countries. 4. Europe, Central–
Economic conditions–1989- I. Szent-Iványi, Balázs. II. Title.
    HF1532.7.Z4D444 2015
    338.9'14–dc23
                    2014042829

ISBN: 978-0-415-87034-4 (hbk)
ISBN: 978-1-138-07916-8 (pbk)

Typeset in Times New Roman
by Taylor & Francis Books

To Áron and Gyöngyi, Ben and Sam

Contents

List of illustrations

Figures

Tables

Acknowledgement

"Where did the idea for your book come from" is a question we have often been asked during the time it has taken to write it. There is unsurprisingly no specific date we celebrate, but the friendship between the two authors dates back to a meeting at the EADI conference in Geneva in 2008. Our research interests overlapped and we went from there! The majority of the research was carried out while Balázs was a Marie Curie Research Fellow at the University of Leeds (project INTDEPNEW) in 2012–2013. The support of this program is acknowledged with thanks, as is the support of other funders: notably the British Academy (SG-46721), the Elisabeth Barker Fund and a Hungarian National Excellence Fellowship program (TÁMOP 4.2.4.A/2-11-1-2012-0001, co-financed by the European Union). The European Office at the University of Leeds, especially Maggie Credland, were instrumental in us getting the Marie Curie IEF, without which the research for this book would have been much, much harder.

The material for the book could not have been gathered without the involvement of numerous interviewees and informants: officials from old and new EU member state governments, representatives of several development and humanitarian NGOs, the officials from the EU institutions, the OECD DAC, UNDP, CIDA, the World Bank, and other bodies across the East Central European region. Due to reasons of confidentiality, their names will remain anonymous, but we really appreciate the level of engagement these people have shown towards our project, even if they may not always agree with our conclusions.

Balázs began researching international development policies during his PhD studies, and has received substantial support in this from various colleagues at Corvinus University of Budapest. His PhD supervisor, Professor Tamás Szentes was instrumental in providing encouragement in dealing with development economics and the politics of development; both considered rather niche issues in Hungarian academia. Together with Beáta Paragi, whose critical thinking has been a constant source of inspiration throughout the years, they started the first university level course in Hungary on international development policy. Teaching this course has been a key source of learning. Other colleagues at Corvinus University who have provided support, mentoring, and were open to sharing ideas and working together, are too numerous to mention. Standing out among them are László Trautmann, Professor András Blahó, István Benczes and András Tétényi.

Simon's interest in the topic can be dated back to an encounter in a corridor with Professor Ruth Pearson. Having just started working at the University of Leeds, she encouraged him to embark on a new research project looking at how the former recipients of aid in East Central Europe had become donors of aid. Without this, and further encouragement and contacts, he would not have embarked upon this fascinating research topic. Once he started the journey, Professor Maja Bučar and Professor Maurizio Carbone offered support and friendship along the way. A 2004 book chapter by Maurizio and Maja's 2007 paper on the ECE donors were the first serious academic studies of the topic he came across and helped shape his research in many ways. In modern academia much is spoken about mentoring and supporting colleagues, yet the reality often falls short. These three people, in very different ways, highlight how influential mentoring and support can be to colleagues. For their help, I am eternally grateful.

Many friends and colleagues went to eleven by providing comments on drafts of the book and helped our thinking enormously: Maja Bučar, Elżbieta Drążkiewicz-Grodzicka, Ondřej Horký-Hlucháň, Erik Lundsgaarde, Péteris Timofejevs Henriksson and Zsuzsanna Végh. Their comments greatly contributed to the final form this project took. Ondřej Horký-Hlucháň has especially been an excellent source of information, critique and friendship over the years for both of us. Some of the ideas in this book have been developed to some extent in various journal articles, and have been presented at several conferences by us. In addition to the people above, Dave Allen, Charlie Burns, Gordon Crawford, Mikaela Gavas, Monika Hellmeyer, Paul Hoebink, Wil Hout, Emma Mawdsley, Jan Orbie, Tsveta Petrova, Michael Smith and Neil Winn all commented on these papers and conference presentations, or have helped us to refine our thinking over the years. Any remaining mistakes are of course, ours.

Our editor at Taylor and Francis, Peter Sowden, showed admirable patience with us as he just listened to what Douglas Adams called the whooshing sound of deadlines flying by. His guidance on everything from the title to the review process was invaluable, as was the excellent editorial support provided by Helena Hurd and Emma Chappell. Sabrina Lacey and her colleagues did a wonderful job typesetting the final manuscript in very quick time. Professor Richard Sakwa, as series editor, has supported the project from day one. Our thanks to all. We are also indebted to Boglárka Angyal and Hungarian Baptist Aid, who have granted us permission to use the photo that appears on the cover of this book, an image highly expressive of East Central European development cooperation.

Our largest debt, of course, goes to our families. Throughout the period of writing the book, Gyöngyi and Sam have provided constant love and support. Simon's son Ben was born just before this project started and throughout the project discussions with him about Star Wars or football (especially Liverpool and Notts. County) have provided a welcome break. Áron came later, and made Balázs a proud father. It is to the four of them this book is dedicated.

Balázs Szent-Iványi and Simon Lightfoot
Birmingham and Leeds
October 2014

Abbreviations

AAA	Accra Agenda for Action
ACP	Africa, Caribbean and Pacific Countries
ADA	Austrian Development Agency
BMZ	Federal Ministry for Economic Cooperation and Development, Germany
BRICS	Brazil, Russia, India, China, South Africa
CzDA	Czech Development Agency
CEE	Central and Eastern European
CFSP	Common Foreign and Security Policy
CIDA	Canadian International Development Agency
CIS	Commonwealth of Independent States
CMEA	Council for Mutual Economic Assistance
CODEV	EU Council Working Group on Development
CONCORD	European NGO Confederation for Relief and Development
COREPER	Committee of Permanent Representatives
CRS	creditor reporting system of the OECD
CSOs	civil society organizations
DAC	Development Assistance Committee
DG	Directorate General
DfID	Department for International Development, UK
EC	European Commission
ECE	East Central Europe
EDF	European Development Fund
EDI	Emerging Donors Initiative
EEAS	European External Action Service
ENPI	European Neighborhood Policy Instrument
ETC	European Transition Compendium
EU	European Union
GDP	gross domestic product
GNI	gross national income
FOND	Romanian NGDO Platform
FoRS	Czech Forum for Development Co-operation

HAND	Hungarian Association of NGOs for Development and Humanitarian Aid
HUN-IDA	Hungarian International Development Assistance Non-profit Company
IATI	International Aid Transparency Initiative
IMF	International Monetary Fund
LDCs	least developed countries
MDGs	Millennium Development Goals
MoE	Ministry of Education
MoF	Ministry of Finance
MFA	Ministry of Foreign Affairs
MP	member of parliament
MVRO	Slovak NGDO Platform
NATO	North Atlantic Treaty Organization
NGDO	non-governmental development organization
NGO	non-governmental organization
ODA	official development assistance
ODACE	Official Development Assistance in Central Europe
OECD	Organisation for Economic Co-operation and Development
OECD DAC	Organisation for Economic Co-operation and Development, Development Assistance Committee
PCD	policy coherence for development
PiN	People in Need
PPP	purchasing power parity
PRTs	Provincial Reconstruction Teams
RPP	Regional Partnership Program of the Austrian Development Agency
SIDA	Swedish International Development Agency
SLOGA	Slovenian NGDO Platform
UN	United Nations
UNDP	United Nations Development Programme
V4	The Visegrád group of countries (the Czech Republic, Hungary, Poland and Slovakia)

1 Introduction

1.1 The changing landscape of international development

The landscape of international development cooperation has undergone significant changes since the turn of Millennium. One of these changes is that many countries which were previously part of the aid system as recipients, have now become donors. The rise of China as a donor, and its engagement in Africa especially, has received much attention both in the scholarly literature and in the daily press. Less spectacularly, a number of other large emerging countries, like Brazil, Russia, India or Turkey have also initiated or strengthened their foreign assistance programs, while at the same still remaining recipients of aid. While many of these aid programs are still relatively small and in their infancies, the potential of these new donors is huge. This newfound plurality of donors means that the "traditional" donors in the global North are losing their dominance in setting the principles, priorities, and goals of the international development system. South-South development cooperation may well become an important theme in the following decades. The increasing diversity of donorship, even if some new donors have received criticism for the way they provide foreign assistance, should generally be seen as positive as it not only increases the resources available for development, but also provides developing countries with a larger selection of knowledge and potential models for development.

A further group of donors has also emerged in the past decade which has received far less attention: the East Central European (ECE) member states that have joined the European Union (EU) since 2004. These states have a history of providing assistance to the South during their Communist regimes, but since the fall of the Berlin Wall, these countries were essentially recipients of foreign assistance until their accessions to the EU. This transition from recipient to donor was not only very rapid but unprecedented in the number of countries undergoing the transition simultaneously. The run-up to EU accession and eventual membership has had a profound influence on these countries in all policy areas. Development cooperation is no different and it is the EU that is often credited as having helped (re-)created this policy. In the past decade, the ECE countries have all embarked on a process of institutionalizing and professionalizing their international development policies, and despite the initial similarities, clear differences have emerged in their trajectories. Volumes of foreign aid provided by them remains relatively small, at least compared to the "traditional" donors, but the ten ECE member states together contributed more than 1 billion dollars of official development assistance in 2012, which is not negligible. The 2008+ economic crisis has had profound effects and as a result, progress may not have been as quick as some observers may have hoped for at the time of accession. The ECE donors face a number of problems and shortcomings to this day, ranging from low public awareness on global development issues, the lack of political support and limited government capacities.

The South-South challenge has increased the relative importance of the ECE new donors, despite their relatively small individual aid efforts. As members of the EU, these countries clearly identify themselves as part of the Global North (despite perceptions of East-West divides which are still strong), and have expressed their intentions on several occasions to adapt their international development policies to the principles and standards laid down by the established donors. This can serve to bolster the failing legitimacy of "traditional" (North-South) development cooperation. The transformation of the ECE member states into fully fledged Northern donors can be seen as symbolically complete in 2013/4, when the Czech Republic, Poland, Slovakia and Slovenia joined the OECD's Development Assistance Committee (DAC), the forum for coordinating the activities of Northern donors. The DAC was extremely keen on admitting these new members (along with Iceland and South Korea who also joined recently), most likely sensing its own possible marginalization if it did not act in response to the changing global landscape of aid donorship.

This book aims to provide an understanding of the paths and trajectories which international development policies have followed in five of the ECE new member states in the ten years after their EU accession. The five countries are the Czech Republic, Hungary, Poland, Slovakia and Slovenia, which can be seen as the most significant donors in the region in terms of foreign aid provided. There are a number of reasons to expect similarities between these countries: they all had expertise in development during the Communist regimes, and they all began re-emerging as donors roughly around the same time. They all joined the EU in 2004, and have thus experienced relatively similar international pressures. The Czech Republic, Hungary, Poland and Slovakia have close cooperation between themselves in the framework of the Visegrád Group (V4). These similarities would imply relatively similar international development policy trajectories among these five countries. As we show in the book, indeed there are many similarities, but there is also an apparent degree of variation among the five countries, which has placed them on somewhat divergent paths. Beyond understanding why development policies have evolved the way they have in the ECE countries, the book also aims to explain this intra-ECE divergence. This introductory chapter continues by briefly presenting the research questions and argument of the book, data collection methodology, the relevance and contribution of this volume to the literature, and also discusses a few issues on terminology.

1.2 An overview of the argument and research questions

Based on the broad aims of the book presented above, we seek to answer two main research questions:

1   To what extent have the international development policies of the ECE states conformed to the "Global Consensus on Foreign Aid?"
2   What factors and dynamics account for the paths and trajectories taken in this policy area?

The first research question is descriptive in nature. We argue however that such description is necessary for several reasons: (1) while the literature often asserts that the ECE countries do not live up to internationally agreed best practices on aid, no study has ever actually examined this in detail, and determined how they perform, what their main deficiencies are, etc. (2) With the exception of more policy orientated reports by non-governmental organizations and think tanks, no detailed comparative mapping has ever been carried out with a view of explaining policy evolution in these countries. While in-depth individual country case studies do exist, these usually do not allow for mapping and comparing cross-country dynamics.

We argue that in the past 15 years, a "Global Consensus in Foreign Aid" has emerged (Chapter 3). Through a series of international conferences and high level meetings, including the UN Millennium Summit in 2000, the Monterrey Conference in 2002, and the Paris, Accra and Busan High Level Forums on Aid Effectiveness, a consensus has emerged on how to make foreign aid work better in combating global poverty. The elements of this Consensus include commitments from donors on increasing aid with the view of reaching the widely cited 0.7 percent aid/GNI target and increasing the effectiveness of aid through implementing principles in their policies like ownership, alignment, harmonization and coordination. The European Union has been one of the drives behind this process, and has done much to implement the Global Consensus into its own body of soft law, and has even gone beyond it in some aspects. The Global Consensus serves as a point of reference for donor countries on how to change their international development policies with a view of increasing effectiveness. While compliance is clearly problematic even with established donors, the fact that all donor countries, including the ECE countries, have made political commitments to the Global Consensus means that its elements can serve as benchmarks for evaluating donor policies and practices.

We thus use the elements of the Global Consensus on Foreign Aid as an ideal type against which we measure the performance of the five ECE countries (Chapter 4). This comparison reveals three important conclusions. First, overall, the ECE donors do not comply with most of the requirements of the Global Consensus, with shortfalls in the fields of aid volumes, untying aid from exports, using program based aid modalities like budget support and working together with other donors. Second, despite this general non-compliance, the past ten years have shown some degree of progress towards the Consensus. The ECE countries have mostly managed to create stable legal and strategic backgrounds for their international development policies, and have firmly placed development cooperation into the wider frameworks of their foreign policies. Third, there are significant differences between the five countries. The Czech Republic seems to stand out as the front runner, as it provides increasing amounts of aid to the poorest countries, has a well established legal and strategic framework, and has done clear efforts to concentrate its aid allocation. Slovenia and Slovakia also show good performance in certain issues. Poland has done some reforms, but these are far from spectacular. Hungary on the other hand seems to be a laggard, it is the only country which does not have any legal framework for development, has hardly made any efforts to implement reforms to increase effectiveness, and is the least transparent. We argue that the trajectories of the five countries are rather clear and there is a clear divergence between them, which may make differences more visible in time.

Why have the ECE countries not done more in implementing the elements of the Global (and European) Consensuses on Foreign Aid? They basically emerged as donors the same time as these Consensuses were formed, and had little expertise in "modern" development policy. Thus one could rightfully expect them to seek international best practices and recommendations as sources of inspiration on how to manage their new policies. Also, what are the reasons for the observed divergence between the five countries? Why has the Czech Republic (and to a lesser extent, Slovakia and Slovenia) done relatively better than Hungary or Poland? We turn to answering these questions in Chapters 5, 6 and 7.

The second research question aims to explain why ECE international development policies took the trajectories they did and are in the state they are in as identified by the first research question. In order to explain the performance of the ECE countries in meeting the requirements of the Global Consensus, we develop an actor-based theoretical framework for understanding how international development policy, as a subfield of a country's foreign policy is made (Chapter 2). Modeling such policy-making can be highly complex due to the large number of variables involved, but we argue that a parsimonious yet insightful model is possible. As a basis, we use the governmental politics model of foreign policy analysis developed by Allison (1969), but expand it and adapt it in several ways. We argue that development policy-making in the ECE countries is mainly dominated by technocratic bureaucracies, with little attention from the legislative or chief executive levels. Thus, conceptualizing the core of our framework as a bureaucratic bargaining process, in-line with Allison's model, can be valid. The most important actors included in this bargaining process are the ministries of foreign affairs (MFAs), the international development departments within these ministries, and any implementing agencies. In most ECE countries however, a number of other line ministries are (or were) also involved in foreign aid policy-making and implementation, thus arises the need for a model of government bargaining. These agencies will all have somewhat different interests in the policy area, and the final development policy outcome will depend on a process of bargaining between them.

However, government bureaucracies do not work in isolation, as they are subject to numerous influences from the international environment and society. We therefore conceptualize two sets of actors that influence the process: international actors and domestic stakeholders. International actors are mainly international organizations like the EU or the OECD DAC, which both have strong roles in the global and European development systems, and have clearly attempted to influence ("socialize") international development policies in their members and accession countries. A third organization, the United Nations Development Programme (UNDP) has also played an important role in the ECE context. These organizations directly attempt to convey the Global Consensus on Foreign Aid and its European interpretation to their members and beyond. Just how strong their influence will be however depends on a number of factors, most importantly the mechanism through which they attempt to socialize members. Two main mechanisms have been identified in the literature, conditionality and social learning, both of which may be at play.

Domestic stakeholders are non-state actors in each country which are, for some reason or another, interested in influencing development policy. These stakeholders may have normative agendas based on moral and other considerations, or they may be interested in the "aid business" as project implementers, contractors etc. The main domestic stakeholders are non-governmental organizations (NGOs) active in development and humanitarian aid. These organizations and their associations play an important role in advocacy in all ECE countries, and are usually rather transparent in their reform demands towards governments. How much they will be able to get their demands through however will again depend on a number of variables, including issues like structure of the development NGO sector, finances, capacities, and government attitudes towards them.

Our model therefore has three channels of interaction and influence: from international actors to the government, from domestic stakeholders to the government and within the government. Within each of these channels, we formulate a set of variables which can explain how strong influence is in each case. The different constellation of the three sets of explanatory variables in the five countries allows us to come to informed conclusions on why one country has been able to approximate its international development policy more strongly towards the Global Consensus than others.

Applying this model, we first focus on international influence (Chapter 5), and discuss how major international actors in the global development system have attempted to shape the nascent international development policies of the ECE donors. We focus mainly on the EU and the OECD DAC, but also discuss the role of the many organizations that have provided capacity-building assistance to the ECE donors, most notably the UNDP and the Canadian International Development Agency (CIDA). These agencies have used strategies based both conditionality and social learning to shape ECE development policies. EU accession conditionality played a key role in restarting development policies in the region, but conditionality was formal and led to minimal compliance only. The EU was not really able to provide assistance to the accession countries in formulating their new policies, and this void was filled by other established donors, mainly the UNDP and CIDA. These capacity development programs were important in creating the initial institutional infrastructures and "getting the policies going," but they were unable to fundamentally shape the directions each country took. In the post-accession stage, the EU could only rely on promoting social learning, these channels however seem to have been rather ineffective and have only led to "shallow Europeanization" (Lightfoot 2010). Similar conclusions emerge for the OECD DAC. The ECE countries were observers in the committee up to 2013, when four of them joined. Interactions and participation in the OECD DAC's work was thus rather limited, providing limited possibilities for social learning. Accession conditionality to the OECD DAC was not credible and thus also had little effect on most of the countries which joined, with the potential exception of the Czech Republic. However, the OECD DAC may have longer term socialization effects, and membership will definitely lead to increasing the transparency of ECE foreign aid.

The effects of domestic stakeholders are discussed in Chapter 6, with a focus on development NGOs. The impact of these organizations on development policy-making has clearly varied among the five countries. EU accession has empowered development NGOs *vis-à-vis* their national governments, but has also distorted the ways they work, as opposed to their counterparts in more developed donors countries. Most importantly, they rely mainly on grants from their national governments and international organizations to secure their operational expenses, as opposed to raising grassroots funding. This not only has important implications on just how critical they can be towards the government, but also constrains their funding and capacities and biases their skills development. None the less, development NGOs in all five countries have created their national advocacy platforms for more effective engagement with the government, and governments have acknowledged these platforms as official partners. The NGO platforms all publish regular AidWatch Reports in which they list their reform demands towards the government, most of which correspond with the Global Consensus. How effective they are however is difficult to assess. NGOs in the Czech Republic seem to have developed relatively high capacities to engage the government, and they are also the most successful in securing international grant financing. Slovak NGOs are in a special situation as their platform is the only one to receive direct funding from the MFA, which most likely weakens their propensity to criticize the government and push for reform. Hungarian NGOs on the other hand seem to have a highly confrontational relationship with the MFA, and have not been able to achieve much until recently.

Chapter 7 deals with dynamics within the governmental bureaucracies, and uses the insights from Chapters 5 and 6 to explain the state of international development policies in the five countries. We present a brief example below of the explanatory power of our framework, the case of the Czech Republic. The country clearly stands out in terms of adopting many elements of the Global Consensus on Foreign Aid. Czech development aid has undergone a spectacular transformation between 2007 and 2011, which resulted in a streamlined and centralized institutional system, the creation of a development agency, and a new law on international development. Most aid funds were centralized in the MFA, making the many other government agencies involved in development clear losers of the reforms, which they therefore all strongly opposed. We argue that the Czech reform was made possible due to smart coalition-building by the MFA and especially the development department within it. International organizations may have achieved some results in socializing Czech development policy decision-makers, and the department used the OECD DAC and domestic NGOs to argue for reform towards the wider government. The department commissioned a Special Review from the OECD DAC in 2007, which pointed out the necessary reforms that needed to be done and called greater centralization. This external evaluation gave the MFA's development department credible support in the policy-making negotiation game with other government agencies. The MFA also used the development NGO sector to lobby the wider government, who were interested in increasing the effectiveness of Czech aid and supported many of the conclusions of the OECD DAC Special Review. This constellation greatly empowered the MFA's development department and allowed the reform to go through, although various concessions were also needed to gain support from line ministries and the Ministry of Finance in particular.

Similarly, the framework is used in Chapter 7 to explain the other four country cases as well, including a similar, although not as ambitious centralization reform in Slovenia, partial reform and in Slovakia, only minor adaptation in Poland, and long-term muddling and stagnation in Hungary.

1.3 Relevance and contribution

This book contributes to the literatures on foreign policy and development studies in several ways. First, it develops a model for understanding how countries make international development policy. While understanding why donors provide as much aid as they do, how they allocate it among recipients, and what national characteristics donors possess have been long standing questions in political science (Lancaster 2006; Hoebink and Stokke 2005; Hoebink 2010; van der Veen 2011), but the literature has only sparingly relied on theoretical models to guide such analysis. Our theoretical model can be adapted and expanded to explain decision-making in other donor countries as well. Second, the book places an important emphasis on understanding external influence and the impact of global norms on how international development policy is made in countries. So far, the international socialization framework has not been applied in a systematic manner to the development policies of the ECE new donors, nor has it been widely tested empirically in this policy area. Third, aside from policy orientated surveys by NGOs and think tanks (see, for example Kiss 2007; Zagranica Group 2011; CONCORD 2013; CRPE 2013) and individual country case studies (see Horký-Hlucháň and Lightfoot 2012), no similar in-depth comparative academic research on the ECE donors, concentrating on explaining change and drawing conclusions for future policy evolution, has been carried out so far.

Gaining a better understanding on the driving forces behind international development policies of the ECE EU member states and likely dynamics of change is relevant for a number of further reasons as well. First, this is an unprecedented historical experiment. Never before in Europe have so many countries turned from being aid recipients to aid donors at the same time. Second, by getting a deeper understanding of the dynamics of ECE foreign aid policies, one also has greater scope to formulate policy recommendations both on the national level and on the EU-level, related to quantitative aid targets, aid quality, aid allocation, and cooperation between EU donors. This can contribute to making European aid and development policies more effective in combating poverty and building good governance in less developed countries. Third, the research identifies potential longer term differences and complementarities between the ECE donors and the older EU Member States. The longer term comparative advantages of ECE donors are identified, but there is also considerable scope to indentify some ECE practices which could be beneficial for the old Member States to adopt.

1.4 Data collection methodology

This book is a culmination of research carried out by the authors between 2007 and 2014,[1] both jointly and individually on the ECE new donors. Throughout these eight years, we have not only carried out a large number of interviews, but have also worked rather closely with many of the actors involved in ECE development in various research, consultancy and educational projects, and thus have managed to gather firsthand experience as well on how these policies have evolved.

As detailed information on development policies in the ECE countries can often be difficult to access, much of the data required for this exercise needed to be obtained directly from those working in the policy area. Throughout the years we have carried out more than 70 face to face semi-structured (qualitative) interviews with representatives of various stakeholders in ECE development policies. These include officials from Ministries of Foreign Affairs (both in national capitals and foreign missions), development agencies, and various other government ministries and agencies, as well as officials at international organizations such as the various EU institutions, the OECD, the UNDP, and the World Bank. We have also conducted interviews with representatives of other, more established donor countries, as well as a number of experts working in development NGOs, advocacy groups, epistemic communities and academia. The interviews were all of qualitative nature, and mostly involved a set of pre-formulated questions on which respondents could elaborate. The interviews covered a large number of topics, but most generally we were interested in finding out issues on dynamics: how policies have changed throughout the years, how policy related decisions are made, and how various actors interact with each other, etc. In some cases, we interviewed the same officials on more than one occasion, but several years apart. This allowed for potential comparisons on how a person's views changed throughout the years. Finding such people however was rather difficult, and most people we managed to interview twice were non-governmental experts, as fluctuation among government officials was rather high. For reasons of confidentiality, all our respondents remain anonymous. When citing interview data, we will sometimes refrain from giving exact details on respondents. The reason for this is that often there are very few people working in international development policy in various ECE countries, and respondents may be identifiable even if their names are not given.

A second source of data were the various evaluative reports and reviews carried out by international agencies (mainly the Special Reviews of the OECD DAC) and NGOs (mainly the national AidWatch Reports, and their European-level counterpart published by CONCORD, the European Confederation of Relief and Development NGOs), and, to a lesser degree, by various think tanks. For obtaining numerical data on the foreign aid of the ECE countries, we relied on the OECD DAC's online statistics database. A third source of data included official written government sources, such as government declarations on aid strategies, relevant laws and legal documents, and government reports on the implementation of development assistance.

1.5 What's in a name? Some notes on terminology

Labels can often be misleading or oversimplifying, and can be a major source of disagreement between observers. Accordingly, there is sensitivity over the terms used to describe the donor status of the states from ECE that have joined the EU since 2004. To give a flavor of the debate it is worth highlighting some of these issues. A common label is "new donors." For some states, such as the Baltic States or Slovenia, this label is relatively accurate as they did not exist as independent states until the end of the Soviet system or the break-up of Yugoslavia. For the other states, the term is more contentious, as the Czech and Slovak Republics, Hungary, Poland, Romania and Bulgaria, had a long history of providing aid bilaterally or via the Council for Mutual Economic Assistance (CMEA) (Browne 1990: 227). The terms "emerging" or "re-emerging" donors are also often used. While the former term is not much different from "new donors," the latter is often invoked to show that these countries are actually not new-comers to the field of development and have some amount of previous knowledge and expertise, even if from a very different context. As we discuss later however, the relevance of this experience is questionable.

The term "non-DAC donors" has also been applied to this group of donors (see Mawdsley 2012) although this term is now increasingly irrelevant as the ECE states gradually started becoming full-fledged OECD DAC members, with the Czech Republic joining in May 2013, followed by Slovakia (September 2013), Poland (October 2013) and Slovenia (December 2013). Another term that has been used is "new EU/OECD donors." This distinction is important as China, India or Brazil are also non-DAC donors (as they are not members of the OECD), and there are non-EU OECD members such as Mexico and Turkey which are not OECD DAC members either (Kharas 2009; Rowlands 2012). It seems that ECE countries do not like to be confused with other non-DAC or emerging donors, as evidenced by the following quote from an MFA official from Hungary:[2]

> We do not like the term 'emerging donors'. China and other emerging donors are doing a lot of harm, and we do not want to be grouped with them. If you need labels, call us 'new EU/OECD donors'.

But even this is inaccurate. Kragelund (2008) created a classification in which he distinguished between OECD and non-OECD EU states, but since the publication of his article, further heterogenization has taken place, as now we can actually distinguish three groups within the ECE states. There are EU and OECD DAC members (Czech Republic, Poland, Slovakia and Slovenia), EU and non-DAC OECD members (Hungary and Estonia) and then finally non-OECD EU members, which is made up of Latvia, Lithuania, Bulgaria, Romania and Croatia.

A further term that has been used is "EU-12" donors, but this also includes Cyprus and Malta, and since Croatia's accession in 2013, EU-13 would be more accurate. However, there are differences in both history and politics that limit the scope of comparison between the ECE states and either Cyprus or Malta (Calleja-Ragonesi *et al.* 2014). "New member state" donors is also an option, but since the first wave of ECE countries joined more than ten years ago, this also seems a little dated and also people do not tend to talk, for example, about the "1973 accession states" today as a group either! There is also a sense that now that the ECE states are members, they should be treated as members and not singled out as newcomers. None the less, the term is helpful as it distinguishes between the EU states that have a 0.7 percent of GNI as a target for aid volumes (the EU-15) and those that have the 0.33 percent target (the EU-13, see Chapter 3).

Using geographical terms like Central and Eastern European (CEE), or East Central European donors can also be contentious, and opens the issue of where exactly the boundaries of Europe lie, and even if there are boundaries within Europe (see Volgy *et al.* 2012). The CEE region can conceptualized to be much larger than just the new donors under scrutiny, and include Germany or Austria to the West, and the Ukraine, Belarus, and potentially even Russia to the East. ECE, or the "Eastern part of Central Europe" is perhaps more accurate, but also open to interpretation. What is exactly Central Europe, and where does its Eastern part begin? Simply using Eastern Europe is problematic because most people in the countries examined in this volume do not consider themselves to be from Eastern Europe, but rather think in more "Central European" terms.

There are some further terms coined by academics, which also include a certain degree of normative judgment on the nature of the new development policies. Murphy and Gray (2013) use the concept of "recruited donor." Although they developed the concept for Russia (see Gray 2014), it applies to the new EU/OECD donors as well, and implies that these countries have been "recruited to a DAC-style model of development donorship" through the efforts of the international development community, and not necessarily their own will. In a similar vein, Szent-Iványi and Tétényi (2013) talk about "premature donors," countries which became donors of foreign aid before they were actually ready for it, mainly due to external pressure and without any strong domestic constituency for foreign aid. Both of these heavily normative terms are of course rejected by policy-makers.

Neither label therefore is perfect. In most cases, the book will simply use "ECE donors," as it is neutral and perhaps the least contentious among the geographic terms, but we acknowledge the limitations that even this label may have.

On further terminological issues, we use international development policy and foreign aid policy interchangeably as synonyms. While international development clearly refers to a much wider set of tools and actions than foreign aid, we argue that in the ECE context there is not much point to make a difference. The ECE countries are still new to international development, and their international development policies do not go beyond the usage of foreign aid. Issues like "beyond aid" and policy coherence for development, which have gained increasing popularity in international development discourses and also on the policy level, have only penetrated development policy-making in the ECE countries marginally. When talking about foreign aid in terms of numbers and statistics, we use the OECD DAC's statistical category of Official Development Assistance (ODA).

Notes

1 Data collection was closed in May 2014.
2 Interview with ECE official A, February 2012.

2   Theoretical framework

The domestic politics of foreign aid decision making remains poorly understood in the literature. Much of the empirical research on aid quality and allocation fails to tie the identified determinants of a country's bilateral aid flows together with the interests of domestic actors and processes in domestic politics that shape these into policy outcomes. Some have argued that creating a model of these processes is not feasible due to the large and diverse number of actors and interests. Those that do try to explain foreign aid decision making focus almost exclusively on the established donors, and there are no models on the domestic politics of aid in 'new' donor contexts. This chapter presents a model for understanding aid policy decision making in the ECE countries, where due to the low profile of foreign aid policy, actors, their interests, and their interactions are easier to model in a parsimonious and insightful way. The model builds on the governmental politics model of foreign policy analysis, but also incorporates two sets of actors which have had profound influence on shaping ECE foreign aid policies: international organizations like the EU and the OECD DAC, and domestic non-governmental organizations.

2.1 Opening the black box

Academic research has done much in the recent decade to provide an understanding on the determinants of foreign aid policies and also how aid is allocated among recipients. There is a clear consensus in the literature that donors pursue rather egoistic political, strategic, security or economic goals with foreign aid, evidenced especially by quantitative studies on how bilateral aid is allocated (Alesina and Dollar 2000; Younas 2008; Hoeffler and Outram 2011). There is little evidence of donors acting altruistically. Often, pursuing self-interested goals even decreases the effectiveness of aid in terms of its contribution to reducing poverty in recipients (Alesina and Weder 2002; Collier and Dollar 2002). This general picture however is nuanced by the well documented fact that the foreign aid policies of donor countries differ to a great extent (Schraeder *et al.* 1998; Berthélemy 2006). Some countries, such as the Nordic states, are usually seen to have a clear poverty focus and allocate much of their aid to countries where poverty is high, driven by "enlightened self interest" (Lumsdaine 1993). While there is evidence that these countries also take foreign trade considerations into account (Danielson and Wohlgemuth 2005), this is much less pronounced as in the case of countries like Japan which put a strong emphasis on economic interests and much of their aid is allocated to their trading partners. Others again have been shown to be especially keen on favoring their former colonies and using aid as a tool to maintain these links (France or Portugal). The United States has been frequently accused of having an aid policy which primarily serves its foreign policy interests and not the poverty reduction needs of its recipients (see Meernik *et al.* 1998), although more recently, with the Obama administration's National Security Strategy there seems to be a greater alignment between the two (see Gibler and Miller 2012). Differences however are not only apparent between countries, but also within donors over time: during Tony Blair's government, the United Kingdom transformed itself from being an ex-colonial master interested in maintaining strong economic ties with former colonies into a globally responsible donor with an emphasis on aid effectiveness in terms of poverty reduction (Morrissey 2005).

It is beyond doubt that the political, social and economic contexts, as well as the different historical trajectories of donor countries have profound influences on how they give foreign aid, how much they give, and who they give it to. These interior dynamics, or, in other words, the domestic politics of foreign aid decision-making, however remain poorly understood in the aid literature. Much of the empirical research on aid allocation fails to tie the identified determinants together with the interests of domestic actors and processes in domestic politics which articulate these interests (Kleibl 2013). Researchers for example may find that a certain donor gives more aid to its trading partners, but they will usually not go into details explaining which domestic constituency this benefits, how they lobbied for this, or why the government decided to support these particular interests as opposed to others, which may, for example, favor allocating aid along poverty reduction criteria. Most of the quantitative aid allocation studies cited above do not use any formal theoretical models to explain why aid is allocated the way it is, and those that do tend to neglect the dynamics of domestic policy-making and treat the state as a unitary, utility maximizing agent (Younas 2008). In other words, the "black box" of aid policy-making is left unopened.

A more qualitative approach to understanding aid policy-making in donors relies on case studies (Hoebink and Stokke 2005; Lancaster 2006; Hoebink 2010; Horký-Hluchán and Lightfoot 2012; Lundsgaarde 2013a). These studies often provide important insights into how various aid policy outcomes in different donors are reached, buy they very rarely use any theoretical background that would allow cross sectional comparison between donors or longitudinal comparison within a single donor over time, with perhaps Lundsgaarde (2013a) being the only notable exception. In her book on the domestic determinants of the aid policies of some major donors like the USA, France and Japan, Lancaster (2006) readily acknowledges that she has no theory, arguing that there are far too many variables affecting aid policy decisions to allow for a parsimonious and insightful model. This lack of theory is true for qualitative donor studies in general, and is especially surprising given the amount of attention which has been directed to understanding the determinants of aid policies in the donor countries.

We disagree with Lancaster and think that theoretical models are necessary in order to better understand the drivers of why aid policies differ among donors and to allow meaningful comparisons. We also argue that a workable and insightful theoretical model is not impossible to develop, provided that the scope of the model is limited to some extent: a model formulated for the special characteristics of the ECE donors may be relatively parsimonious and at the same time remain insightful and relevant. Aid policy in these countries is relatively low profile compared to the more established donors, meaning less actors involved and thus less complex interactions. Lundsgaarde (2013a) has adopted a similar approach by limiting his model to the determinants of poverty focused aid in donor countries.

In order to create a theoretical model to better understand the making of foreign aid policy in the ECE countries, we first take one step back to models of foreign policy-making in general. Aid, after all, is a tool of foreign policy, and as such, it can be understood as having the goal of promoting the various foreign policy interests of the donor country. The analysis of foreign policy has a large and highly influential theoretical and methodological literature (see Mintz and DeRouen 2010 or Marton and Eichler 2013 for an overview), and we argue that at least some of the models used in foreign policy analysis may easily be adopted to provide insights on how foreign aid policy is made, with a focus on the ECE setting. Foreign policy analysis, by its nature, relates to case studies on explaining the determinants of how various countries have reacted to specific immediate foreign policy challenges, or how they have formulated longer term strategies in various areas of foreign policy like security, economic diplomacy or even foreign aid. In the remainder of this chapter, we first introduce the various models used for understanding foreign policy decision-making. We argue that the governmental (or bureaucratic) politics model is especially suitable for explaining foreign aid policy-making, and thus we adapt this model to the context of the ECE countries, which includes expanding it with the influence of international and domestic non-governmental actors. We then explore the dynamics of this model and formulate theoretical insights on the determinants of aid policies of the ECE countries.

2.2 Models in foreign policy decision-making

The field of foreign policy analysis aims to understand the factors that determine how a country makes decisions in given foreign policy situations. To guide the empirical analysis of various foreign policy situations, several theoretical models have been formulated. These models can be grouped into rational or cognitive approaches (Mintz and DeRouen 2010). Rational models emphasize actors making rational decisions based on cost-benefit analysis, while cognitive models focus more on the psychological side of decision-making, and argue that resulting foreign policy decisions may not always be rational. The three basic and highly influential models of the rational school were formulated by Allison (1969, 1971) in his classic works on the Cuban missile crisis. We first review these.

Model I in Allison (1969), often termed as *the* rational model, assumes that foreign policy decisions are made by rational actors making decisions in order to maximize some utility function. The model supposes that the government's actions are driven by clear, rational goals The main decision maker is the somewhat abstract "leader" of the country, like the president of the United States or a unified national government. This leader receives several inputs (policy options) from a variety of domestic actors such as bureaucracies, various stakeholders and the public opinion, and ultimately makes a decision by carrying out cost-benefit analyses on all possible options, and selects the one which yields the highest level of utility for the country. The main problem with the rational model is that it neglects that the various interest groups within a state will not only provide policy options, but will actively lobby the government to implement their proposed option. Looking at states as unitary actors can also be misleading because interest groups and other actors may have different, and at times even conflicting utility functions, and it is not clear how these should be aggregated into a country-level function that the decision maker can maximize. None the less, this model has proved highly influential to explain decisions in crisis situations where national security is threatened, the decision is in the hand of highest executive level, and national interest can be clearly identified.

A second model, also originating from Alison's classic work, is the organizational politics approach, which takes the organizations where decisions are made and their procedures into consideration. Foreign policy decisions are not made in vacuum, but are made in agencies and these agencies have standard operating procedures. Most of the foreign policy decisions a government makes are not taken in crisis situations and do not reach the attention of the highest executive level, but are rather standard and can be done on the basis of pre-existing governmental guidelines. One strategy that agencies may follow is incrementalism: organizations will tend to fine tune previous decisions and will refrain from exploring new policy opportunities (Mintz and DeRouen 2010).

A third model, called the governmental politics or bureaucratic politic model, elaborated in Allison and Halperin (1972) and Halperin (1974) and also within the rational framework, gives up the assumption of a unified government. It assumes that governments are composed of different bureaucracies such as ministries, agencies and departments, as well as subdivisions within them, and these all have their own interests and goals related to foreign policy. Instead of having one national utility function, the model assumes that each player has a different function it wishes to maximize: "where you stand depends on where you sit," a maxim which has become known as Miles' Law (Miles 1978). The governmental politics model tries to understand the process through which the utility functions of the individual bureaucracies are aggregated. In this sense, foreign policy outputs are the result of bargaining and interactions amongst several players within government, each with different objectives, different constituencies, and also differing degrees of influence. Each bureaucracy will tend to "jealously protect its own turf" (Mintz and DeRouen 2010: 71), and thus the ultimate decision is usually not cut and dry, but rather involves negotiations between the agencies, coalition making and bargaining. The final decision, even though the individual bureaucracies are seen as rational agents, may be far from optimal, as it may be reflection of something that all agencies accept as opposed to what maximizes utility for the country as a whole. A commonly used method for applying the governmental politics model is by using two-level games (Putnam 1988), where both the domestic bureaucratic decision-making process and the subsequent international negotiations can be modeled in a single framework.

Krasner (1971) has strongly criticized the governmental politics model, arguing that the chief executive has a key role in foreign policy-making and the model tends to under represent its power. Bendor and Hammond (1992) echo this conclusion and argue that the model is only useful for explaining mid-level policies, on which there is little attention from higher level politics. The model is clearly most reliable in the case of mid-level issues that are not pressing and thus there is time for political debates and negotiations between agencies. Another issue relates to the portability of Allison's models: developed to understand policymaking in the United States, how useful is it in other contexts? It seems that there are a large number of non-US applications of the models in the literature, ranging from explaining India's decision to start building nuclear weapons (Sagan 1996) to German foreign policy (Rittberger and Wagner 2001). Thus the models appear highly versatile both in terms of countries and foreign policy issues.

The three rational models have been complemented by various cognitive approaches, which introduce the psychological aspects of how individuals make decisions into the foreign policy analysis process. Mintz and DeRouen (2010) provide a detailed overview of these theories, we only mention some of the more important ones for the sake of completeness. One such model is bounded rationality (Simon 1957), which assumes that decision makers have limited information and face other constraints, thus instead of searching for the utility maximizing solution, they look for ones that are "acceptable." Prospect theory (Kahneman and Tversky 1979) introduces the concepts of risk aversion and risk acceptance to decision-making, and shows that decision makers accept or avoid risk to varying degrees in different situations. Poliheuristic theory (Mintz 2004) can be seen as an attempt to combine the rational and the various cognitive approaches, and assumes that decision-making is a two step process: first, the decision maker eliminates many of the options using cognitive procedures, and then makes a rational choice using the remaining ones.

Foreign policy analysis therefore offers several possible models which could be adapted to understanding foreign aid policy decision-making in the ECE countries. We argue that the *government politics approach* is the most appropriate candidate for such a model. One reason is that designing foreign aid policies, as well as designing and implementing foreign aid programs and projects requires a broad range of expertise, in areas like healthcare, rural development and agriculture, private sector development, education, infrastructure and govern-ance. These issues cut across several government agencies in terms of mandates, constituencies and expertise. Lundsgaarde (2013b: 37) quotes that in the USA in 2011 a total of 27 public entities were involved to some degree in the country's foreign aid program. The case is no different in most ECE countries, meaning that several government actors will be involved in the foreign aid decision-making process. A second reason is that aid policy formulation, as opposed to formulating foreign policy responses to often urgent situations, is a rather slow process without any hard deadlines, thus there is more time for negotiations between the government agencies involved. Third, foreign aid can be seen as a mid-level policy area, and a country's aid strategy is clearly a long term issue. As argued above decision-making in such issues is ideally explained by govern-mental politics. Forth, aid is a low salience issue (Lundsgaarde 2013a), which is especially true in the ECE countries, meaning that the attention of the higher executive levels to it may also be lower, giving greater room for bureaucratic politics to hammer out the necessary solutions. In the following section we adapt this model to the characteristics of foreign aid in the ECE countries.

2.3 Governmental politics and foreign aid in the ECE countries: actors and interests

When adapting the governmental politics approach to foreign aid policy-making in ECE, the most important questions to address is who the main governmental actors are in the policy area, and what their views, values, and interests are. The main actor in development policies in the ECE countries is the Ministry of For-eign Affairs (MFA), which in all five countries is charged with being the agency responsible for policy formulation and coordinating the activities of the other line ministries and agencies involved. No ECE country has an independent develop-ment ministry like the Department for International Development (DfID) in the UK or the Federal Ministry for Economic Cooperation and Development (BMZ) in Germany, which is justified by the fact that they spend relatively low amounts on foreign aid. Development is therefore one of the MFA's many responsibilities. The bureaucratic location of aid policy actors in the government is important, although it does not directly determine policy outcome. For example, in Denmark aid is connected to the MFA yet this has not weakened the development purpose of aid (Lancaster 2006: 221; although see Engberg-Pedersen 2014 for a more recent view). Martens (2008) suggests that aid agencies can be understood as actors that play a mediating role between the interests of partner countries and the interests of individual donors. Within donor countries, they may be considered the actors that defend the interests of partner countries and support the promotion of development goals against a host of other national interests, such as diplomatic or commercial objectives (Faust and Messner 2012).

In general, most bureaucracies aim to maximize their budgets (Niskanen 1968) and prestige, although foreign affairs represent a different kind of bureaucracy compared to other ministries. While diplomatic actors may be less interested in budget maximization as opposed to other (related) goals like increasing the MFA's global network of embassies, greater interactions with international organizations etc., it is difficult to argue that an MFA would not be interested in increasing resources for foreign aid as well as increasing staff numbers and capacities. Indeed, aid bureaucracies can play a major role in maintaining spending as they push to protect their institutional territory (Van Belle *et al.* 2004). The incentive to increase their budget however may be at odds with pursuing the most effective and efficient development policies and strategies (Lundsgaarde 2013b). Besides budget and capacities, MFAs usually also have a vision on how the country's foreign policy should look like, at least in terms of strategic goals, and what role foreign aid should play in this policy.

What this vision actually is however is by no means clear as it emerges as a result of bureaucratic politics *within* the MFA. The MFA itself is far from being a monolithic structure. The main unit responsible for foreign aid policy-making is the international development cooperation department, and some ECE countries (most notably the Czech Republic and Slovakia) have also created aid implementing agencies as semi-autonomous bodies of the MFA, but these are not engaged in policy work. Conflicts of interest may often arise between foreign policy goals and international development goals: the latter may advocate giving more aid to poor countries, while foreign policy goals, such as building alliances or maintaining regional stability can divert aid from the poorest, thus the need for bargaining between various units is already present within the MFA. The international development cooperation department or the aid agency may be a champion of development goals, but it may have a difficult time getting this through in face of opposition from other MFA departments, which may prefer to promote the more traditional foreign policy goals of the country. All MFA units are likely to agree that bigger budgets and larger staff numbers are in there interest, especially since larger aid budgets will lead to staff increases not only in the Aid departments, but also in the bilateral and multilateral relations departments. The main strategic goals or visions of foreign aid articulated by the MFA as a whole however will depend on the bureaucratic policy-making processes within the MFA.

This vision of development policy-making within the MFA does suggest a large degree of bureaucratic autonomy and technocratic policy-making. We of course do not wish to imply that the executive or national parliaments do not play a role, and indeed the literature on the domestic politics of aid has attempted to develop an understanding of the role of parliaments. Gibson *et al.* (2005) conceptualize the issue in a principle-agent framework, where the parliament is the principal and the MFA is its agent to conduct its foreign policy in the desired manner. Lancaster (2006: 219–220) argues that "informed and engaged legislatures can affect aid's purpose," and in countries where legislatures are not involved, such as France and Japan, aid policy decisions are opaque and not subject to public scrutiny or influence. Round and Odedokun (2004) agree as they argue that constitutional checks and balances on the government are important. They argue that if the government (and, hence, the aid agency) is under constitutional or political constraints and subject to veto players, such as parliament, then aid policy must satisfy not only the interests of government but also those of the veto wielders. An unengaged legislature can lead to the public being little informed about the uses of aid.

Much of literature on ECE development policies shows that the involvement of the legislative or chief executive levels is much less significant than in the case of many other policy areas, and development policy-making is indeed often (but not exclusively) characterized by bureaucratic autonomy. In case of Hungary for example, Paragi (2010: 201) argues that:

> ... no budget lines, no country selection, and no organisational questions have ever been debated at the plenary sessions of the legislative council. Details of the Hungarian [international development cooperation] activity are regularly presented to the Foreign Affairs Committee of the Parliament by [the] MFA ... However, this practice is more reminiscent of a compulsory procedural matter than a reflection of a substantially innovative and initiative decision-making process.

The following account by Drążkiewicz-Grodzicka (2013: 66) on a conference held for Polish MPs in 2008 reveals a similar story:

> As it was anticipated that all structural and legal changes of the ODA would eventually have to be approved by the Parliament, the basis of the conference was to provide Polish parliamentarians with information on how other countries organize their national ODAs. This catalogue of 'good practice' would eventually allow the MPs to make informed decisions when recreating Polish ODA. ... MPs ... came in very few numbers, with none staying at the conference for the whole day.

Parliamentary and executive attention may be higher in the Czech Republic, but there is evidence to the contrary even there. Horký (2010c: 235) for example notes that the "Parliament, or at least the Chamber of Deputies, a common agent of change in policy coherence issues in experienced donor countries, has never tackled the issue." Low level executive attention in the Czech Republic is signaled by the fact that the "Inter-ministerial Commission [for coordinating aid policy] almost never met at Deputy Ministerial level because of the low priority of the development agenda" (Horký 2010c: 234). These quotes are also supported by interview data: for example, an official from of an ECE MFA argued that "what is lacking is backing from the Parliament and from politicians in our country."[1] A Polish NGO representative complained about the "lack of interest in development from government and parliament."[2]

Based on these findings, we think it is justified to conceptualize development policy-making in the ECE countries as a primarily bureaucracy driven process. Beyond the formal approval of policies, strategies, budget lines etc., intervention from the legislative and the chief executive levels into international development policy seems to have been highly ad hoc and sporadic.

We now turn to identifying actors beyond the MFA in this policy process. All five ECE countries started off after the turn the Millennium with international development policies that gave some role to many line ministries beyond the MFA. One reason for this was the limited presence of sectoral expertise in the MFAs. Two line ministries may be especially important: the Ministry of Finance (MoF) and the Ministry of Economy (MoE). We conceptualize these as two separate actors, although they may not actually be separate ministries in some of the ECE countries. Foreign aid is not a key mandate for either of these two ministries, as opposed to the MFA, and therefore internal divisions over aid are less pronounced. Therefore, for the purposes of this study and to avoid unnecessary complications in the theoretical framework, we treat these organizations as homogenous in terms of their interests towards foreign aid.

The MoF, as the agency responsible for preparing the government budget has an important role in suggesting the amounts allocated to each budget line. In case of low salience issues like aid and no members of the legislative who champion aid (as often the case in ECE countries, illustrated above), suggested amounts on the draft budgets may well become final with formal approval from Parliament. Officials and technical experts in the MoF may well be aware of issues like the alternative costs of foreign aid and may put little value on aid, especially if it is perceived by them as ineffective. The MoE is important because in most ECE countries it is responsible for external economic relations such as trade development and investment promotion. As aid can be seen as a tool to stimulate exports, especially through the usage of tied aid and export credits, the MoE's main interest will be to use aid as much as possible to achieve its own mandate of export promotion and "assist" national companies in gaining access to foreign markets. Further line ministries may also have a stake in foreign aid, and be mainly interested in promoting their sectors in international development. The Ministry of Agriculture for example may be keener on aid projects focusing on rural development, while the Ministry of Education may prefer giving scholarships to students from developing countries.

Government bureaucracies do not work in isolation, but are subjects to outside influence. Bureaucracies are generally not isolated from the societies and international environments they work in, and resulting government policies should be seen to some extent as reflections of societal preferences and international effects. In order to make the governmental politics model relevant for foreign aid, we propose expanding it with two sets of actors outside of the national government, which both try to influence the decisions made through the governmental politics process: international actors and domestic stakeholders. We therefore conceptualize these actors as sources of influence on how the interests and perceptions of various government agencies are shaped, and not as organizations that would directly take part in the bargaining process among government agencies.

International actors are mainly multilateral organizations which try to influence their members into implementing certain practices in their foreign aid policies and refraining from others. The most important such institutions for the ECE countries are the EU (especially the European Commission), the OECD DAC, and to a lesser degree the UNDP. These organizations can attempt to influence government agencies either through setting explicit conditions that the government must fulfill in order to gain some benefit from the organization (such as membership or access to increased financing), or through prolonged interactions, moral authority, or setting an example may try to engage the country in a process of social learning (Checkel 2005). The interests of international actors are rather easy to identify. The international organizations mentioned above will have a clearly defined agenda to promote in member states, mainly related to aid effectiveness and aid volumes, along the lines of what we term the "Global Consensus" on foreign aid, discussed in the following chapter. The EU has played an especially important role in "convincing" the ECE countries to restart their international development policies during the accession negotiations. The EU has also developed a large body of soft law along the lines of the global consensus that provides a whole set of recommendations for member states on how to give aid, who to give it too, how much to give, how to work together, etc., while also acknowledging the fact that member states are sovereign in formulating their bilateral foreign aid policies. The OECD DAC has also been active in formulating tailored recommendations for its members or accession countries through its peer review system, but it also produces a wide range of thematic recommendations for member countries. The contents of these also aim at making aid more effective, and many recommendations are similar to those of the EU, although the OECD DAC focuses more on effective institutional structures. The UNDP mainly exerted influence early on with its capacity-building program, also in terms of institutions, and is thus unique for the ECE region.

Another set of international actors are the developing partner countries of the global South. While development cooperation has traditionally been a highly donor driven area, the concepts of ownership and partnership have increasingly become key aid effectiveness criteria in recent decades (see Chapter 3). These concepts imply that it is the developing partner countries' interests which should drive donor policies. None the less, we do not conceptualize partner countries in our model, quite simply because it is almost impossible to find any example of their policy-level influence in the ECE countries. We do not wish to say that ECE development practice is formulated without consultation with developing partners. Indeed, governments often refer to the needs of the partners, and how partners are the ones that request specific forms of assistance. However, the ways they interact with governments in terms of policy formation is not clear or transparent at all. In ECE development discourses partner countries are often portrayed in a paternalistic manner: they are passive, vulnerable recipients, who are happy to receive any assistance that comes their way and never ask questions (see Mawdsley 2012 for a discussion). These discourses have an influence on government mentalities and how policy-making processes work, most likely not allowing any entry points for developing country interests.

In terms of domestic stakeholders, one must begin with the general societal environment and how the public relates to foreign aid. The case of foreign aid is interesting from this perspective, as it is usually seen as an area in which the public may express preferences, but these often have little impact on policy-making (Otter 2003; van der Veen 2011). Individual support for aid mostly comes from the principle of solidarity and identification with vulnerable populations, a moral and religious obligation to give charitably and support others less advantaged than oneself (Paxton and Knack 2012). Opinion polls have shown that publics in ECE countries are much less interested in, and aware of foreign aid policies, and are also more volatile in their support than in the more established donors (Eurobarometer 2007, 2010, 2012). Harmer and Cotterell (2005: 14) argue that moral obligation was a "significant factor in the first post-independence humanitarian responses by the Central European countries," and more recent opinion polls also confirm the importance ECE publics tie to moral obligations (Eurobarometer 2010). Still, foreign aid, unless seen as an alternative cost to other government expenditures, is seen to have little direct impact on the lives of people in a country. As stated by Otter (2003: 116): "aid is seldom a domestic political issue: put simply, there are no votes in foreign aid." Therefore, the wider public in these countries may not have any clear preference on how aid policies should be formulated and may not even care about it, giving the government large space to formulate aid policies. The crucial issue here though is the need for civil society organizations that could translate moral feeling into acts and channel public opinion towards policy-making.

The group of domestic stakeholders therefore includes non-governmental organizations active in development and humanitarian issues. These organizations are not only important for channeling public opinion into foreign aid policies, but they are also stakeholders are beneficiaries in the "aid business" in a sense that they are often the ones to implement government financed projects. NGOs may also be driven by moral considerations and be highly supportive of alleviating poverty in developing countries. NGOs will attempt to influence the various government agencies and actors through their advocacy work (see Kim, Y. 2014) and lobbying, and can also serve as "watchdogs" of government policy.

NGOs will also have a set of interests related to foreign aid that they will try to promote. It is usually assumed that NGOs are a voice of the global South within donor countries and thus represent the interests of people in developing countries (Lewis and Kanji 2009). Therefore, they will campaign for an increase in aid volumes, and also more effective aid in terms of poverty reduction, along the lines of the Global Consensus. The world of NGOs active in development in any country is usually highly heterogeneous, both in terms of organizational sizes and activities. Some organizations may focus on delivering development or humanitarian projects in the field, others may prefer development education and awareness-raising activities within their home countries, and again others may be more involved in advocacy. Some may have several different sets of activities. Organizations may also be specialized on some specific area or issue within development.

A main dilemma however concerning NGOs is related to their dual role in foreign aid policies as implementers of government financed aid projects (or, in effect, subcontractors of the government) and watchdogs of the government's foreign aid policy. At least two contradictions arise from this dual role, which make it difficult to determine what the actual interests of the NGO community are towards national foreign aid policies, and how these actually diverge from the Global Consensus. For one, if an organization receives some part of its funding from the government (and this part can be much more significant in the ECE context than in the more established donors), it will be less inclined to criticize it. NGOs may therefore practice self-censorship and refrain from strong criticism. Second, NGOs may have different interests as project implementers as opposed to their interests in their advocacy roles. As project implementers, NGOs are interested in having stable and predictable access to government financing. In their advocacy role however they mainly promote the interests of the global South in their home countries, and this may require them to lobby their government for aid practices that undermines their access to financing. One area where this conflict is clearly shown is the issue of aid effectiveness. In order to make aid more effective in reducing global poverty, reforms such as untying aid, greater coordination and harmonization between donors, and a better division labor is required. But, if national governments untie their aid or engage in joint programming with other donors, national NGOs will have to compete for government financing with actors from other countries as well, undermining their access to funding. While all groups of NGOs will agree on the need to increase aid to developing countries, there may be disagreements on issues related to aid effectiveness.

A second group of domestic actors are private businesses, who are mainly involved in aid policy as implementers. Business interests in foreign aid in the ECE countries are very weakly present and so far business has failed to exert any significant influence on aid policies. In order to keep our model as parsimonious as possible, we refrain from conceptualizing the interests of business actors. Also, the MoE can be seen as a promoter of national business interests within the government.

Having an overview of the main governmental and outside actors and their interests, it is possible to sum up the interactions between them into a theoretical model. The theoretical model is depicted in Figure 2.1. Aid policy-making is conceptualized as a bureaucratic negotiation game within the government, both among the departments of the MFA, and between the MFA and line ministries, with only sporadic intervention and only formal approval from the legislative or chief executive level (marked by a dashed lines). However, the interests of the government actors are influenced through the advocacy work of domestic stakeholders, mainly NGOs (which themselves may or may not be influenced by public opinion, again marked with a dashed line), as well as international actors like the EU and the OECD, which may use explicit conditionality and socialization strategies to modify policy outcomes. The bureaucratic bargaining process, influenced by outside pressures, takes place within an institutional framework, which provides formal channels for channeling societal and

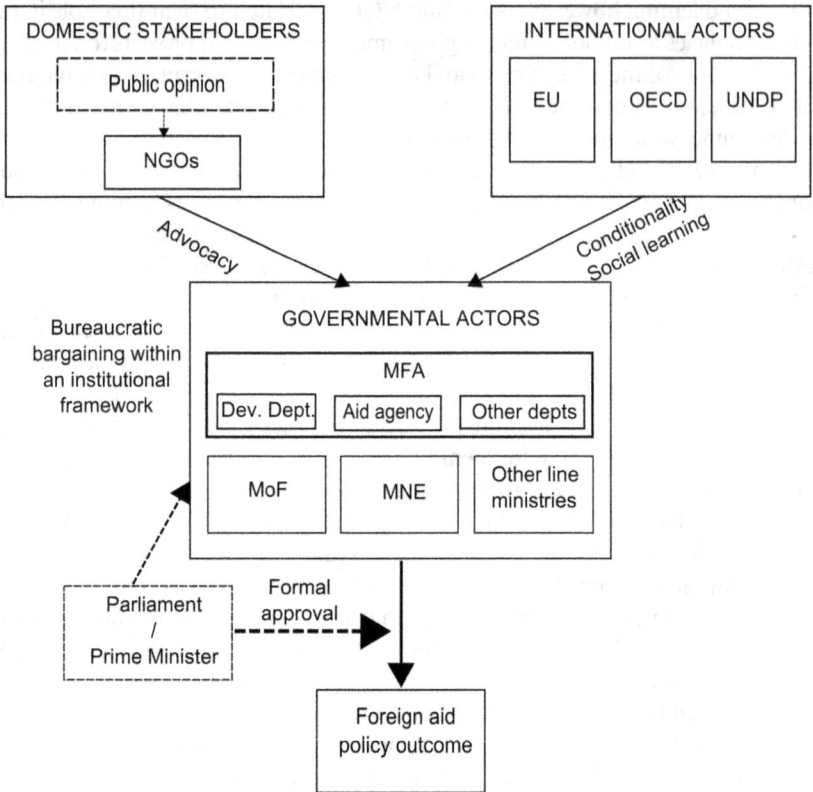

Figure 2.1 Theoretical framework for understanding foreign aid policy decision-making in the ECE countries

international interests into policy, and also for negotiations between government agencies. The result of this process is a foreign aid policy outcome.

In order for the model to be of use in our empirical analysis of how aid policy is made and how it changes (or remains the same) in the ECE countries, describing the actors and their interests is not enough, as we must also understand the dynamics between them. In order words, we must formulate theoretical expectations on what determines the success of (1) conditionality and socialization by international organizations; (2) advocacy by NGOs; and (3) the policy outcome of the governmental bargaining process. We address these three issues in turn in the remaining three sections of this chapter.

2.4 Determinants of the influence of international actors

The literature on international socialization (Checkel 2005; Schimmelfennig *et al.* 2006) aims to explain how international organizations can influence domestic politics. A significant branch of this literature, the theory of Europeanization, explicitly deals with the domestic impacts of the European Union (Schimmelfenning and Sedelmeier 2005; see Sedelmeier 2011 for a recent review of the literature). Although the EU has been the key international actor in influencing ECE foreign aid policies, other organizations like the OECD DAC or the UNDP have also played a role, and so have some bilateral partners, most importantly CIDA (see Chapter 4), thus we favor the term international socialization as opposed to Europeanization. The proposed mechanisms and theories of how international influence translates into national level politics and policies are highly similar in the two approaches anyway.

The basic model of international socialization (and Europeanization) states that laws in a wide sense, including institutions, methods, processes, norms and behavioral rules, originating from the international level may be incongruous with relevant legislation of the nation states (Risse *et al.* 2001: 6–12). This gap between the international and domestic level may lead to pressures for the nation state to adopt these international rules. Two main mechanisms for explaining this adoption process have been put forward: conditionality and social learning, both of which been documented extensively in the literature (see for example Checkel 2001; Schimmelfennig and Sedelmeier 2005; Juncos 2011). Conditionality is based on a rational institutionalist approach, where domestic actors make decisions whether to adopt rules originating from the international level based on a rational analysis of costs and benefits. International norms and legislation will therefore be adopted if the costs of this are outweighed by the potential benefits. The approach focuses on the explicit use of conditionality by international organizations, and assumes that they are able to set conditions for nation states that they must adapt to. International actors should be able to provide rewards if nation states comply, and punish them (or at least withhold any reward) if they fail to comply. The rewards that international organizations can provide clearly depend on the mandate of the organization. The EU for example had a rather clear hierarchy of rewarding the compliance of non-member countries in adopting EU legislation: possibilities of cooperation, foreign aid, trade integration and (for a select group of countries) membership. An organization like the OECD DAC has much more limited tools to reward compliance, with membership being perhaps the only one, and the UNDP or CIDA will have even less. It is not surprising therefore that much of the literature on conditionality has focused on the EU context.

The exact size of the costs and benefits, as well as how they are perceived by the nation state and thus the outcome of the cost-benefit analysis will depend on several factors. Sedelmeier (2011: 13), in the context of EU accession, groups these variables into international and domestic facilitating conditions. The domestic facilitating conditions relate to national players, power relations and institutions, which our theoretical framework already models. Transposing international rules to the domestic level may change national power configurations and empower certain actors. Thus, certain national actors may have a strong interest in implementing international rules, while others may be opposed. These "domestic mediation" processes of international socialization effects are crucial, and the government politics model of foreign policy decision-making we have adapted as our framework incorporates them. The international facilitating conditions are the following:

- *Clarity of the international demands.* Do the nation states know what is exactly expected of them? A major source of uncertainty here that makes cost-benefit analyses difficult is that the international rules themselves may be constantly changing, or international actors may not agree on the exact set of rules to be adopted.
- *Credibility of conditionality.* Just how credible are the conditions set by the international actors? The effectiveness of conditionality increases if the international actors apply it consistently (Schimmelfennig and Sedelmeier 2005), meaning that rewards are sure to be given once conditions and met, and they are only given when conditions are met. This also relates to the ability of the international actor to withhold rewards or even punish if conditions are not met.
- *Temporal proximity of rewards.* The more immediate rewards are after compliance, the higher the likelihood that countries will adopt the rules.
- *The capacities of the international actors to monitor compliance.* If the international actors can effectively monitor how each state is performing in transposing the international rules to the national level, then there will be fewer possibilities for free riding. If non-compliance can easily be detected, states will have no possibilities to engage in "rhetorical only" compliance.

The second mechanism, social learning, is based on constructivist institutionalism. It argues that nation states will adopt international norms and laws not because the costs of adoption outweigh the benefits, but because these rules become internalized and a conviction gradually develops that they represent the only proper way to act. The main channel through which this happens is that a large variety of national actors, including politicians, civil servants and civil society become engaged in the activities of the international actors, and a dense set of interactions between them develops. National actors are exposed to the international way of doing things, and through a longer process their identities may gradually shift. Social learning is better equipped to understand the long term processes leading to identity change through prolonged interactions with international organizations. As it argues that these processes may happen even without material incentives (as these material incentives themselves change), it is ideal for explaining national level policy change induced by international organizations which have little capacity to dish out rewards, like the OECD or the UNDP, but even the EU in a post-accession setting, where its abilities to use conditionality towards member states greatly decrease, at least in some policy areas (Epstein and Sedelmeier 2008; Sedelmeier 2012).

Sedelmeier (2011: 13) notes two important international facilitating conditions for social learning, both revolving around the legitimacy of the international demands. The more legitimate international rules are perceived, the more likely that actors will internalize them in the long term. Legitimacy can have two sources. It can either be derived from the normative content of the rules, in which case we speak of *substantive legitimacy*, or the process through which the rules are made, which can be interpreted as *procedural legitimacy* (see Clark 2007: 196). Substantive legitimacy derives legitimacy from the content of the rules: if they are normatively consistent, effective at a solving problems in the issue area, are acted out in practice by authoritative actors, or a broader consensus exists on their appropriateness, they will be seen as legitimate regardless of how they were made (Sedelmeier 2011: 15). Procedural legitimacy argues the opposite: rules will be seen as legitimate, regardless of their content, if the process through which they were made is seen as democratic, inclusive and participatory. Inclusiveness of the international rule making process does not only refer to formal participation of nation states in the process, but also to their capacities to participate in a meaningful way. They must actually feel that their voices and interests get heard in the process. The characteristics of the rule making process also matter beyond a strict understanding of perceived procedural legitimacy. Social learning is more likely to occur in less politicized settings, and its likelihood also increases the more contacts member state officials have with the rule promoters (Beyers 2005; Lewis 2005).

Two further, domestic facilitating conditions for social learning may also be indentified: *domestic policy resonance* and the *presence of norm entrepreneurs* (Sedelmeier 2011). Domestic policy resonance is a related, but different concept from perceived substantial legitimacy. How well do the specific rules advocated by the international actors resonate with target country decision makers? Do they have any ingrained, prior beliefs on the issue? Are these compatible with international rules? Domestic actors may perceive rules to be substantively legitimate, but this does not necessarily mean that they will also resonate with their own beliefs. They may feel that their country's situation is different and would require special rules, different from those advocated on the international level. The second domestic factor is the presence of norm entrepreneurs, who themselves act as (additional) socializing agents and try to educate the governments. Such norm entrepreneurs in the case of development policy may be the European Commission, the OECD DAC or national NGOs and any EU-wide epistemic community they may be linked to.

International socialization through conditionality can be rather explicit and quick, and has been widely applied in a European context to explain the transformation and integration of the ECE countries (see Schimmelfennig and Sedelmeier 2005). Social learning however is a slow process and often difficult to identify in practice. However, as mentioned, it can play a role even if conditionality is not present due to the inability of the international actors to offer rewards. Scholars in the international socialization literature have long argued however that the two mechanisms should not be seen as mutually exclusive, but rather complements to each other, even though they lie on different paradigmatic bases (Johnson 2006; Sedelmeier 2011: 10). Zürn and Checkel (2005) even go as far as to argue that the two approaches have strongly "fertilized" each other, and scholars examining social learning are increasingly using terms like "scope conditions" (independent variables) and "causal mechanism," which are not traditionally associated with the constructivist paradigm.

In order to explain the influence of international actors like the EU, the OECD and the UNDP on the foreign aid policies of the ECE countries, we therefore rely on both conditionality and social learning and use the scope conditions that determine the effectiveness of these processes identified above.

2.5 Determinants of successful advocacy by domestic stakeholders

There is little systematic research on what factors determine how influential development NGOs will be on the government international development policy, especially in the ECE context. The general literature on interest group influence (Olson 1971; Gerber 1999) can be helpful, but there is also a growing literature on the influence of civil society groups in various sectors in the ECE countries which may provide more direct insights. Much of this latter literature relates to environmental NGOs (Kerényi and Szabó 2006; Carmin and Fagan 2010; Císař 2010), but there are examples from a few other sectors as well (see Roth 2007 on gender and O'Dwyer 2012 on gay rights). The insights from these two literatures can be used to generate theoretical expectations on the conditions that could determine the influence of NGOs on foreign aid policies in the ECE countries. We argue that the ability of NGOs to influence government decisions in foreign aid policy will depend on five factors: (1) the composition of and power relations among the development NGOs; (2) organizational capacities of the NGOs; (3) their abilities to mobilize international allies for specific causes; (4) foreign donor assistance in the form of financing and knowledge transfer; and (5) attitudes and administrative capacities of state actors.

The literature on the influence of environmental pressure groups in the ECE countries argues that much depends on the structure and power relations of the movement (Doherty and Doyle 2006: 701). Power relations and structure in a given sector affects to what extent the NGOs can speak with a single voice towards the government. Problems of collective action (Olson 1971) may emerge if the sector is composed of several small organizations, many of whom are competing for funds (see Sloat's 2005 study on women's NGOs). Relatively strong and large organizations are needed to drive the process and pay for the most of the costs, but strong organizations may also "hijack" the agenda. Therefore, it is expected that influence will be maximized if the development NGO sector represents a healthy balance between small and large organizations, which are able to articulate clear demands towards the government. The potential to influence the government will be lower if the sector is composed of several small organizations, or they fail to speak with a single voice.

Issues related to organizational capacity will also clearly affect how much influence NGOs will have on ECE governments (see Börzel and Buzogány 2010; Bruszt 2008). Staff capacities are not only required to analyze policy and coordinate the position of the NDO community on these, but also to communicate responses and engage the MFA and other government agencies on a sustainable basis. In order to be influential, it is assumed that NGOs or their associations must have dedicated policy staff with sufficient expertise, who regularly produce reactions to official policy changes. NGOs must also have ample financing to cover policy work.

NGOs can supplement their potentially weak capacities by mobilizing international support for their cause. Parau (2009) has shown how weak Romanian environmental and cultural NGOs were able to mobilize international support for specific issues and ultimately force the Romanian government to concede. Therefore, NGOs may be more influential if they have strong international partners which they can alert to unfavorable policies, and these in turn can put credible pressure on the respective national governments.

While relying on foreign donors and the lack of grassroots fundraising is often seen as a disadvantage (Fagan 2005), Císař (2010) argues this actually empowers Czech environmental NGOs to engage in policy-making, freeing them from the "the constraints of mass membership and public opinion" (Carmin and Fagan 2010: 701). In a similar vein, Kerényi and Szabó (2006) conclude that it was foreign advice and techniques learned from abroad and adapted to domestic contexts which allowed Hungarian environmental NGOs to successfully campaign on high profile issues. Increased access to foreign funding for development NGOs, including the ability to successfully tender and win international grants, as well as a wider network of international contacts and more learning opportunities can therefore increase influence on official policy-making.

Last but not least, the influence of civil society also depends on the receptiveness of the government. Due to the legacy of Communism, governments in the ECE countries were not accustomed to involving civil society in the policy-making process, and have often regarded it as a time consuming burden. Also, due to political and administrative instability leading to frequent changes in institutional setups and policies, the state was often not able to act in a predictable manner, sending mixed signals to environmental NGOs on how much their input is valued (Börzel and Buzogány 2010). State actors also seem to have failed to create meaningful forums for the involvement of NGOs in EU Structural Funds monitoring (Batory and Cartwright 2011). The influence of NGOs on development policy will therefore likely be larger if the government is open to consultations with them, provides legal safeguards on involving them in policy-making, and has formal or informal procedures in place to channel their inputs into policy outcomes.

Clearly, these five factors are not independent from each other. Being more successful in obtaining foreign financing and access to international networks contributes to increasing NGO staff capacities, for example. None the less, the five sets of variables provide a useful frame of analysis. Having established the determinants of external influence, both from international organizations and domestic stakeholders (mainly NGOs), we now turn to examining the determinants and the dynamics of bargaining among government actors.

2.6 The dynamics of governmental politics and decision-making

The final policy outcome from the governmental decision-making game will depend on the interests and relative power and influence of the various bureaucracies involved. The interests of these agencies in the ECE context have been discussed in section 2.3. Thus, the question is what determines the likelihood of an agency getting its interests through. We argue that the power and influence of each governmental actor is determined by three sets of variables: (1) institutions, i.e. the rules of the decision-making process; (2) capacities of the given agency; and (3) its ability to form coalitions and mobilize allies both within and outside of the government. We first discuss these, and then examine the time dimension of our model.

Institutions. Policy-making processes in governments are regulated by the institutional environment. Institutions are defined as the "rules of the game," i.e. all formal and informal rules, procedures, organizational cultures that have an impact on how a decision is achieved (see Helmke and Levitsky 2004). This definition therefore includes both formal legislation, but also more informal methods related to "ways of doing things." We understand "action channels" defined by Allison (1969) as "the established processes for aggregating competing perceptions, preferences, and stands of players in making decisions" to be part of the institutional setting. Institutions are not only important because they provide a setting for decision-making, but because they also distribute advantages and disadvantages among the various actors, and thus ascribe different levels of influence. The institutional setting gives different mandates to the actors, and some may have a more important role in the given policy area than others: a given agency may be formally named the coordinator of government activities in a policy area, or the head of agency may chair a relevant governmental committee, etc.

There are several potential institutions in the governmental aid policy decision-making game in the ECE countries which may be of interest. These may vary from country to country, but it is possible to identify two potentially common institutions that distribute power: government strategic documents and decision-making mechanisms. A broader government strategy on foreign relations may exist in a country, and indeed it has, in some form or another for most ECE countries in the past decade. Such a strategy sets a vision, broad goals, principles and tools for the country's foreign policy, of which development policy is one element. The MFA will have to align itself to these goals, and such a strategy can give a basis for reference in governmental bargaining. Depending on its contents, the foreign strategy may give advantages to the international development department within the MFA, or the MFA within the government, if it mentions issues related to foreign aid by providing a basis for reference. If foreign aid is not mentioned or is only marginal in broader foreign policy strategies then that will weaken the position of the international development department.

Second, intra-ministerial and inter-ministerial decision-making mechanisms and procedures can also distribute advantages and disadvantages. The international development department will most likely be the initiator of aid policy, but its policy drafts go through a consultation process, with many other departments within the MFA and in other governmental agencies commenting on it. Who is involved exactly? National legislation is crucial here, as it assigns different roles to different actors. As mentioned, foreign aid is recognized to be a part of foreign policy, thus the MFA must have a key role, and is the coordinator of the international development related activities of the other line ministries. However, this coordinating role can mean very different things depending on the exact legal mandate. The MoF can also have a key role in terms of the budget. Formal interactions between the government agencies will play out in inter-ministerial committees, both on the expert level and ministerial level (see Lundsgaarde 2013b).

Capacities. A second set of variables relate to the capacities that the various bureaucratic players may have. The international development department's capacities will depend on many variables, including its staff numbers, the number of staff engaged in policy work and their expertise in preparing well researched, convincing proposals. Clearly, this would call for well trained development professionals, something which was missing from the ECE countries during the recreation of their international development policies, and development departments were often staffed with career diplomats. The relative prestige of international development will also matter, which can often be seen as rather low in ECE MFAs compared to "traditional" foreign policy areas like security policy.[3] Towards other ministries, is the MFA able to present itself as the agency with authoritative expertise on international development? Is it able to provide arguments that resonate with the interests and beliefs of the other ministries? Finally, one must also consider access to the chief executive: does the Minister of Foreign Affairs have access to the Prime Minister, who may make the ultimate decision (at least formally).

Coalitions. In order to get their interest through, the various governmental players may look for allies, either temporary ones for the given issue, or longer term relationships with other "like-minded" actors. Much depends however on the specific issue: governmental agencies, can be seen as allies when it comes to increasing resources devoted to aid, but rivals when determining how it is allocated between them. However, building coalitions can go beyond the government: in many issues, the interests of the MFA's international development department may correlate strongly with those of development NGOs, and these actors can develop cooperative strategies. Using NGOs can increase the legitimacy of arguments made by the international development department by providing an example of societal demand for the reforms it wishes to pursue. The international development department or the broader MFA may also invoke international obligations and commitments and point towards the international organizations.

A final issue that needs to be discussed in terms of our theoretical model is the *time dimension*. If the time dimension is not specified correctly, the model could allow for circular reasoning: the model aims to explain foreign aid policy outcomes, but an important independent variable in explaining governmental bargaining is the existing institutional and policy setting. This existing setting, in turn, can be seen as an outcome of a previous governmental bargain. The existing system will empower certain governmental actors, and thus already bias any policy outcome.

In order to overcome this issue, we assume that the recreation of ECE development policies in the late 1990s and early 2000s represents a "clean slate." We assume this initial ($t = 0$) state of the policies and institutional set-ups to be exogenously determined. This is not unreasonable. As we will detail in Chapter 4, most ECE countries, with the exception of the Czech Republic, had a ten year plus hiatus in their international development policies after 1989. During this time, governmental decision-making mechanisms have been completely overhauled as part of the transition processes from one-party states to democracies. Most experts working in the field of development have left the field. The ECE countries recreated their international development policies due to external pressure, and had little domestic expertise on how to do it, thus they seem to have rather mechanically adapted highly similar initial institutional and policy setups, assisted by international actors like the UNDP and CIDA. Our model can therefore be used to track the subsequent evolution and individual country trajectories after this initial exogenously determined stage. The model should be seen as iterative, where institutional set-ups and existing policies in period t will have an impact on the policy (and institutional) outcome in $t + 1$. With a clearly identified starting point and an iterative procedure, we are able to avoid circular reasoning.

2.7 Summary

The book's theoretical model, as depicted in Figure 2.1, builds on the governmental (or bureaucratic) politics model of foreign policy decision-making, which is especially suitable for explaining foreign aid policy, but we adapt it to include the influence of international and domestic non-governmental actors. The model thus includes three key sets of interactions: (1) international actors and national governments; (2) domestic stakeholders and national governments; (3) between government agencies. The sets of variables that determine the outcomes in these interactions are summed up in Table 2.1.

Some of these variables are constant in all country contexts (such as socialization pressures from international organizations), while others vary. Thus the model is well suited to explain the variation and increasing heterogeneity among the ECE donors that has emerged in the past decade.

Table 2.1 Summary of the main variables that determine the influence of various actors in ECE foreign aid decision-making

Influence of international actors	*Influence of domestic stakeholders*	*Relative power and influence of government agencies*
Conditionality • (Domestic facilitating conditions) • International conditions: • Clarity of the demands • Credibility of conditionality • Temporal proximity of rewards • Monitoring capacities	The NGO sector • The composition of the sector and power relations • Organizational capacities • Abilities to mobilize international allies • Foreign donor assistance	Institutions • Broader foreign policy strategy • Intra-ministerial and inter-ministerial decision-making mechanisms
Socialization • Domestic facilitating conditions: • Policy resonance • Norm entrepreneurs • International conditions: • Procedural legitimacy • Substantive legitimacy	The government • Attitudes and administrative capacities of state actors	Capacities • Staff numbers and expertise • Ability to convince other actors • Access to the chief executive level Coalitions • Existence of like-minded actors • Alliance with development NGOs • Existence of international commitments

Source: Authors.

Notes

1 Interview with ECE official B, October 2008.
2 Interview with ECE NGO representative A, July 2010.
3 It is worth noting the lack of prestige is not confined to ECE states. A very good example is that of Belgium, as shown by Breuning (2013).

3 The Global Consensus on Foreign Aid

After the turn of the Millennium, a 'Global Consensus' emerged on what constitutes good practice in foreign aid. Through a series of international summits and conferences, ranging from the UN Millennium Summit through the Monterrey Conference to the Paris, Accra and Busan High Level Forums, a number of internationally accepted documents have emerged which form a 'code of conduct' of sorts for donor and recipient countries, with the view of increasing both the quantity and quality of foreign aid and the effectiveness of development. The European Union has been especially active in driving this process, but it has also done much to translate this Global Consensus into its own body of law, the *acquis communautaire*. This chapter discusses the main elements of the Global Consensus and its European translation, and creates a set of ten benchmarks against which the aid policies and performance of the Central and Eastern European (and potentially other) donors can be measured.

3.1 Shifting donor priorities

The perceptions on how foreign aid should be channeled to recipients, what modalities donors should use, what sectors aid should support, what conditions donors should attach to it (if any) have been constantly changing in the decades since the birth of the modern aid system after the end of World War Two. From the focus on physical capital accumulation in the fifties, through the "Basic Needs" approach of the seventies and structural adjustment in the eighties, all the way to the focus on governance, institutions and political conditionality today, donors have often shifted their preferences on what constitutes effective aid (see Degnbol-Martinussen and Engberg-Pedersen 2005 for an overview). These shifts have been influenced on the one hand by changes in economic thinking on what the determinants of economic growth are (Easterly 2003; Szentes 2005), and thus how foreign aid should assist this process. On the other hand, the changing donor practices are also reflections of shifting donor interests on what to use aid for. While during the Cold War aid was an important tool in supporting allies and buying political influence, the last two decades have seen a shift in donor interests towards using aid to combat direct and indirect security threats caused by global poverty (Woods 2005).

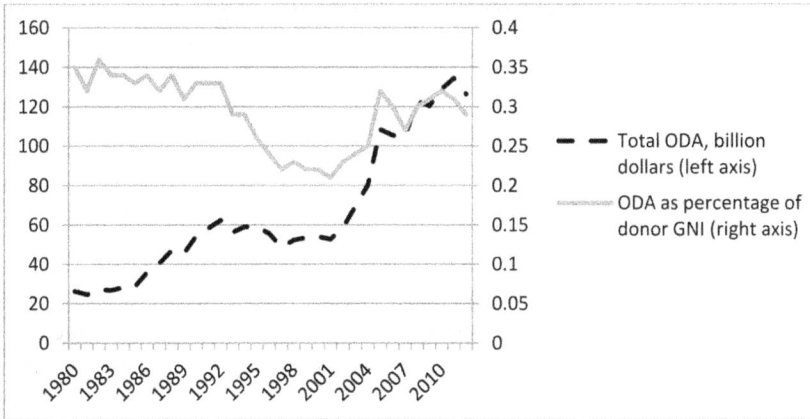

Figure 3.1 Annual flows of ODA from OECD DAC members between 1980 and 2012 (billion dollars in constant 2011 prices and percentage of donor GNI)
Source: OECD (2013).

Donors have not only shifted the ways they spend aid, but also the relative size of aid volumes has been shifting. This is especially true with the 1990s marking a decade of "aid fatigue" after the Cold War, when the average aid effort of donors decreased from 0.33 percent ODA/GNI in 1990 to 0.21 percent in 1999 (see Figure 3.1). This aid fatigue has been well documented in the literature (Boschini and Olofsgård 2007), and may have been fuelled by three main factors. First, the end of the Cold War also meant the end of Soviet aid and Soviet influence in the developing world. Propping up corrupt, but staunchly anti-Communist dictators like Mobutu in Zaire suddenly lost its appeal to countries like the United States. Second, public opinion in developed countries seems to have become disillusioned with the little visible impact that aid has managed to achieve in developing countries, and has become increasingly hostile towards aid. Third, the triumph of neoliberal economic ideology, which, in its most orthodox form denies that any form of state intervention into the economy, can be effective. Thus, any efforts to aid developing countries in centrally planning their economies and financing public investments from foreign aid are doomed to failure (Lal 1996). The ideology especially became influential in the United States and the international financial organizations dominated by it, like the World Bank and the IMF. The neoliberal set of policy recommendations for developing countries, the well-known Washington Consensus (Williamson 1990) advised developing countries to cut their public expenditure, liberalize international trade, privatize state owned companies, adopt low marginal tax rates and de-regulate their economies. The message was that developing countries have failed to develop because the state has over-expanded and has strangled the private economy with bad policies and over-regulation. Reforming the heavily interven-tionist state policies would automatically set these countries on paths of economic growth, and foreign aid is only needed marginally to support this process in the form of structural adjustment lending provided by the World Bank and the IMF (Collier and Gunning 1999). The state does not have the necessary information to allocate foreign aid effectively in the economy, thus it will inevitably lead to waste.

With the end of the Cold War, donors lost an important political reason to give aid, tax payers were disillusioned, and the dominating economic theory at the time suggested that aid is wasteful and even counterproductive. Thus the decline in aid volumes during the 1990s should not be a surprise, which is especially pronounced when compared to the GNIs of donor countries (see Figure 3.1). By the end of the decade however, an increasing number of economists and social scientists began questioning the rationale and the effectiveness of the Washington Consensus (Stiglitz 1998; Gore 2000), and while some refined and expanded versions of the consensus have emerged under names like Post-Washington Consensus or Washington Consensus Plus, these have not given any new legitimacy to the neoliberal development agenda or foreign aid either (Rodrik 2006). Throughout the 1990s, donor agencies and ministries of foreign affairs struggled to find a new rationale for giving aid, and this led to a change in the content of aid, as donors increasingly began attaching political conditions to aid and using it as a tool to promote democracy, better governance (Hout 2010) and the respect for human rights (Burnell 2005: 4), goals that were strikingly absent from aid policies during the Cold War.

A clear resurgence in the importance of aid began after the turn of the Millennium, and this can mainly be explained by the changing global political landscape. Burnell (2005) argues that the two main reasons behind this resurgence of aid are globalization and the terrorist attacks against the United States in 2001. 9–11 can be thought of as highly visible evidence of how problems rooted in global poverty can have their impact felt in developed countries as well. Combating security threats, broadly understood, like terrorism, "illegal" and mass migration, epidemics, drug trafficking etc. has given a new rationale for foreign aid, something donors were struggling to find during the 1990s. Many donor countries may have recognized that foreign aid can serve as a tool for addressing these threats directly, or by tackling their root causes, poverty and state weakness in the developing world (Brainad 2003; Rotberg 2002). With the new rationale for aid identified, absolute amounts spent on aid accordingly underwent significant growth between 2000 and 2005. The resurgence of the importance of foreign aid has led to intense debates, both on the political and academic levels on what role aid should play in developing countries, how it should be allocated, and what forms are the most effective in tackling poverty or supporting economic growth (see for example Burnside and Dollar 2000, 2004; Collier and Dollar 2002; Dalgaard *et al.* 2004; Sachs 2005; Easterly 2006b). The academic debate mainly focused on the determinants of aid effectiveness, and an influential strand in this research argued that aid works in countries where the policy or institutional environment is "good" (Collier and Dollar 2002; Burnside and Dollar 2004).

Although these findings were disputed (Hansen and Tarp 2000; Easterly *et al.* 2004), they resonated well with the mainstream of development economics which increasing embraced institutions as the "fundamental cause of long term growth" (Acemoglu *et al.* 2005; Acemoglu and Robinson 2012), and thus became influential themselves in academic circles. While openly donors talked little about heeding this advice and giving more aid to countries with better institutions and policies (with the exception of the USA, which created the Millennium Challenge Corporation in 2002 to reward good performers, see Hook 2008), some shift towards these better performers is apparent in aid allocation (Dollar and Levin 2006; Claessens *et al.* 2007). Debates in policy-making circles generally focused on increasing aid and on how the existing aid system could be tweaked in order to avoid some of the well know inefficiencies such as the lack of coordination between donors, the proliferation of donors and projects, uncertainty caused by the volatility of aid, administrative burdens that aid places on recipients, and combating corruption.

We argue that due to these debates on increasing aid volumes and making aid more effective, a "Global Consensus on Foreign Aid" has emerged by the second half of the first decade of the 2000s. This consensus should be understood in a sense that all major donors, as represented by the OECD's DAC, many non-DAC donors, multilateral agencies and most recipients have signed up to the various international declarations and documents that constitute the consensus. The consensus is therefore mainly reflected in political commitments, and implementation is another matter. It is clear that the Global Consensus on aid does not have a uniform influence on the practice of all donors, but there seem to be no strong voices arguing against it either. Nor do we wish to argue from a normative standpoint that this consensus is the holy grail of development policy and will solve all problems of the developing world—as discussed later, it does have flaws. The global economic crisis which erupted in 2008 and seems especially persistent in Europe, has hit many donor countries rather hard and provided an impetus for them to decrease the emphasis on aid quantity and focus more on improving effectiveness. There has also been a recent shift in donor rhetoric from aid effectiveness to development effectiveness, reflecting on how aid, as a tool to promote development, should not be seen in isolation (Alonso 2012; Gore 2013). None the less, we prefer the phrase Global Consensus on Foreign Aid as most of the international documents which constitute the consensus relate explicitly to foreign aid.

The remainder of this chapter seeks to identify what exactly the elements of the Global Consensus on Foreign Aid are. We first identify the most important global summits and conferences and the resulting political documents, and then proceed by examining how these have been translated to the EU level, as the European level may represent a more meaningful frame of reference for the ECE donors. We then use this to derive a set of benchmarks which will allow us to gauge how the ECE countries perform against the Global Consensus on Foreign Aid and its EU-level translation.

3.2 Elements of the Global Consensus

It is difficult to dispute that the Millennium Development Goals (MDGs) have had a profound effect on the discursive level of the international aid system (Manning 2010), even if achieving the goals has not been successful in many areas. The MDGs should be viewed as the basis of the Global Consensus on Foreign Aid. The set of measurable poverty reduction targets, later evolving into the MDGs, was originally recommended by the OECD in 1996 (OECD 1996). Accepted unanimously by the UN Millennium Summit in 2000 in the form of the Millennium Declaration, these goals aimed to achieve substantial global progress in a number of poverty related targets by 2015. These targets were grouped into eight main goals, including the reduction of (income-based) poverty, famine, improving child and maternal health, improving educational enrolment, promoting gender equality, eradicating various diseases, ensuring sustainability and transforming the global development system. The main novelty of the MDGs was to put poverty reduction and pro-poor policies like education and healthcare into the focus of the development efforts of bilateral donors and multilateral agencies, and also give this approach widespread legitimacy by getting most of the world's heads of states and governments to agree. This widespread legitimacy is what has allowed the MDGs to act as the cornerstone of the Global Consensus on Foreign Aid.

The eight goals require a rethinking of how donors approach aid, and in more general, their relations with developing countries. While the Millennium Declaration itself does not put a large emphasis on foreign aid as the main tool to achieve the MDGs, it was more or less implicit from the very beginning that aid should play a key role. This was shown rather clearly in the conclusions of the Millennium Project's work (UN Millennium Project 2005), a multidisciplinary team of experts led by economist Jeffrey Sachs, who were commissioned by UN Secretary General Kofi Annan to draw up a practical plan to achieve the MDGs. The Project's most widely cited conclusion calls for doubling foreign aid from the amount around 100 billion dollars in 2005 to 200 billion, in order to give developing countries the "big push" that they need to make adequate progress towards meeting the goals. Sachs even popularized these findings in a bestselling book, The End of Poverty (Sachs 2005).

While progress towards the MDGs was highly uneven, with many developing countries, especially in Sub-Saharan Africa, falling short of most goals, while others being spectacular overachievers, it did have a substantial impact on the rhetoric and aid strategies of donor countries (Manning 2010). In the decade following the acceptance of the MDGs, most OECD DAC member countries adopted references to the MDGs in their aid policy documents, and many have made poverty reduction a central goal of their international development policies, some even enshrining this is legislation. In the post 9–11 setting, most donors were clearly faced with the need to increase their aid spending to address various security concerns, and in the MDGs they found a perfect framework for doing this and selling it to the wider public as alignment with an internationally agreed consensus, with the goal of creating a poverty-free world.

While the countries which made the most significant efforts in reducing poverty are actually the ones which receive relatively little aid, such as China and India, in rhetoric achieving the MDGs clearly became tied to donor countries increasing their foreign aid efforts (Easterly 2009). The UN International Conference on Financing for Development, commonly known as the Monterrey Conference was organized in 2002 in order to generate political will among donors to actually increase aid with a view of meeting the MDGs. Finance ministers from all UN members participated and several heads of state and government did as well. The emerging declaration, the Monterrey Consensus (United Nations 2003) revived an age old (and heavily criticized, see Clemens and Moss 2007) UN aid target, calling for donors to spend 0.7 percent of their GNIs on aid. US President George Bush made significant aid pledges on behalf of the USA and announced the creation of a new aid agency, the Millennium Challenge Corporation (see Hook 2008), while the EU member states committed themselves to drawing up roadmaps on how to achieve the 0.7 percent target by 2015. The Monterrey Consensus also stressed that "recipient and donor countries, as well as international institutions, should strive to make [official development assistance] more effective" (United Nations 2003: 15). It also included provisions on mobilizing private financing for development, reducing the debt burdens of developing countries and making the international financial system more development friendly.

A further significant step towards increasing the amount of foreign aid was the 2005 G8 summit in Gleneagles, Scotland, where leaders of the eight countries pledged to provide a 50 billion dollar increase in aid, of which 25 billion would go to Sub-Saharan African countries. The summit also re-affirmed a previous agreement by G8 finance ministers to cancel 40 billion dollars worth of debt for 18 heavily indebted poor countries. However, it was never made clear how these new commitments related to previous ones, and many speculated that it would be difficult to ensure that they are additional to the Monterrey commitments (Doward 2013). A follow-up conference to the Monterrey Conference was organized in 2008 in Doha, but this failed to achieve any significant impacts other than reaffirming the Monterrey Consensus and emphasizing that donors must not falter in their commitments despite the emerging global financial and economic crisis (United Nations 2009).

As shown in Figure 3.1, the relative aid effort of donors did increase substantially after the turn of the Millennium. Average official development assistance (ODA) provided by donors as compared to their GNI's increased a full 0.1 percentage points, from 0.22 in 2000 to 0.32 in 2005. The increase is also substantial in absolute numbers: total foreign aid in 2000 was 53 billion dollars, which increased to 108 billion in 2005 and 123 billion in 2008 and has remained around that amount since (OECD 2013). Thus, there is evidence of a significant increase in donor aid spending, up to the emergence of the global financial and economic crisis, but it seems that the crisis has put a stop to reaching the ambitious 200 billion target foreseen by the Millennium Project, and there is not much sign of the additional 50 billion promised at Gleneagles either. While the increase in relative donor aid efforts was also evident, 0.32 percent is still a long way from 0.7. Among the donors who did not already fulfill the 0.7 percent aid target (Denmark, Luxemburg, the Netherlands, Norway and Sweden), only the United Kingdom made significant steps towards it, achieving the target in 2013. Thus Nunnenkamp and Thiele (2013) can talk about a significant "gap between words and deeds since Monterrey."

Critics of the MDGs and the Monterrey Consensus were quick to point out, that increasing foreign aid, as good as it may sound, may not be the best solution to the problems of developing countries. Academic research pointed out that there are significant possibilities to use current aid levels to achieve substantial poverty reduction, all that is needed is to change its allocation (Collier and Dollar 2002) and improve effectiveness. Many arguments also emerged that more aid may actually cause harm to developing countries that lack "absorption capacities" by weakening institutions and causing macro-economics distortions (Moss *et al.* 2006; Rajan and Subramanian 2008, 2011). The Millennium Project and Jeffrey Sachs also received severe criticism from academic circles, most of which argued that his idea of a big push to achieve the MDGs are based on outdated and invalid economic concepts from the 1950s (Easterly 2006a). Others pointed to the problems of the way the aid system is structured and the problems emerging from it, such as being heavily driven by donor priorities, the lack of coordination between donors, the proliferation and fragmentation of aid projects (Aldasoro *et al.* 2010), the administrative over-burdening of recipients (Easterly 2007; Knack and Rahman 2007). While none of these issues were new and have been analyzed by previous academic research (Cassen *et al.* 1986), the increase in foreign aid after the turn of the Millennium clearly exacerbated them, and the regained popularity of research on aid led many academics to revisit these issues. Most critics argued for a reform of the aid system with a view of increasing effectiveness, but some even went as far as to call for abolishing foreign aid, arguing that inefficiencies are inherent in the system, making it unreformable (Moyo 2009).

Clearly, policy makers could not ignore the calls for more effective aid, and the emerging Global Consensus on Foreign Aid, initially focusing mainly on increasing aid, needed to be complemented with a second element aimed at increasing the effectiveness of aid. Building political will to increase aid effectiveness, and setting out the tasks to be done was undertaken by a process of successive high level fora, including ministers and heads of development agencies from recipient countries as well as bilateral donors and multilateral organizations. The process was driven by the OECD DAC, but the EU also played a key role in setting the agenda (Holland 2008). The first such forum took place in Rome in 2003 and resulted in a short and highly general declaration on harmonizing donor practices and urging donors to base their assistance on the priorities of the countries receiving it. Breakthrough however came with the second high level forum in Paris in 2005. The resulting Paris Declaration on Aid Effectiveness has since become the most widely cited element of the Global Consensus on Foreign Aid relating to aid quality. Its main novelty is that it included a set of clear, highly specific, in some cases even heavily technical targets, together with an action-oriented roadmap on achieving them by 2010 (UKAN 2011). The Paris Forum also created a mechanism for monitoring progress, with the OECD DAC in charge.

The goals of the Paris Declaration are organized into five fundamental principles (OECD 2008):

1 Ownership: developing countries set their own strategies for poverty reduction, improve their institutions and tackle corruption.
2 Alignment: donor countries align behind these objectives and use local systems.
3 Harmonization: donor countries coordinate, simplify procedures and share information to avoid duplication.
4 Results: developing countries and donors shift focus to development results and results get measured.
5 Mutual accountability: donors and partners are accountable for development results.

Within these five principles, twelve specific targets were also elaborated, which include untying aid, building and using reliable recipient country public financial management systems, creating operational development strategies, recording aid in recipient budgets, better coordination of technical assistance, reducing parallel implementation units, providing more predictable aid, etc. This was the first time in the history of foreign aid that donors and recipients agreed on a shared set of goals to make aid more effective and also established a mechanism to actually monitor progress towards these goals.

However, as its name shows, the Paris Declaration was not an international treaty, but only soft law at best, and as such does not need to be transferred to the domestic legal systems of the countries that signed up to it and thus cannot become legally binding. The enforcement mechanism relied on peer pressure and "naming and shaming" non-complying countries, which clearly proved inadequate, and thus the third high level forum in Accra in 2008 mainly called for accelerating the implementation of the Paris targets. The resulting Accra Agenda for Action (AAA) took stock of progress and proposes specific ways of implementing the Paris targets. Accra also represented a significant step in broadening the Global Consensus on aid by involving representatives not only from donor and recipient governments and intergovernmental organizations, but also from civil society. The OECD's website on the history of the high level forums argues that "[t]he principles put forward in the Paris Declaration and Accra Agenda for Action have gained support across the development community, changing aid practice for the better." By 2011, 160 countries and 52 international agencies had signed up to the Paris Declaration and the AAA,[1] and there are almost no voices criticizing the need and rationale of the goals.

Critics mainly focus on the lack of political will of donor countries to implement the targets (Martini *et al.* 2012). In fact, as Chandy (2011) argues:

> [t]he Paris Declaration put forward a bureaucratic solution to a problem that is largely political. Certainly, most of the inefficiencies in today's aid system are manifested as bureaucratic failings ... But many of the underlying causes of aid inefficiency concern politics and the incentives these create for determining aid allocations and modalities ... which donor agencies have been largely unable to resolve.

Thus, while the targets of the Paris Declaration truly address real existing problems, they remain on the technical level and do not consider the political reasons which cause the problems in the first place. Increasing ownership, as well as harmonizing aid with other donors and aligning it with recipient systems, may seem like technical issues, but they clearly decrease the level of control donors have over their aid policies. Donors therefore seem to regularly profess commitments, but rarely fulfill them (Chandy 2011), which is supported by data as well. The last report the OECD published on monitoring the Paris goals states that only one target was achieved universally by the original deadline of 2010, and all the others were off track (OECD 2011a). Figure 3.2 shows a breakdown of individual donor performances in meeting targets—the majority of donors have not met more than three of the targets. Nunnenkamp *et al.* (2013) even argue that coordination among donors has become worse since 2005.

The fourth high level meeting in Busan in 2011 should be noted for attempting to broaden the Global Consensus. With more than 3,000 participants, it was the largest such forum to date, and has attempted to incorporate emerging (non-DAC) donors, with a strong emphasis on the BRICS countries, as well as civil society and private funders of development into the aid effectiveness framework. Emerging donors like Brazil previously saw the aid effectiveness processes as based on the experiences of developed countries and unsuitable for the realities of new donors (Cabral *et al.* 2014). The Busan high level forum introduced

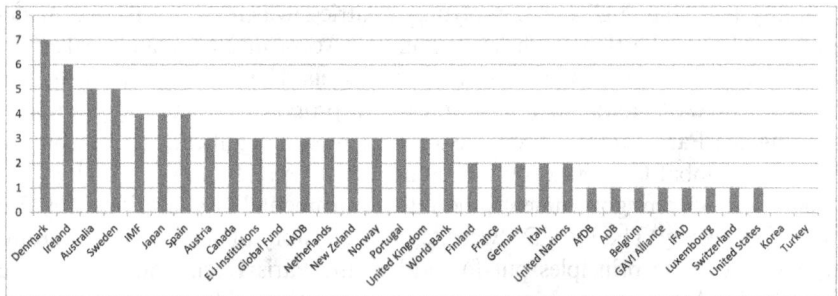

Figure 3.2 Number of Paris declaration targets met per donor
Source: UKAN (2011).

the vague concept of "differential commitments," meaning that emerging donors do not have to subscribe to the same commitments as members of the OECD DAC do, thus making the global aid effectiveness agenda more acceptable to these countries (Purcell *et al.* 2011). The inclusiveness of the Busan forum was also manifest in the fact that it marked a change in language: instead of talking about aid effectiveness, the emphasis shifted towards development effectiveness, implying a degree of broadening in the scope of the agenda. As with Accra, Busan also attempted to generate political will for countries to continue with implementing aid effectiveness efforts.

While there is a clear rhetorical consensus surrounding the Rome to Busan process, evidenced by the widened participation and frequent references to the documents by donors, clearly it is plagued by the same problems that are apparent in the half-hearted efforts of donors at increasing aid. These findings again underline the fact that the Global Consensus on Foreign Aid should be seen mainly as a rhetorical consensus with varying effects on donor practices.

After the turn of the Millennium, a series of international conferences have created an international framework for increasing the size and quality of foreign aid, which we have termed the Global Consensus on Foreign Aid, reflecting the fact that these conferences all aimed for wide participation and unanimous decision-making, which has given the results a wide legitimacy, even if the implementation of the decisions has been uneven. The two pillars of this consensus are quantitative (increasing aid volumes) and qualitative (increasing aid effectiveness), and have resulted in a set of recommendations to countries on how much aid to give and how to give it. The Global Consensus has clearly had some impact on donors and their aid policies, although as discussed above there are many shortfalls from the ambitious targets. The EU, and the European Commission in particular, have acted as champions of the Consensus not only in being the main driving force behind the process (Holland 2008), but also in translating and even expanding it on the EU level. Since 2000, the EU has developed a "European version" of the Global Consensus on Foreign Aid, which, in many issues, is even more ambitious and includes detailed and specific recommendations for the foreign aid policies of the EU member states. We now turn to analyzing this.

3.3 The Global Consensus and Europe

The EU has done much in the past decade to translate the Global Consensus on Foreign Aid into its own body of law, the *acquis communautaire*, and even go beyond it in some aspects. In a broader sense, the EU's common development policy has undergone a spectacular change since the turn of the millennium (Carbone 2007; Holden 2009; OECD 2012), which most observers agree has made EU aid more effective in reducing poverty. It is not only the effectiveness of aid disbursed by the European Commission (EC) from the common budget or the European Development Fund (i.e. the EU's common development policy) which has increased, but the Lisbon Treaty (and the Treaty of Maastricht before it) gave the EC a role as a coordinator of the bilateral development activities of member states as well. Article 210 of the Lisbon Treaty states the following, which is broadly similar to Article 130x of the Treaty of Maastricht:

> 1. In order to promote the complementarity and efficiency of their action, the Union and the Member States shall coordinate their policies on development cooperation and shall consult each other on their aid programmes, including in international organisations and during international conferences. They may undertake joint action. Member States shall contribute if necessary to the implementation of Union aid programmes.
> 2. The Commission may take any useful initiative to promote the coordination referred to in paragraph 1.

The EC has been trying to make as much of this role as possible by formulating and promoting a wide range of recommendations for member state bilateral development policies, in line with the Global Consensus on Foreign Aid. The EC presents these recommendations in the form of "Commission Communications," which are then debated in the relevant working groups of the Council and finally adopted in the form of Council Conclusions, Statements, or Resolutions. These form a body of soft law, which are clearly non-binding, "and rest solely on moral force" (Carbone 2007: 50). This soft law *acquis* includes important recommendations for member states on issues related to aid quantity, aid quality and aid allocation, which the member states are "invited to act upon," or should "strive" to implement. Wording and language used in these documents is crucial, leaving many aspects voluntary and also leaving much to the discretion of the member states (Schrijver 2009: 181).

The most important element of this body of soft law is a document whose name expresses its centrality in the EU system: the European Consensus on Development (European Consensus 2006). The title is a reflection of many issues. First, it indicates that European countries have reached a consensual agreement on the main principles that guide European development policy (covering both aid disbursed by the EC and by member states, which constitutes more than half of global official development assistance). Second, it implies that Europe is special. Europe has different ideas on how to promote development in poor countries as opposed to other donors. Specifically, the title implies a reflection towards the Washington Consensus, and signifies the ways in which EU aid differs from the policies advocated by the US and the international financial institutions dominated by it. Third, it may be understood as representing a European level interpretation of the Global Consensus on Foreign Aid.

Accepted in 2006, the European Consensus mainly discusses principles, practices and approaches for the common development policy managed by the EC, but also lays down several general recommendations on how member states should behave with regards to their bilateral development aid. Member states for example are required to make poverty reduction an explicit goal of their national aid policies, with a clear reference to meeting the MDGs. The

European Consensus also points to the Monterrey Consensus, and reaffirms the quantitative aid target of 0.7 percent, which the EU pledged to achieve by 2015. It also introduces separate targets for the new member states: 0.17 percent for 2010 and 0.33 percent for 2015, taking into consideration the fact that they are relatively new donors and also relatively poorer than the old member states. The Consensus should also be seen as a key policy coordination tool in terms of putting operational significance to the article in the founding treaties quoted above: it emphasizes the need to enhance coordination and complementarily: "Where appropriate, the EU will establish flexible roadmaps setting out how its Member States can contribute to countries' harmonization plans and efforts" (European Consensus 2006: C46/6). There are even explicit references to the broader goals of the Paris Declaration, clearly linking up European Consensus with the Global Consensus. But, it also goes beyond the Global Consensus, one aspect of this is that the European Consensus emphasizes the need for the division of labor between the EC and the member states, with each actor concentrating on areas where they have "comparative advantage," and also requires that member states strive to ensure the coherence of other policies with their development policies. On the global level, such division of labor between donors has not been strongly discussed. But, on the European level, with a central coordinator among the member states like the EC, it can at least enter political rhetoric, though implementation may not be easy.

Even several years after its acceptance, much of the European Consensus can still be seen as relevant. None the less, in order to bring the strategic framework of EU aid closer to changing realities, the Consensus was updated by a document entitled Agenda for Change in 2012 (Council of the European Union 2012a). The Agenda mainly seeks to answer the question of how the EU should react to the global changes that have happened since the European Consensus was accepted, such as the shift from aid effectiveness towards development effectiveness (apparent in the Busan outcomes), the rise of new emerging donors like the BRICS countries, and how the EU should relate to potentially disrupting events of democratization in partner countries, such as the Arab spring (Koch *et al.* 2011). The Agenda attempts to find the role of the EU in the global development system, and argues that the EU should focus on strengthening its unique face as a donor, with a clear focus on inclusive and sustainable growth (and not poverty reduction!), and also become a more consistent actor in promoting and strengthening democracy. Reassessing the allocation of EC aid is also mentioned, with a view of focusing more on the poorest countries. The Agenda formulates little new recommendations for the bilateral development policies of member states, but it does call for "joint programming, single EU contracts for budget support and common EU frameworks for measuring and communicating results" (Gavas *et al.* 2012).

The European Consensus and the Agenda for Change are complemented by a plethora of further EC communications and Council conclusions, mainly in specialized areas, but also detailing, operationalizing, and reaffirming the commitments in these two main papers. Many of these include further or more detailed recommendations on what member states should implement in their aid policies. We present the most important ones briefly below, focusing only on what recommendations they make for member states, and how they relate to the Global Consensus on Foreign Aid.

1   In 2002, well before the European Consensus was adopted, a Commission document stressed the untying of aid from exports both on the Community and the bilateral level (European Commission 2002). This need was reaffirmed by the European Consensus (which even talks about going beyond OECD recommendations, see paragraphs 29 and 50), and is also one of the targets of the Paris Declaration.

2   In the EU's Africa Strategy, the member states are encouraged to focus their development policies on Sub-Saharan Africa (Council of the European Union 2005). This is related to the provision of the European Consensus that members increase their aid to least developed countries, most of which are in Sub-Saharan Africa (European Consensus 2006: paragraph 24). The Monterrey Consensus calls for allocating at least 0.15–0.2 percent to least developed countries (United Nations 2003: 14), and the EC recommends that member states allocate at least half of any increase in their aid volumes to Africa, which is reminiscent of the Gleneagles G8 conclusions. Member states are, of course, free to choose which countries they want to assist in development.

3   In trying to convince members to increase aid, the EU sees legally binding aid growth trajectories as a good tool. Therefore, it recommends member states to set out timetables on how they plan to achieve the quantitative aid targets agreed in Monterrey, and reaffirmed in the European Consensus (European Commission 2007a: 8).

4   The EU has accepted a voluntary Code of Conduct on the Division of Labor for bilateral development policies in 2007 (European Commission 2007b), which along with other documents has emerged as an Operational Framework on Aid Effectiveness (Council of the European Union 2011a), with close links to the Paris Declaration and its follow ups. This framework focuses on operational complementarily between donors and includes, among others, broad guidelines on sectoral concentration (each donor should not be active in more than three sectors in a given recipient), delegated and joint partnerships, focusing on comparative advantages of donors and also improving recipient ownership. Guidelines on sectoral concentration can be seen as relatively specific recommendations on the implementation of the harmonization principle of the Paris Declaration.

5   The EU urges member states to make increased use of the budget support modality in their bilateral aid policies (Council of the European Union 2012b). Budget support, as opposed to traditional, project based aid modalities means that donors provide aid as a direct contribution to the recipient country's budget, giving the recipient much larger control over

how the money is spent. This is seen as a tool that promotes recipient ownership, as well as decreasing the problems caused by donor fragmentation, and it automatically entails the usage of recipient public financial management and other systems, as well as recording aid flows in budgets, all of which are Paris targets (Schiltz and Bichler 2009).

6   Policy coherence for development (PCD), i.e. making sure that the effects of other donor policies act in synergy, or at least do not go against the goals of development policy has not been a strong element of the Global Consensus on Foreign Aid, although the eighth MDG clearly talked about pro-development policy reform in areas like trade, finance, debt and intellectual property rights. Despite the lack of emphasis globally, within the EU it figures prominently in aid and development effectiveness discourses. PCD is mentioned in the Treaty of Maastricht, and the European Consensus includes an explicit requirement for EU common policies like trade (see Udvari 2011) and the Common Agricultural Policy to be coherent with development. Since 2007 the Commission also publishes an annual report on progress in the area, in which the performance of the member states is also assessed and evaluated (see European Commission 2013a). A 2012 Council Conclusion has an explicit call for member states to ensure coherence in other related policy areas (Council of the European Union 2012c).

7   Member states must also increase the transparency of their bilateral aid programs (Council of the European Union 2011b).

As mentioned, this rather large and continuously expanding body of development *acquis* must be considered as soft law, as they have mostly taken the form of Council Conclusions or communications from the Commission. The Council can only create "hard law" in the field when it regulates the common development policy. Very few aspects of this are directly applicable to member states, the most important is the European Development Fund (EDF), which is an extra-budgetary fund financing cooperation with the African, Caribbean and Pacific countries (Council of the European Union 2007). The *acquis* on the EDF obliges the member states to contribute financially to the fund, which is in addition to their contributions to the EU's common budget, and also lays down the rules for decision-making related to the programs financed by the fund. Other, more indirect references can be made by hard law, for example the tying of aid to national exports can violate the basic rules of the internal market, including European rules on public procurement (European Commission 2002: 9–10), and thus this can serve as a legal basis for untying aid. No member state however has faced legal consequences for tying its aid to date, and the EC has shown no intention of starting such legal proceedings.

The EC therefore has few tools to enforce compliance with the development *acquis*. While member states accept the conclusion documents when voting in the Council, they often see these as political documents and not something that should actually be implemented into their national legal systems on development. The EC has initiated a monitoring system called the EU Accountability Report on Financing for Development in 2002, which assesses each year how the member states stand on their commitments (European Commission 2013b). Originally designed to monitor progress towards the Monterrey commitments, the contents of the reports have become increasingly comprehensive over the years and now cover all major aspects of the development *acquis*. The report is based on questionnaires filled out by the member states without any verification by the EC. The reports are publicly available, and so are the individual member state questionnaires, but beyond this the EC has no possibility to impose sanctions in case of non-compliance. The influence of the EC on the ECE member states is discussed more in Chapter 5.

The EU has made important steps in translating the Global Consensus on Foreign Aid into the European context. The resulting European Consensus (understood here in a broad sense referring to all development *acquis*) now includes a wide range of recommendations for EU member states to implement in their bilateral aid policies. Compliance however is voluntary. The concluding section of this chapter operationalizes the elements of the Global and European Consensuses into a set of qualitative and quantitative benchmarks, against which the performance of the ECE member states can be assessed.

3.4 Summary—benchmarks for ECE development policies

The Global and European Consensuses include several elements that bilateral donors should implement in order to increase the amounts and effectiveness of their development aid. As discussed in this chapter, a strong political consensus has emerged around these measures, even if implementation remains uneven among donors. The ECE countries have all participated in the UN Millennium Summit and thus accepted the Millennium Development Goals. Their finance ministers were present in Monterrey (in case of Romania even the head of state was present). Most ECE countries, while not being among the states that originally drove the agenda, have since declared their confirmation of the Paris declaration and the Accra Agenda, with the exception of Slovenia, Lithuania and Latvia (OECD n.d.c). As members of the EU, the *acquis* on development policy also clearly applies to them, and they have accepted all the relevant conclusions in the Council.

The wide set of recommendations based on the Global and European Consensuses therefore clearly apply to the ECE countries. The question, which the following chapter aims to address, is to what degree they've actually implemented these regulations. In order to create a framework of analysis to judge the performance of ECE foreign aid policies, we derive ten benchmarks from the global and European documents against which ECE performance can be measured. Undoubtedly, many more indicators could be derived from the numerous documents discussed in this chapter, but our aim is to keep our framework concise and usable in practice. Our indicators incorporate some on the Paris indicators, but are much wider as they also refer to the MDGs, the Monterrey Consensus and the EU development *acquis*. We have opted for less technical indicators than what is included in the Paris Declaration in order to ensure a relative ease of measurement, and also include a number of qualitative benchmarks in order grasp the richness and complexity of the Global and European Consensuses. The ten benchmarks are the following:

1 An increasing volume of foreign aid, with a clear growth timetable set out with the view of achieving the 0.33 percent ODA/GNI target by 2015.
2 The existence of foreign aid policy documents which clearly make poverty reduction a central goal, with reference to the achieving the Millennium Development Goals.
3 An increasing share of bilateral aid allocated to least developed countries and countries in Sub-Saharan Africa.
4 A decreasing share of aid that is tied to procurement from national actors.
5 An increasing share of the budget support modality in bilateral aid in order to ensure ownership, harmonization and alignment.
6 The existence of country strategy papers which guide how aid is allocated within a recipient, and have been drafted through consultations with the respective recipient governments in order to ensure ownership.
7 Transparency of aid policies and predictability of resource flows, including the usage of multiannual programming.
8 Establishment of a "realistic" number of partner countries to ensure harmonization and reduce donor fragmentation.
9 Limiting activities to three sectors in each partner to promote harmonization and reduce fragmentation.
10 Use of country systems to ensure alignment, and coordination and cooperation with other donors through joint programming and other means.

The following chapter provides an overview of the history and main characteristics of foreign aid policies in the ECE countries, and discusses how these countries perform along the ten criteria above. Have the ECE countries embraced the Global Consensus on Foreign Aid and its European interpretation?

Note

1 See www.oecd.org/dac/effectiveness/countriesterritoriesandorganisationsadheringto theparisdeclarationandaaa.htm for a full list of adherents.

4 New development policies in the ECE countries

Chapter 4 focuses on describing development policies in the ECE new donors and evaluating their policies along the lines of the ten benchmarks identified in Chapter 3. It first provides an historical overview of the emergence of international development policies in these countries. This is followed by the description of the main characteristics of development policies today in these countries through the presentation of their performance along the ten benchmarks. The main conclusions arising from this comparative exercise are that (1) the Global Consensus on Foreign Aid and its European interpretation have yet to have a major impact on the development policies of the ECE countries, but (2) development policies in some of the countries (most notably the Czech Republic and Slovenia) are more aligned to it than those of others, leading to a heterogenization of ECE development policies. Explaining the general lack of compliance with the Global and European Consensuses, as well as the varying performance of the five countries will be the topic of the following chapters.

4.1 "And if you know your history"

Given the controversy over labels we highlighted in the introduction, and especially the issue of whether "re-emerging" donors is an appropriate name in terms of the relevance of past donor experiences, it is worth here revisiting development assistance in the ECE region under Communism.[1] While there was some research carried out during the Cold War on aid provided by the Soviet Union (Nayyar 1977; Kanet 1981), aid from the ECE countries during that time is still heavily under-researched and may be a fertile topic for political and economic historians. While we do have a good overall picture of the main drivers, directions, and approaches of Communist era ECE development policies (see for example HUN-IDA 2004 for Hungary, or Oprea 2012 for Romania), not much has been published on how political decisions were made, how much money foreign aid actually meant, and to what extent these aid policies in general are comparable to aid policies today (Waisová 2011: 88). This section cannot attempt to fill this gap as it is not the focus of this volume, rather it only presents a brief overview of pre-1989 development policies and their relevance today.

During the period of Communist rule, the former Soviet bloc tended to provide support to "socialist brother" countries or "friendly regimes" throughout the developing world (Grimm and Harmer 2005: 8). The "Second World" rejected any responsibility for the situation of the Third World, and the formal position was that supporting developing countries was the responsibility of the former colonial powers in the First World (Burnell 1997: 137). The state-led rapid advances in industrialization of the Eastern Bloc countries in the 1950s and 1960s acted as a model for many developing countries and resulted in the copying of centralized economic planning policies in several developing states. Aid from the Eastern Bloc was concentrated on countries pursuing a socialist development model and a foreign policy which was at least neutral or sympathetic to the Soviet Union. Aid was therefore characterized by a "strong and strategic orientation, concentrating on political allies and friendly countries which were pursuing socialist goals" (Carbone 2004: 244). This approach to aiding developing countries (many of them newly independent at the time) was in-line with the geopolitical and ideological interests of the Soviet Union based on the logic of the Cold War, and the members of the CMEA had little option but to follow. The Eastern Bloc countries had a limited scope of maintaining sovereign foreign policies in the shadow of Soviet domination, although some countries, most notably Romania did manage to diverge more than others (Oprea 2012). Other countries, such as Hungary, saw absolute loyalty to the Soviet Union in foreign affairs as a way to get some maneuvering space in domestic issues.

While ideology and the general opposition to what was seen as Western imperialism ran strong, aid was not meant to secure converts, but rather gain political and military influence, trade gains and, even, more altruistic development objectives (Burnell 1997: 138). The aid programs at the time did not make a difference between development aid or export credits, and all had significant military dimensions. This meant that comparisons to data on official development assistance from the OECD DAC donors are difficult because different definitions of aid were used (Browne 1990: 225). In a more general sense, blurring the boundary between development and military aid is only one reason why it is difficult to compare the pre-1989 foreign aid policies to modern day Western practices (see Dauderstädt 2002 for an overview of this process and the challenges). The values and practices of development cooperation have clearly changed: as one interviewee stated, "it is true that development cooperation had already existed in a lot of new member states but in a very different way."[2] Carbone (2011: 153) argues that "in terms of quality of aid, most of these countries made extensive use of project aid (instead of program aid or budget support) and of tied aid." Technical assistance, which of course is clearly important in the Western way of doing foreign aid as well, had perhaps an even greater prominence in pre-1989 ECE aid. In fact, aid provided by Hungary for example was officially termed "technical and scientific cooperation" (HUN-IDA 2004). Another important component was a rather massive number of higher education scholarships to students from friendly developing countries, with the vast majority of these students returning to their home countries after obtaining their degrees, which implies that brain drain was not a motivation for giving aid. The dominance of technical assistance and scholarships can be explained by the fact that the ECE countries, their national currencies being unconvertible, had little hard currency to spare, as most of it was needed to pay for imports from the West, and thus any economic assistance given was usually granted "in forms other than hard currency disbursements" (Després 1987: 157). Foreign aid was also heavily monopolized by the state, with state agencies being responsible for all aspects of implementation.

Little exact and reliable data is available on the level of resources the ECE countries actually devoted to foreign aid, and the sporadic data that can be reached is not comparable between countries, or even in time within a specific country. Czechoslovakia was seen to be second only to the USSR in terms of the aid it provided for developing countries (Starr 1982: 82), with some estimated suggesting it gave up to 0.74 percent of its GDP as aid (Després 1987: 156). Sporadic data for Hungary indicates that aid in general was around 0.2–0.3 percent of the country's national income in the late 1970s, but higher amounts were not rare either, with aid reaching 0.7 percent in 1980 and 0.45 percent in 1981 (HUN-IDA 2004: 10).

It was also worth noting that deep ties existed between the socialist states in ECE and less-developed capitalist states (Nayyar 1977). These relations were interconnected with trade issues, especially for goods that could not be produced in Europe, and the need to promote exports in order to obtain hard currency (Nayyar 1977; Kanet 1981). In fact, the economic hardships and increasing indebtedness of the ECE countries led to a decline of the ideological edge of foreign assistance in the 1980s, and also a gradual decay of the policy area.

It is of course a simplification to treat all ECE countries the same, even if their foreign aid policies were under heavy Soviet influence. Yugoslavia and Romania had more independence in their relations with developing countries than the "loyal five" of Bulgaria, Czechoslovakia, the German Democratic Republic (GDR), Hungary and Poland. Whilst these five states had autonomy over which states to support, their policies towards the developing world were "directly subordinated to the long-range goals" of the Soviet Union (Radu 1981: 13). Yugoslavia was part of the Non-Aligned Movement, and the country's leader, Josip Broz Tito was one of the main drivers behind it along with Jawaharlal Nehru and Gamal Abdel Nasser. Yugoslavia established the Solidarity Fund for Non-Aligned and Other Developing Countries in 1974. In terms of strategic policy, this fund had much of what is still considered "good practice" for aid donorship today: an articulation of principles and goals; a definition of comparative advantage, and clear selection criteria, with the aim of giving at least two-thirds of its grants to Sub-Saharan Africa and 20–25 percent to Asia (Grimm and Harmer 2005: 8). Romania's Nicolae Ceaucescu was also highly active in the Developing World, and engaged frequently on high profile multi-country tours, with little regard to whether the country was a friend of the Soviet Union or not (Oprea 2012).

Due to the differences between the Communist-era development policies and what constitutes modern aid, it is no surprise that an interviewee talked about "un-learning the old ways as a major priority."[3] Other observers concluded that "these countries have no great tradition of development aid and no development cooperation policy in the modern sense" (Michaux 2002) or that most ECE states "were novices in the field of modern international development cooperation" (Adanja 2007). In general, there was little talk among ministries of foreign affairs about building on past experiences, and rather the rhetoric used implied the need to build a new development policy from scratch in order to catch up with the West (Oprea 2012; Lightfoot and Lindenhovius Zubizarreta 2011).

With the collapse of the Eastern Bloc in 1989, the dual process of political and economic transformation happened at rapid speed. Regime change and revolutions, transformations of states and secessions from larger entities took place throughout East Central Europe. Political systems and economies were fundamentally and rapidly changed; so was the position of the entire region in the international system (Grimm and Harmer 2005). With the collapse of the Soviet Union, the ideological and political motives behind development policy to the Developing World countries disappeared. During the first half of the 1990s, the focus of the ECE countries was on domestic system transformation, which absorbed the major part of the domestic resources (Vencato 2007: 135). Due to economic crisis caused by the transition, poverty rates in the ECE states soared. The attention of Western donors quickly turned towards the region, turning the ECE states from donors of aid into recipients. Multilateral donors like the EU and the World Bank, as well as bilateral donors like the United States, Canada, Germany or the Netherlands all initiated assistance programs to the regions. The EU started the *Poland and Hungary: Assistance for Restructuring their Economies* (PHARE) program in 1989, which despite its name was extended to cover all ECE transition countries. But while Poland for example briefly became one of the world's largest recipients of aid in the early 1990s (Drozd 2007), these aid programs fell short of the expectations of people and governments in the ECE region, and did not turn into a "new Marshall Plan" as many had hoped for (Agnew and Entrikin 2004).

This transition period undergone by all ECE states saw their engagement with the developing world and any aid programs dramatically reduced (Carbone 2007: 47). Most aid programs that existed were terminated at the beginning of the transition processes in 1989/1990. However, some small degree of foreign aid was maintained. Scholarship programs to developing country students for example, while suffering heavy reductions in financing, remained intact (Szent-Iványi and Tétényi 2008: 577). Most ECE countries also maintained *ad hoc* cooperation with various multilateral United Nations agencies (such as the World Health Organization, UNICEF, or the UNDP), as well as humanitarian assistance. In the case of Hungary or Poland, supporting their respective ethnic minorities in neighboring countries emerged as a new form of aid, although it was usually not discussed in terms of international development policy, rather concepts like "nation-building" or "national unity."

4.2 A return to donorship

All ECE countries expressed aspirations early in the 1990s to become members of the Euro-Atlantic community and join the international organizations that represent this community, mainly NATO, the OECD and the EU. In the mid-1990s, some countries became eligible for OECD membership. The Czech Republic became a member in 1995, followed by Hungary and Poland in 1996 and Slovakia in 2000 (Slovenia only acceded in 2010). The OECD is often referred to as the "club of rich countries" (see Woodward 2009). Its Development Assistance Committee is the main forum for coordinating donor activities, sharing best practices and creating harmonized aid statistics (see Eyben 2012). While joining the OECD did not mean automatic accession to the OECD DAC, it did provide an increasing, although rather implicit international pressure towards the ECE countries to take a larger share in aiding poorer countries. Exactly how much impact this implicit pressure had will be explored in detail in Chapter 5; for now we just note that it is often referred to in case of the Czech Republic: the country often claims to have been the first state of former communist Central Europe to re-institute an official foreign aid program in 1995 (Hancilova 2000: 5). However, the rationale for an international assistance program probably first occurred to officials in newly-independent Slovenia. Slovenia's close proximity to the war in Croatia and Bosnia resulted in large-scale population flight to Slovenia in the early 1990s. This refugee crisis marked the first phase of Slovenia's (re-)entry into official donorship through humanitarian aid (Mrak 2002).

The "break with the past" in all ECE states had weakened the bureaucratic support for development aid (Drążkiewicz-Grodzicka 2010), and most observers agree that it was the accession process to the EU that had the single most decisive impact on the re-emergence of ECE development policies, which we discuss in more detail in Chapter 5 (see also Lightfoot 2010; Lightfoot and Lindenhovius Zubizarreta 2011). Some argued that creating (bilateral) international development policies was an explicit requirement for accession (Fodor 2003; Drozd 2007), but there is little evidence of this in any official accession negotiation documents. Development assistance was part of the accession negotiation chapter on External Relations (Chapter 26), which was provisionally closed between late 1999 and early 2000 and formally closed in Helsinki in 2002. This was unsurprising given that the regular Progress Reports of the EU did not indicate any substantial conflict (Dauderstädt 2002; Lightfoot 2008), and they voiced few specific issues. Annual progress reports published by the Commission usually gave brief descriptions of the state of development policies in the candidates, and summed up conclusions in sentences like "Hungary should have no difficulties in applying the *acquis* in the field of development policy" (European Commission 1999: 53) or "Alignment to the *acquis* is progressing satisfactorily [in the Czech Republic]" (European Commission 1998: 34).

Driven by these reports, the ECE accession countries all launched their official bilateral development policies between 2001 and 2003. However, the

European Commission's final monitoring reports in 2003 identified inconsistencies of the development policies of the new member states with EU principles (see for example the report on Poland: European Commission 2003: 57–58). It called for a revision of the development cooperation policies and increased attention to the EU's agreed principles and guidelines. More appropriate policies needed to be designed, which would combine the comparative advantages, specific experience and planned foreign policy priorities with the development co-operation strategies of the ECE countries (Bučar *et al.* 2007). Schmidt (2004: 5) argued that the states involved "have hardly any properly functioning organizations that could implement this policy; the legal basis and substantive definition of the issues are inadequate; and the financial resources available are below the average for the 15 states that were EU members up to May 2004." Despite this, "the final report produced by the European Commission in 200[3], nevertheless, concluded that all candidate countries had aligned their policies with the *acquis* in the field of external relations" (Carbone 2011: 153). It is therefore clear that the development *acquis* was not a deal breaker. The EU clearly had development on the accession agenda, "but considering the many essential political topics and policies that were discussed during accession negotiations, one cannot expect development to receive disproportional amounts of attention" (Carbone 2011: 153). The European Commission demanded rather minimal administrative and legal standards and the ECE states were able to show achievement of these standards or at the very least a clear direction of travel towards them.

In setting up the new development policies and approximating these as much as possible to EU and OECD principles and standards, the ECE countries received substantial capacity-building assistance from several established donors (Szent-Iványi and Tétényi 2012, 2013). These projects aimed at sharing knowledge with the new donors on issues like reporting ODA figures to the OECD DAC, project cycle management, efficient institutional structures, tendering and contracting, monitoring and evaluation, etc. Ministries of Foreign Affairs had little expertise in these fields, and thus this assistance was highly welcomed, even though the actual impact is not clear (see Chapter 5). Table 4.1 lists the capacity development programs in the region. The two most important programs were the "Official Development Assistance in Central Europe" (ODACE) program, carried out by the Canadian International Development Agency (CIDA) and the UNDP's "Emerging Donors Initiative." Both of these programs offered a wide range of capacity development activities, including traditional knowledge transfer through training, mentoring, workshops and on-site consultancy, as well as allowing the new donors possibilities for "learning by doing" through joint programming (CIDA) and setting up dedicated UNDP Trust Funds, essentially money from national governments, but programmed according to UNDP rules. The Western donor community therefore not only required the acceding ECE countries to start international development policies, but also gave them assistance in this through the transfer of knowledge and some limited resources.

Table 4.1 Major capacity-building programs for the ECE donors

Donor	Title of the program	Duration	Beneficiary ECE countries*
Canadian International Development Agency (CIDA)	Official Development Assistance in Central Europe (ODACE)	2001–2008	Cz, Es, Hu, Li, Lt, Pl, Sk, Si
Irish Aid	Irish Aid Mentoring Programme	2005	EU12 + Cr
Austrian Development Agency (ADA)	Regional Partnership Program (RPR)	2005–2007	Cz, Hu, Sk, Si
United States Agency for International Development (USAID)	Emerging Donors Initiative (EDI)	2006–2009	Bu, Cr, Cz, Hu, Pl, Ro, Sk, Si
Japan International Cooperation Agency (JICA)	no systematic program	2006–2008	Pl
Ministry of Foreign Affairs of the Netherlands	Strengthening the Implementing Capacity for ODA	2006–2007	Hu
Foreign Ministry of Finland	Twinning Light	2007	Hu
Swedish International Development Agency (Sida)	Partnership Program	2009–	Offered to all, with Es, Pl, Ro, Sk, Si being more involved
United Nations Development Program (UNDP)	Emerging Donors Initiative	2003–	Cr, Cz, Es, Hu, Li, Lt, Pl, Ro, Sk, Si, Tk
European Commission (EC)	Emerging Donors Capacity-Building Schemes I–IV	2004–	Bu, Cz, Es, Hu, Li, Lt, Pl, Ro, Sk, Si
Council of Europe North-South Centre (CoE-NSC)	Strengthening Global Education in the Visegrad countries	2004–2005 and 2009–2011	Cz, Hu, Pl, Sk in the first phase, later all others

Source: Szent-Iványi and Tétényi (2013: 824) and OECD (2005: 25).

Note: * Country abbreviations are the following: Bu—Bulgaria, Cr—Croatia, Cz—Czech Republic, Es—Estonia, Hu—Hungary, Li—Lithuania, Lt—Latvia, Pl—Poland, Ro—Romania, Sk—Slovakia, Si—Slovenia.

The transition process, as well as the international pressure to restart official development policies raises a number of important questions. Firstly, were the ECE countries economically ready to be donors? By the time of accession, they were classified as high income countries and many of them were members of the OECD, thus the answer must be yes. However, as Granell (2005: 10) argued there are real differences between the EU-15 and some of the new and future member states in terms of income levels: in 2000, Bulgaria's GDP per capita in purchasing power parity (PPP) terms was only 23 percent of the EU average; Latvia, Lithuania, Romania and Turkey were also below 30. Even the more advanced countries like Hungary or the Czech Republic were only around 40 percent. Some ACP, Mediterranean, Latin-American and Asian EU partners receiving EC assistance actually had higher incomes than the accession countries did. This then raises a further question. Were they socially ready to become donors? The self-perception of the societies at the start of the EU accession process was that they themselves are poor and that support should be given first at home. A significant part of the populations would argue that their country itself is in need of aid, and is not ready to provide aid to others. Political support for aid is also crucial (see Lancaster 2006). It seems that the politicians in the ECE countries were slow to grasp the uses of aid and politicians see aid as "difficult to justify to the public." To a large extent, the conclusions of a report commissioned by the European Commission sum up the situation prior to accession:

> [G]overnment commitment to development cooperation in the countries we visited is in general rather low, reflecting in part the lack of a significant constituency for development cooperation, as development NGOs are few and far between and the public supports mainly humanitarian aid to neighbouring countries.
>
> (Development Strategies and IDC 2003: 19)

It is easy to overlook now the political and economic challenges associated with creating a new political order in the region (see Elster *et al.* 1998). We can point to states such as Spain or Ireland who had taken a number of years to progress towards donor status. For example, Ireland joined the OECD DAC in 1985, whilst Spain joined in 1991. Greece, an EU member since 1981 only joined the OECD DAC in 1999. However, given the nature of the accession process and the nature of the EU action in the field, it is clear that more was expected from the ECE countries in this regard than in previous enlargement rounds. This issue, and the fact that the ECE countries were not necessarily ready to become donors supports the usage of normative labels like "premature donors" or "recruited donors" as discussed in the introduction of this book.

Although there is debate on how explicit EU pressure was, it is without doubt that the accession process was a key driver in re-creating international development policies in the ECE countries. As a senior Hungarian MFA diplomat put it in an interview: "Don't have any illusions. If the EU didn't require us to do development policy, we wouldn't be doing it. The returns are just too small."[4] But, the EU gave little indication as to how the acceding ECE countries should formulate their development policies, beyond references to vague EU principles. The EU's development *acquis*, and especially its body of soft law recommendations for member state development policies (as discussed in Chapter 3) was much less developed at the time of the accession negotiations between 1999 and 2002 than it is today, and there was little practical guidance on what member states should implement beyond general principles embodied in the founding treaties like complementarity and coordination (see Lightfoot 2008). This lack of substance, and more importantly the low political priority attached to development policy as opposed to key issues like regional policy or the Common Agricultural Policy, meant that development was seen as an "easy" issue. The accession states duly created their own bilateral development, but for the time being at least, did not attach any weight to it and did not see it as more than a technical hurdle. While the UNDP, CIDA and other donors attempted to assist making these new development policies meaningful by providing technical assistance, and they did play a key role in supporting the creation of the initial institutional structures and first aid projects, much of their longer term advice went unheeded. The impact of international influence on ECE development policies is discussed in more detail in Chapter 5.

These dilemmas surrounding the creation of the new aid policies in ECE are reflected well in the characteristics of the emerging policies, as well as their subsequent evolution. The following section examines how the new ECE development evolved in the decade after EU membership, and whether they have converged towards the recommendations of the Global Consensus on Foreign Aid and its European interpretation. Specifically, we analyze the evolution of aid policies in the region along the lines of the ten quantitative and qualitative criteria identified in Chapter 3.

4.3 Evolution of ECE development policies between 2004 and 2014

4.3.1 Aid volumes

The European Consensus explicitly states that "Member States which joined the EU after 2002 will strive to increase by 2015 their ODA/GNI to 0.33%" (European Consensus 2006). An interim goal for the new members of 0.17 percent was also set up for 2010. The wording ("strive to increase") can hardly be taken as a legal commitment, none the less it has become a frequent point of reference for the new members, and is invoked regularly, both by political decision makers, and NGOs engaged in advocacy (see for example CONCORD 2013). It is telling however that many of the new states wanted no reference to the 0.33 percent target in the European Consensus, not even in this highly soft form.[5] Table 4.2 provides an overview of how aid volumes per GNI have actually evolved in the ECE countries since accession, and also includes absolute ODA figures.

While there is a clear run-up in the first years after accession in the case of many countries, aid volumes in most cases seem to be marked by sporadic decreases and stagnation after 2006. This increase can be attributed to several factors. First, the ECE countries all started their bilateral programs, which though small in amounts, were none the less a significant addition to what they did previously. These were also assisted in the beginning by co-financing from CIDA, and the UNDP also obtained significant commitments from governments

Table 4.2 Aid disbursements in million dollars and as a percentage of gross national income in the ECE countries, 2003–2012

	2003	2004	2005	2006	2007	2008	2009	2010	2011	2012	2013
Czech Republic	145.0	152.2	177.4	198.4	191.9	224.2	206.8	223.7	230.2	219.6	209.3
	0.10	0.11	0.11	0.12	0.11	0.12	0.12	0.13	0.12	0.12	0.11
Hungary	29.5	83.6	114.9	174.4	99.9	93.8	113.6	111.9	128.9	118.4	115.9
	0.03	0.06	0.11	0.13	0.08	0.08	0.10	0.09	0.11	0.10	.
Poland	42.0	163.7	246.4	341.0	353.8	311.0	384.5	370.0	389.6	421.0	457.3
	0.01	0.05	0.07	0.09	0.10	0.08	0.09	0.08	0.08	0.09	.
Slovakia	28.0	43.4	82.4	74.1	74.4	86.8	72.0	73.6	80.5	79.7	81.6
	0.05	0.07	0.12	0.10	0.09	0.10	0.09	0.09	0.09	0.09	.
Slovenia	.	.	41.2	50.7	54.9	62.4	66.0	57.7	58.2	58.5	58.1
	.	.	0.11	0.12	0.12	0.13	0.15	0.13	0.13	0.13	0.13
OECD DAC average	0.25	0.26	0.33	0.31	0.28	0.31	0.31	0.32	0.31	0.29	0.3

Source: OECD (2014).

Note: Absolute figures are net disbursements in constant 2012 dollars.

through its Trust Fund schemes (Szent-Iványi and Tétényi 2013). Second, as national contributions to the development share of the EU's budget can be reported as ODA, EU accession had a direct statistical effect on ECE ODA flows. Third, the ECE donors at the time knew little about how to report their ODA statistics according to the standards of the OECD DAC.[6] CIDA and UNDP, as well as other capacity development programs included providing training on reporting ODA statistics, and due to these trainings ministry officials in the ECE countries were able to "find" several government expenditures which could be classified as ODA, again leading to increased statistics.

However, the shortfall from commitments, especially the interim goal of 0.17 percent for 2010 is rather spectacular for most countries. CONCORD's 2011 AidWatch sums this up perfectly:

> As for the EU12, no single country (except for Cyprus) has managed to reach its interim target of 0.17% of GNI. The worst performers in 2010 include Latvia (fulfilling only 35% of its 2010 obligations), Romania (41%), Poland (49%), Slovak Republic (50%) and finally Bulgaria and Hungary (both fulfilling merely 53% of their 2010 obligations). […] The EU12, in turn, account for only 5.6% of the shortfall (or less than Greece alone), due mainly to lower targets (0.17% of GNI) and smaller economies. Poland and Romania (with gaps of €295 and €119 million respectively) contribute to more than 50% of the funding gap of the EU12.
>
> (CONCORD 2011: 5)

The 2012 AidWatch Report reaches similar conclusions, but the ECE states were part of a group of 18 EU states that did not meet their target or show progress towards the target—a group that also included Germany and France as well as Greece and Spain (CONCORD 2012). The most often cited reason for this shortfall is the 2008 economic crisis, which put severe strains on government budgets in the region. As has been argued elsewhere "because there are few lasting [multiyear] governmental instruments, [ECE] development assistance has been very shock-prone and sporadic" (Horký and Lightfoot 2012: 8). The downturn of 2008–2009 demonstrates this fragility; "whereas 13 out of the EU-15 member states were able to raise aid from 2007–2008, only 4 out of the EU-12 states raised their levels" (see Horký and Lightfoot 2012: 8). Aid was seen as an issue where cuts could be made easily, due to the low political priority attached to the area. In the Slovak parliamentary discussion following the first reading of the Development Act for example, the former Minister of Foreign Affairs Eduard Kukan could state that: "Nobody will get mad if we will not fulfill the targets and we have to defend it internationally that we cannot be compared with Scandinavian and other countries active in this area for years and that we can reach required percentages gradually" (quoted by Drążkiewicz 2008).

The crisis not only meant lower aid figures because of explicit cuts. The Czech Republic for example managed to avoid cutting bilateral ODA up until

2013. Decreasing national incomes automatically cut contributions (and thus those that can be reported as ODA) to the EU, as they are capped as a percentage of GNI, thus lower GNI means lower EU contributions. The decrease in multilateral aid is a significant component of economic crisis-induced decreases in ECE ODA, as multilateral contributions mean the bulk of ECE aid, at times reaching 75–80 percent of total ODA expenditures, as opposed to 30–40 percent in the more established donors (see Table 4.3).

A final issue concerning aid volumes is that most ECE countries have not made an explicit commitment or formulated a legally binding roadmap on how it plans to reach the 0.33 percent target by 2015. The exception is the Czech Republic, which established "a multi-annual indicative timetable/minimum aid level commitment, approved by the national government" in 2010 (European Commission 2011: 25), but it is not available publically. Although politicians have frequently expressed aspirations to reach the target in all countries, not much has been written on how they would plan to do this. This lack of written commitment again shows how politicians have been reluctant in actually meeting the target. Hungary's 2014 ODA strategy is perhaps one document from the region that does include a certain roadmap, but it only promises modest annual increases of HUF 100 million (about €330,000) in the bilateral aid managed by the MFA (Hungarian Ministry of Foreign Affairs 2014: 32). The lack of written roadmaps in the region is especially striking when compared to some more established donors, such as the UK, which have formulated clear, legally binding agendas of reaching their own (0.7 percent) targets.

4.3.2 Aid strategies and poverty reduction

In terms of creating strategic and legal frameworks for foreign aid policy, the ECE countries have generally done rather well, and all have made poverty reduction a goal to some extent, at least on the legal/strategic level. Laws on development cooperation provide a framework in a sense that they detail the main goals and priorities of the policy area and mainly deal with setting down the responsibilities of actors in system. They all call on the government to create strategies that operationalize the principles embodied in the laws by specifying modalities of support, target countries, priority sectors and other

Table 4.3 Share of multilateral aid in total ODA per country, 2007–2013, in percentages

Country	2007	2008	2009	2010	2011	2012	2013
Czech Republic	54.7	46.9	47.0	65.2	69.4	69.8	73.3
Hungary	68.1	85.6	74.7	75.3	76.3	81.2	76.0
Poland	57.0	76.5	76.5	73.5	77.1	73.5	75.3
Slovakia	58.9	55.6	73.8	73.0	75.2	76.2	81.1
Slovenia	60.4	56.7	64.6	61.9	69.7	67.3	66.2

Source: OECD (2014).

Table 4.4 Legal and strategic documents on development cooperation in force in the
ECE donors in 2014

Country	Legal framework	Operational strategy	Poverty reduction made a goal?
Czech Republic	Act 151/2010 on Development Cooperation and Humanitarian Aid, and Amending Related Laws	The Development Cooperation Strategy of the Czech Republic, 2010–2017	Yes, but also other goals: democracy promotion, human rights, good governance and environmental protection
Hungary	No law on development cooperation	Government Resolution on the Framework strategy for Hungary's International Development Cooperation, 2014–2020	Yes (achieving the MDG's), but also other goals including creating markets for Hungarian firms
Poland	Development cooperation act of 16 September 2011, amended on 11 October 2013	Multiannual Development Cooperation Programme 2012–2015	Yes, but is not emphasized strongly. Democracy promotion and long-term social and economic development *leading* to poverty reduction are the two main goals.
Slovakia	Act No. 617/2007 Coll. on Official Development Assistance	Medium-Term Strategy for Official Development Assistance, 2009–2013	Yes, but also other goals: sustainable development, peace, economic cooperation.
Slovenia	Act 70/2006 on the International Development Co-operation of the Republic of Slovenia	The Resolution on International Development Cooperation of the Republic of Slovenia for the period 2008–2015	Yes, but also other goals: peace and human security, health, gender equality, sustainable development

Source: Compilation of the authors.

issues on the medium term. The relevant national laws and latest aid strategies
are summed up in Table 4.4.

The Czech and Slovak laws both include strong references to both the Global
Consensus (mainly the MDGs) and EU level documents such as the European
Consensus. Poverty reduction is a central goal in both cases, but a large number
of other goals are also mentioned, ranging from the promotion of human rights
and democracy to sustainable development. The law in Slovenia is similar in
terms of goals, but it does not make any reference to the MDG's, only to EU
level provisions. The Polish law is the only one where poverty reduction is
mentioned only as an indirect goal. In fact, the primary goal of Polish

development assistance is democracy promotion, and the secondary goal is long-term social and economic development *leading* to poverty reduction. The Polish law only includes a vague reference to "relevant provisions ... set by the European Union," and no explicit reference to the MDGs.

Hungary is the only country among the five which does not have specific legislation on international development policy. The necessity for such a law has been raised repeatedly by both official practitioners and the NGO community (see Hódosi 2012), and work has been carried out preparing various drafts, but none of these has ever been presented to Parliament. Hungary was also rather late in creating a strategic ODA framework, with the first such document (aside from a short 2001 concept note) only presented by the MFA in 2013 and approved by the Government in early 2014. This strategy mainly emphasizes the goal of Hungary's ODA in supporting the achievement of the MDGs (and any set of goals that may take over their place after 2015), but also mentions "gaining markets for Hungarian firms and certain parts of the state sector (e.g. education and health), as well as supporting the development of Hungarian knowledge and technology." While such "selfish" donor interests are often clearly drivers of bilateral aid policies, donors rarely emphasize them in written strategic documents. On the more progressive side, the Hungarian strategy also references a number of EU documents, most prominently the European Consensus. It also discusses many issues that the other countries have included in their laws.

The five ECE donors therefore clearly refer to the Global and European Consensuses in their legal and strategic documents on development policy. The extent to which this is merely paying lip service is important here. Preparing laws and papers stating that poverty reduction is a goal of aid policy is of course one thing, whether it is really so in practice is another. One way of looking at the poverty focus in practice is by examining aid allocation and how much resources the five countries devote to supporting the poorest recipients.

4.3.3 *Aid allocation and the share of LDCs and SSA*

There are some strong commonalities among the ECE donors in terms of their aid allocation, which sets them apart from other donors, the two most important issues are their focus on the European neighborhood and their relatively low attention towards the "traditional" target countries of foreign aid in Sub-Saharan Africa. According to the EU Code of Conduct (European Commission 2007b), the direction of bilateral aid, whilst up to the member state, should be used to support EU priority states and areas. In practice however there exists "a significant disjunction between the bilateral programmes of the new EU members ... and the approach being pursued at the EC level and by existing member states" (Granell 2005: 10).

Using aid allocation regressions for data between 2001 and 2008, Szent-Iványi (2012a) has identified three major groups of recipient countries of the Visegrád states (the Czech Republic, Hungary, Poland and Slovakia), which points to strong commonalities among them, and also supports previous evidence. The first group includes countries where the four donors are present due to international obligations, mainly their alliance with the US and NATO membership. Iraq and Afghanistan were the two major countries in this group, with the latter being more important. The Czech Republic, Hungary and Poland have operated Provincial Reconstruction Teams (PRTs) in Afghanistan, putting them in charge of coordinating reconstruction efforts in their respective provinces (see Hynek and Marton 2012; Marton and Eichler 2013), which also placed large pressure on the governments to provide disproportionately large amounts of aid to the country. Between 2006 and 2010 for example, a quarter of Hungarian bilateral ODA went to Afghanistan. However, the importance of this group has waned in recent years, and the PRTs have ended in 2013. While many ECE NGOs have signaled their intention to stay on in the country, large scale official assistance programs are most likely over.

The second group of recipients are countries in the immediate neighborhood, mainly in the Balkans and the CIS region. Stability and the promotion of democracy, as well as eventual accession to the EU are vital foreign policy interests for the ECE donors towards the region, and they are using their foreign assistance funds to pursue these goals. In 2012, Ukraine and Serbia were the two largest recipients of Hungarian aid (receiving almost 40 percent of bilateral ODA), which can also be explained by the fact that both these countries have sizable Hungarian minorities, which successive Hungarian governments have all made a priority in terms of support. In case of Poland, neighboring Belarus and Ukraine were among the top three recipients with 25 percent of bilateral ODA. Polish minorities (Rehbichler 2006), as well as democracy aid (mainly support to political NGOs) play an important role here. Slovenia's bilateral ODA focuses on six main countries: Albania, Bosnia and Herzegovina, Serbia, Montenegro, FYR of Macedonia and Moldova. These recipients are set down in law, which also stipulates that 80 percent of Slovenia's ODA "should be channelled in support of a geographic or thematic priority, and half of this should support both a geographic and a thematic priority" (Bučar *et al.* 2007). The importance of European partners for most of the ECE donors is illustrated well in Table 4.5 (with the exception of Slovakia, to which we return later).

The third group of recipients shows a degree of path dependence from the legacy of the Communist past of the ECE donors (Szent-Iványi and Tétényi 2008). This is an interesting conclusion as to a large extent the ECE states lost much of their development policy expertise and capacities during the transition period of the 1990s, but it seems that with the re-emergence of these policies, many of their pre-1989 partners also saw a comeback. A major group of recipients of the ECE donors are (former) Communist allies from the developing world. Official partners of the Czech Republic included Ethiopia, Cambodia, Palestine, Vietnam, Yemen and Mongolia. The first four are also official partners of Hungary. These countries all had ties with the Soviet

Table 4.5 Aid allocation of the ECE donors, 2008–2012, in percentages of total bilateral aid

	Czech Republic	*Hungary*	*Poland*	*Slovakia*	*Slovenia*
Europe	25.4	37.6	35.0	17.8	57.1
North Africa and Middle East	6.3	0.7	0.4	0.5	0.2
Sub-Saharan Africa	9.5	2.1	6.4	26.9	2.9
America	3.9	0.8	0.6	0.4	1.3
Far East Asia and Oceania	11.8	7.4	34.0	1.8	0.5
South & Central Asia	33.2	24.0	17.4	6.4	2.9
Unspecified	10.0	27.5	6.1	46.2	35.0
Memo: LDCs	35.8	24.7	13.0	25.7	4.2

Source: Calculations of the authors based on OECD (2014).

block at one time or another during the Cold War, either by having clear-cut Communist regimes (Mongolia, Vietnam, Cambodia) or governments, which at least rhetorically committed themselves towards leftist ideology and socialism (Ethiopia during the Mengistu regime, South-Yemen, Palestine). The importance of Communist path dependency is less evident today in case of Poland, although Vietnam is an important recipient, and the country had strong aid relations with Angola as well. One of the few major non-European partners of Slovenia, Cape Verde, also had a strongly socialist government during parts of the Cold War and ties to Yugoslavia. Slovakia is perhaps the country which has diverged the most from this past, as in 2012 it had no major "ex-Cold War" partners, which implies that the legacy of Czechoslovakia had a smaller impact on Slovak foreign aid policy than it did in the case of the Czech Republic.

It would therefore seem that aid allocation is not driven by poverty reduction considerations, as much of ECE aid goes to middle income European countries (Szent-Iványi 2012a), and not low income countries. This focus on specific regions is problematic. The overarching aim of EU development policy is poverty reduction, and therefore there is a steer that member states should concentrate on least developed countries and Sub-Saharan Africa where much of these countries are concentrated. As one interviewee from an old member state argued "what we see is that [the ECE states] have another type of perception of the world. Their history is in another part of the world. Not in Africa, but Moldova and other old Soviet states where old MS don't have any expertise."[7] This was reinforced by a statement from an ECE official: "for us the priority lies in the Western Balkans and the Neighborhood. We specialize in order to become competitive. There is a need to create added value. For us it is costly to have bilateral relations with Africa, therefore we rely on multilaterals in that region."[8] Indeed, most ECE countries argue that they already support Sub-Saharan Africa through multilateral means, such as contributions to the EU's European Development Fund, which provides aid solely to the ACP group of countries. In interviews it was clear that most new member states supported the EU's focus on Africa as long as support was also provided for countries they regarded as priorities.[9] ECE countries also argue that this is more effective than each of them being present in the region. One interviewee noted that there is "no need for everyone to be every-where."[10] This statement actually resonates well with the principles of division of labor among donors, also advocated by the EU's development *acquis* (European Commission 2007b).

As shown in Table 4.5, countries in Sub-Saharan Africa have a rather low share of ECE aid, with the exception of Slovakia, which, interestingly, has prioritized Sub-Saharan Africa in recent years, with Kenya emerging as the major partner. Figure 4.1 shows how the share of Sub-Saharan Africa in ECE bilateral ODA has evolved by donor between 2003 and 2012. In case of Hungary and Poland, there are periodic spikes in aid to the region, which reflect one-off debt forgiveness, mainly on debt originating from the Communist past. Hungary for example forgave a large debt of Ethiopia, and also one of Nigeria. After forgivable debt ran out, the share of SSA in case of both countries has remained almost negligible. In case of Slovakia, there was a constantly high share of SSA between 2004 and 2008, which was due to government commitment through the UNDP Trust Fund, which prioritized

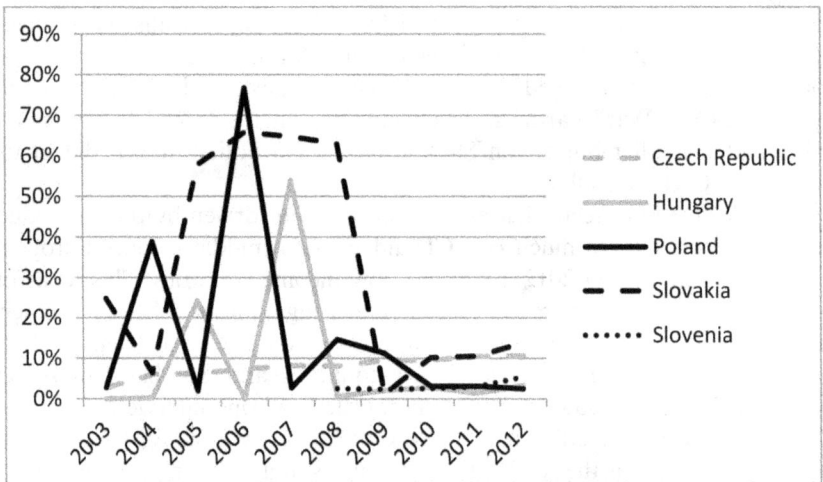

Figure 4.1 ECE aid to Sub-Saharan Africa (percentage of total bilateral aid, 2003–2012)
Source: Calculations of the authors based on OECD (2014).

aid to Sub-Saharan Africa. Aid to the region was reduced with the eruption of the economic crisis, but is still higher than in all the other countries and also shows a slow upward trend. A longer term upward trend is also visible in case of the Czech Republic and to a lesser extent, Slovenia.

Summing up, it is difficult to argue that Sub-Saharan Africa and LDCs are a priority for the ECE donors in their aid allocation, as recommended by the EU. No ECE country has taken any specific measures to ensure that any increase in their aid budgets will be channeled to Africa (European Commission 2011). Slovakia is clearly an exception here, which requires further explanation (see Chapter 7). Also, there is evidence of steadily increasing relative importance of Sub-Saharan Africa, mainly in the case of the Czech Republic. ECE countries justify their relative neglect of the region by pointing to another EU principle, the division of labor among donors.

We now turn to issues affecting the quality of ECE aid.

4.3.4 Tied aid

Exact data is very hard to find as to what percentage of ECE bilateral aid is tied, and under what conditions. While this practice can be found in all EU member states to some extent, due to efforts of the OECD DAC it has been cut back severely in the past decade: "from 1999–2001 to 2008, the proportion of untied bilateral aid rose progressively from 46% to 82%" (OECD 2009b: viii). It however seems highly pronounced and noticeable in the ECE region. Observers agree that most of ECE bilateral aid is tied (CONCORD 2007, 2013). For example, tied aid is seen to be a "business secret" in Hungary due to its importance to Hungarian businesses and export promotion (Lightfoot 2010). In case of Slovakia, "development co-operation is implemented solely by Slovak entities" (OECD 2011a: 16). In its Special Review of Slovenia, the OECD noted the following:

> The current business model maximises the role of Slovenian personnel, agencies and firms in the delivery of bilateral ODA. This model, based as it is on calls for proposals within Slovenia, limited to foundations or NGOs registered in Slovenia, does not promote alignment with developing country-owned strategies, harmonisation, mutual accountability or the use of developing country systems.
>
> (OECD 2011b: 15)

Without any clear time series data, it is extremely difficult to tell whether the ECE countries are decreasing the share of their bilateral aid which is tied or not. Government statements however show that the situation may not change quickly. Hungarian authorities have often proudly emphasized the benefits tied aid has for national businesses (CONCORD 2007: 35), and Hungary's 2014–2020 ODA strategy actually encourages the increased use of "tied aid credits." Indeed, most other countries also point to national business interests and the need to gather support for aid as the main justification for tying bilateral aid. Another frequent justification for tied aid is similar to the classic "infant industry" argument of trade protectionism: national actors which implement development projects are uncompetitive as compared to actors from say Western Europe, but tied aid will help them improve their skills and become competitive in the long run. Countries which have untied their aid only do so because their NGOs and private businesses are competitive anyway. This argument is illustrated well by the following quote from the Czech Development Agency (2013: 4):

> [The Czech Government is] keen to provide development cooperation through its own practitioners, thus improving their skills and increasing their prospects of involvement in future development activities at an international level, including development projects financed by EU funds.

However, membership of the OECD DAC for four of the ECE donors will place increasing pressure on them to become more transparent and publish data on the tying status of their aid, and the OECD DAC reviews all emphasize the importance of untying (e.g. OECD 2010: 26, 2011b: 5).

4.3.5 Budget support

In general, the ECE countries do not use budget support at all, and sector wide programs are almost non-existent as well. Several reasons for this are communicated. The Czech Development Agency (2013: 4) provides a highly telling quote here as well:

> The Czech Government is legally restricted from engaging in budget support. The Czech Republic prefers other forms of assistance, which, in view of its position as a smaller donor, it believes to be more efficient and more beneficial.

Other ECE countries also argue that they are simply too small to use budget support effectively, and the need for national actors to learn through project implementation is also a common theme. As ECE countries can only give relatively small amounts to recipients as budget support, they feel that this would not give them any leverage over the recipients. Other reasons may also include the fact that tying aid is much more difficult to ensure with the budget support modality, and it also decreases the visibility of national contributions. Project financing is more attractive as it allows member states to "fly the flag" on development aid and therefore can help raise public awareness. "Putting national flags on projects is something we all do. To show how nice and good we are," as one official argued in an interview.[11] The following quote from Slovakia is representative of views in the region: bilateral aid is important because it is a "direct tool of foreign politics, draws on Slovak experience, deepens relations with developing countries and effectively helps Slovak subjects to entrench in developing countries" (cited by Vittek and Lightfoot 2009: 27). These goals would be much more difficult to reach with small amounts of program aid.

As with tied aid, it is difficult to see any signs of this position changing. Membership of the OECD DAC is unlikely to have any impact, as increasing the share of program based aid has not been such a strong area of work of the OECD DAC as untying has. Change most likely will only come once the bilateral aid programs increase in size. However, size may not be an excuse: Luxemburg, which has a development aid budget smaller than that of Poland, does use sector-wide programs, and has been investigating the possibility of introducing budget support due to calls from its recipients (Schiltz and Bichler 2009).

4.3.6 Country Strategy Papers

According to recommendations of the EU *acquis*, a donor's aid allocation *within* a recipient should be guided by a country strategy paper, drafted through consultations with the respective recipient governments in order to implement the ownership principle of the Paris-Accra-Busan aid effectiveness agenda. These papers should be meaningful and specific enough to serve as a basis for programming. The ECE donors have made important steps in developing these strategies, but there are important disparities between the five donors.

The Czech Republic has gone the farthest in terms of elaborating country strategies, and currently has five such papers for its five "program" countries in the 2010–2017 period, Afghanistan, Bosnia and Herzegovina, Ethiopia, Moldova and Mongolia. Each of them is publically available in English. These strategies follow the recommendations of the EU and include all necessary elements. They also clearly draw on national priorities of the partners, although it is unclear to what extent representatives of the partners were actually involved in their development. According to the OECD (2007: 20), Czech development policy is highly donor-driven and the recipients have little influence on planning and programming resources, thus one is rightfully skeptical about recipient "ownership."

Hungary does not have publically available country strategies. The MFA did formulate strategies for three priority countries (Serbia, Bosnia-Herzegovina and Vietnam) in 2006, and made these publically available (although only in Hungarian). These papers have expired in 2010, and no successors have emerged. The three papers have received much criticism, as they were more descriptions of the development situation in the three partners and detailed descriptions of past Hungarian assistance granted to them, and were not really strategies in the conventional sense, as they did not include any clear development goals, or details on how to achieve them. They were not discussed with the partner governments either. Due to this nature, there were not many specific things in the strategies to implement, and most likely they did not have any influence on practice. The Hungarian government has signaled its intention to develop both regional strategies and country strategies between 2014 and 2020, but there is no information on how this process will happen and to what degree recipients will be involved in it.

Poland does not have publically available country strategies (Kugiel 2012a). According to the NGO Minority Rights Group, the relatively recent Polish Law on development cooperation and the related Multi-annual Development Cooperation Programme should provide a push for Poland to development country strategies, as it has the necessary capacities for the process. The lack of country strategies "reduces the impact of Polish aid in the partner countries of the Eastern Partnership as well as in the global South. ... CSPs are missing element in the Polish development cooperation system; they are needed to guarantee effectiveness of the policy" (Kochanowicz 2012a: 3–4).

The Slovak government started work on country strategy papers in 2009 for its three program countries, Kenya, Afghanistan and Serbia (Vittek and Lightfoot 2009: 27). The first strategy however was only published in 2013 for Kenya covering aid to the country between 2014 and 2018 (SlovakAid 2013a), which "builds on the Kenyan national long-term development strategy and it has been designed in close cooperation with all development partners including Kenyan Government and Kenyan and Slovak NGOs" (SlovakAid 2013a: 2). The other two strategies (if they exist) have not been made public.

Slovenia does not have publically available country strategies at all. Official bilateral agreements on development cooperation with individual partner countries however are accessible on the MFA's website, and so are bilaterally signed annual programs with some partners. The agreements are too short and general to be considered as country strategies, and the annual programs, while sufficiently detailed in terms of sectors and projects only cover single years and give no indication as to how the selected projects address the needs of the given partner.

4.3.7 Transparency and predictability of resource flows

The transparency of their aid programs is a severe problem for most ECE donors. Most of them do have government websites where they publish descriptive information which usually reflects government rhetoric. Development strategies are also usually accessible, and they all publish annual reports on their development cooperation, although that of Hungary is only available in Hungarian. Beyond this however, finding information on aid allocation is difficult (it can only be done through the OECD's statistics portal), and it is basically impossible to find project-level data. The main exception is the Czech Republic, which publishes rather detailed project information on the Czech Development Agency's website (although it is unclear whether all projects are presented, or only a selection), and the results of evaluation reports are also made public, some in English.

The 2013 Aid Transparency Index generally ranks the ECE donors as poor or very poor in terms of transparency. The best performer among the five countries is the Czech Republic, which ranks 35th out of 67 donor countries and organizations. Slovakia is 55th, Poland 57th and Slovenia 58th, with Hungary performing the worst at position 64 (Publish What You Fund 2013: 16–17). None of the five countries have joined the International Aid Transparency Initiative (IATI), a voluntary, multi-stakeholder initiative that seeks to improve the transparency of aid, in line with the global aid effectiveness agenda and the commitments of the Busan Partnership. NGOs regularly call on their national governments to become more transparent, publish data regularly, join the IATI and implement its principles (CONCORD 2012).

The Czech Republic clearly stands out in this regard, and according to the Aid Transparency Index, its development policy is more transparent than that of Finland, Luxemburg, or the US State Department. Czech NGOs, while acknowledging the efforts of the government in increasing transparency, call on it "to continue adopting concrete tools towards meeting the ODA transparency standards and signing the IATI" (CONCORD 2012). Hungary also stands out as the least transparent, although to be fair, in recent years the Hungarian MFA has been publishing much more data, even on the project level, but only in Hungarian. None the less, Hungarian NGOs have had several conflicts with the MFA in getting access to data in the past decade (Kiss 2011: 6).

The lack of transparency may not be specific to international development policies, but may be a wider government issue in these countries. ECE countries generally rank lower in the Corruption Perception Index published by Transparency International (2012: 4) than the Western European countries do. Thus, expecting greater transparency in development policy can be to some extent unrealistic. None the less, membership of the OECD DAC will have a clear impact on transparency as countries are required to report much more detailed data, and also data they do not report at all.

The predictability of aid flows is another issue where the ECE countries have severe deficiencies. Multiyear aid commitments to recipients, and more specifically, multiannual programming could greatly enhance this, but this has been difficult to implement as national budgets are typically decided on an annual basis and development cooperation has not been seen as sufficiently important to merit separate attention. Four out of the five countries typically commit funds in programming documents (if they exist) for a single year only (HTSPE 2011), with Slovenia being the exception. This of course does not mean that the other countries do not fund multi-year development projects, but that the budget of these projects for the second and following years is never certain. Hungary for example does not use multiannual programming at all, and in fact even annual planning seems problematic. As highlighted by an interviewee from a development NGO,[12] it has happened on several occasions that the call for proposals was only published in September, and projects had to be implemented by the end of the year. The Czech Republic's 2010–2017 Development Cooperation Strategy mentions "the inadequate fixing of multi-annual financing" as one of the main persistent negative issues hindering the effectiveness of Czech development efforts (Czech Ministry of Foreign Affairs 2010: 10). The situation is similar in Slovakia (OECD 2011b: 21).

None the less, there are some exceptions and attempts to overcome the difference between the short-termism of budgetary cycles and the long term perspective needed for development. Poland's Public Finance Law allows for multiyear financial planning, which ought to make it possible for development cooperation to move to multi-year financing (OECD 2010: 20) No references to this however are made in legal and strategic documents. Slovenia has gone perhaps the furthest, as the Act on Official Development Assistance calls for multi-annual financial frameworks with program countries. The country has a multi-annual program budget, basically a two-year rolling budget with forecasts for two further years, and this has enabled the MFA to program funds across years. The MFA runs multi-annual programs in the Western Balkans, with plans to do the same in Moldova and Cape Verde (OECD 2011c: 16).

4.3.8 Number of Partners

Restricting the number of countries a donor gives aid to and concentrating resources is an issue for almost all donor countries, not just those in ECE. However, as bilateral aid provided by the ECE countries is quite small (the World Bank often funds single projects that are larger than the total bilateral aid of Hungary or Slovakia, and their overall bilateral aid budget is smaller than that of a well-funded Western NGO), it is particularly important that these countries concentrate their resources on a few countries only to avoid fragmentation and ensure impact. According to a report commissioned by the World Bank, "while talking about limiting their number of partners, the ECE emerging donors actually have a wide number of partner countries, which can be comparable to the number of partner countries more established donors have." (Szent-Iványi and Tétényi 2012: 12). What however is a "realistic number" of partners? Is it three? Is it twenty? The EU *acquis* does not give any guidance on exact numbers. All donor countries face pressure to fragment their aid to several countries due to political reasons, thus finding and maintaining a realistic number of partners has not been easy. As expressed by an especially vocal interviewee from an ECE ministry in 2008, "we make *our* decisions on geographical and strategic pathways, and will not tolerate anyone to tell us what to do."[13]

One way of looking at the issue is by examining the number of official partners that a country has, as declared in official aid strategies or other government documents, and how this number has evolved in the past years. Most countries have actually been steadily decreasing the number of official partners. The Czech Republic for example aims for five program and five project countries, and is currently phasing out aid from its other three partners (as advised by the OECD DAC review of 2007). In 2006 the Slovak

MFA started to narrow down the priority countries as it was shown that these were set "too broadly." The country reduced the number of partners from 19 in 2009 to about 12 in 2012 (Kugiel 2012b), and has made significant effort to focus on three program countries (Afghanistan, Kenya and Moldova). Still, as noted by the OECD DAC Special Review, "Slovakia should support fewer bilateral and multilateral aid activities" (OECD 2011a: 7). Hungary had 16 partners in 2003 (Paragi 2010: 207), and while there has been much talk of decreasing this number, there have been few results. The 2014–2020 strategy on development cooperation does not even name partner countries, only three broad target regions (Africa and the Middle East, South-East Asia, Eastern Europe and the Western Balkans). There is no clear trend in reducing the number of partners in Poland either, where the 2012–2015 Multiannual Development Cooperation Programme lists 20 partners, and also mentions a Small Grant Scheme, which provides funds to all developing countries where there is a Polish embassy. The OECD DAC peer review highlights that "the Polish ODA business model was built on generating small-scale support for a large number of countries" (OECD 2010: 33). Slovenia also still maintains a relatively large number of partners with four program and four project countries, although the MFA is planning to reduce the fragmentation of aid by focusing on a smaller number of multi-year programs/projects and fewer partners (OECD 2011b).

Therefore, at least some of the ECE donors seem to follow the word of the *acquis*, but do they follow its spirit? The *acquis* aims to avoid fragmentation by limiting the number of partners, but what if many other countries receive aid besides the officially declared partners? Instead of looking at *de jure* partners, it may make more sense to look at *de facto* ones, and examine how large a share of bilateral aid they received. Table 4.6 shows the share of the top ten recipients in the five ECE countries. If the spirit of the *acquis* were heeded, the shares of the top ten should be increasing, signaling a decline in fragmentation. However, the data actually shows the opposite—ECE aid has actually become much more fragmented between 2005 and 2012! The decreasing share of the top ten is especially striking in Slovakia and Hungary, and there is a smaller decrease in Poland and Slovenia as well. The Czech Republic is the only one that does better, but the 2011/2012 share, while higher than the 2005/2006, is a deterioration compared to 2008/2009. But even the Czech Republic raises questions. In 2012 for example, it gave small amounts of aid to a total of 89 countries. The amounts granted to the 13 official partners were only 61 percent of total bilateral ODA. There were also several large partners that did not figure on the official partner country list, like Ukraine, Myanmar, Syria or Belarus.

4.3.9 Number of Sectors

The same issues arise with limiting sectors as with reducing the number of partner countries. The EU encourages member states not only to reduce aid to three sectors per country, but also to support sectors in which they have a

Table 4.6 Share of top 10 recipients in bilateral ODA, percentage

	2005–2006	*2008–2009*	*2011–2012*
Czech Republic	49.3	64.9	54.1
Hungary	86.2	70.4	62.9
Poland	94.1	88.6	87.9
Slovakia	91.7	60.2	39.2
Slovenia	n.d.	59.4	56.5

Source: Calculations of the authors based on OECD (2014).

comparative advantage. For new member states, these sectors are said to include democratization, market liberalization and managing transition to EU membership, including the transition from aid recipients to donors, offering as they do firsthand experience of the regulative and institutional transition process from centralized planned economy to market economy (Bučar *et al.* 2007). In short, this potentially large body of knowledge has been termed "transition experience" (Horký 2012; Szent-Iványi 2014).

The ECE countries have been rather vocal in emphasizing this unique value added that they bring to the international donor community and have also been calling on the EU to acknowledge and support this (see Czech Ministry of Foreign Affairs 2011). All five countries have made the promotion of democracy in their partners a priority (see the edited volume by Kucharczyk and Lovitt 2008; Pospieszna 2014), and there is much anecdotal evidence of projects featuring the transfer of transition experience. In the Western Balkans for example, Slovakia sees its expertise in the region as bringing "added value" at the European level (Haughton and Malova 2007) and the country has also been very active in assisting the democratic transition in Tunisia and other Arab states (Mikulova and Berti 2013). The Czech Republic is supporting the opposition in places like Cuba and Myanmar, and Hungarian NGOs are active in helping the development of civil society in Serbia and Bosnia.

Most of the ECE countries have even created dedicated programs or organizations to make transition experience a more visible component in their international development policies (Végh 2013) by providing grants to national actors to engage in international experience sharing projects. In the cases of the Czech Republic and Slovakia, these are dedicated programs under the MFA, the Transition Promotion Programme in the former and the Transformation Experience Sharing Programme in the latter. In 2011 the Polish government created the International Solidarity Fund, a re-granting agency aimed to support democracy promotion projects abroad. In Hungary, a government sponsored but independent non-profit organization, the International Centre for Democratic Transition "collects the experiences of recent democratic transitions and shares them with those who are determined to follow that same path" (ICDT 2014).

However, exact data on the extent of transition experience as an actual specialization is hard to come by, as it is multisector in nature and thus not reported in conventional OECD DAC statistics. But even if it were, the Czech Republic is the only donor among the five which publishes sectoral allocation data. Transition experience has also received substantial criticism as to how much it can be seen as actual specialization or a form of comparative advantage. Transition management is often seen as being too specific to EU accession to be of use outside a small number of applicant and potential applicant states, mainly in the Western Balkans. Can the ECE countries build their bilateral development policies on this in other regions as well? Horký and Rusin (2006) argue that, while the ECE experience is not directly applicable to Africa, specific areas of transition (good governance and trade agreements), "would be valuable for African countries, especially the less developed ones." A second issue is whether transition experience is actually transferable or not, and how can it be adapted to the local context? (Horký 2012; Szent-Iványi 2014). A third issue is whether there is actual demand for this experience in the partner countries. Clearly many countries are undergoing economic and/ or democratic transitions in the developing world, but do they need ECE experience, even if it is tailored to their contexts? One cannot help the feeling that transition experience is just a re-branding of supply driven technical assistance. Fourth, transition experience has become an all-encompassing buzzword that MFA officials frequently use when justifying the added value of their international development policies, but there is not much hard data to support claims on just how important it is.

Other sectors and comparative advantages are also mentioned by the ECE donors. In fact, the various legal documents and strategies outlined in section 4.4.2 all list a number of priority sectors. Hungary for example has recently been highly vocal on its expertise in water management, and the 2014–2020 development cooperation strategy expands this to the "green economy" as a major activity cluster. The fact that Budapest hosted the World Water Summit in October 2013 was seen as a major diplomatic success by Hungarian development professionals. No sectoral data is available on Hungarian aid, however it is telling that in 2012 only two bilateral development projects were related to water management. The recent strategy also mentions institutional development (including democracy promotion and the transfer of transition experience) and human resource development as the two other sectors of Hungarian bilateral aid. Listing only three sectors as priorities is highly welcome, even if these sectors are fairly broad. However, it is not clear whether Hungary will actually focus on these sectors.

The OECD DAC peer review of Czech Republic outlined that the "objectives of Czech international development co-operation tend to cover many areas, potentially leading to the dispersion of Czech aid across numerous sectors and themes" (OECD 2007: 9). Part of the problem was that the dispersion of Czech bilateral aid across sectors reflected to a large extent the demand for projects coming from the line ministries involved in development co-operation. This produced a situation in 2005 where the share of individual sectors in bilateral ODA was: 29 percent for environment, 24 percent for industrial development, 12 percent for agriculture, 12 percent for education, 7 percent for development education, and 7 percent for migration. These sectors were different from the ones the Czech Republic claimed to have a comparative advantage in, which included health care, education, energy production (Bučar *et al.* 2007). There is evidence that since the reform of the Czech development cooperation system between 2007 and 2010 the situation has become better. In 2010/11 the main sectors were social infrastructure (including health and education, 50 percent), economic infrastructure (7 percent) and production (9 percent). While the two sector lists are not directly comparable, there is some evidence of increasing concentration. In 2013, the Czech Development Agency published a factsheet that lists supported sectors per partner country (Czech Development Agency 2013). While there are often more than three sectors per country, publishing such data shows some will to meet the EU requirements.

The OECD DAC peer review noted that "Poland's bilateral ODA focuses on ... sectors (governance, democracy and transition) where it has a comparative advantage but which do not necessarily address poverty or the Millennium Development Goals (MDGs) directly" (OECD 2010: 7). The sectors in which Poland highlighted an advantage were health, education, access to potable water, protection of environment, local structures capacity-building support for democratic institutions, improvement of public administration efficiency, development of cross-border co-operation, reconstruction of the economy. The peer review highlighted that by 2010 Poland was focusing on a smaller number of sectors in its seven priority countries, especially in Georgia and the Ukraine, but also that the fragmented nature of Poland's bilateral development co-operation was still an issue.

The priority sectors of Slovak development activities are divided into three areas: developing democratic institutions and market environment; infrastructure; and landscaping, protection of environment, agriculture, food safety and use of raw materials. As the OECD DAC peer review showed:

> A more focused approach will deliver more and better results, higher visibility for Slovakia and greater scope for communication of achievements. The government should take forward its Manifesto commitment to reduce the number of partner countries and to focus more on using the transformation experience of Slovakia for the benefit of partner countries. The country's transformation experience, together with its knowledge of the eastern region of Europe and the Western Balkans, gives Slovakia a comparative advantage relative to other donors in these areas. Slovakia should therefore ensure that its comparative advantage as a donor more consistently informs its policy and selection of priorities and countries.
>
> (OECD 2011a: 7)

Slovak development cooperation focuses on four sector clusters, which are perhaps even broader than what other donors mention: building of democratic institutions; social development; economic development (including the building of market environment, strengthening of macroeconomic environment, public finance management); and infrastructure development. These are very broad sectors, which provide little opportunity for concentration in practice. Slovakia does not publish sectoral allocation data, thus it is difficult to evaluate practice (SlovakAid 2013b).

According to the OECD DAC peer review, since 2010 Slovenia is placing greater emphasis on three thematic areas: i) strengthening good governance, the rule of law and social sectors with a particular emphasis on transition assistance and institution-building, respect for human rights of women and children, education and scholarships; ii) environmental protection with a focus on sustainable water management; and iii) women's empowerment as a crosscutting theme. However, Slovenia does not publish detailed sectoral data either, again making it difficult to tell the actual extent of increasing concentration.

4.3.10 Country systems and coordination with other donors

There is little available data on the extent that the new donors use partner country systems. Due to the way they spend their aid (mainly tied grants to national NGOs), the issue is of relatively little importance, as there is actually little direct contact between national authorities of the ECE countries and those of the partner countries. Accordingly, none of the five countries have formal mechanisms in place to ensure the usage of country systems and implement the relevant provisions of the Code of Conduct on Division of Labour (European Commission 2007b). It is argued by officials that bilateral aid levels need to be significantly increased in order to make the usage of country systems a viable option.[14] Legal impediments are also cited, mainly referring to the fact that legal procedures for spending public money do not allow using non-donor systems. None the less, there is one positive example: 15 percent of Slovenian bilateral aid is delivered via a scheme for co-financing with the partner country and uses partner country systems for tendering (European Commission 2013b).

Donor coordination suffers from similar problems, and the main conclusion is that it is *ad hoc* in all countries, with no formal rules or procedures in place. While the ECE countries usually acknowledge the importance of working together, there seem to be several issues that limit just how much coordination they are willing and able to engage in. Consulting with other donors is made even more difficult due to a rather limited field presence of ECE countries, although many of them have assigned diplomats who are responsible for development in embassies in key countries, and the Czech Development Agency has also recently begun to create its own representative offices. *Ad hoc* donor coordination, which also involves joint or trilateral programming in some instances, is mainly driven based on the initiatives of more established donors. Sida, the Swedish International Development Agency for example initiated a capacity-building program for the ECE donors in 2009, which had a joint programming element.[15] The following excerpt from Szent-Iványi and Tétényi (2012: 79), based on interviews with Sida staff, shows the problems that this exercise faced:

> First Sida had to investigate where there was already existing interest among the new EU member states to work in partner countries through joint / trilateral programming. ... The initial response rate was low from ECE countries, which Sida attributed to the fact that at the time of the launch of the Partnership Programme there were severe budgetary issues in all these countries due to the financial crisis. Also, Sida formulated a number of criteria which had to be met in order to form partnerships, mainly related to procurement rules and certain standards set forth by the OECD DAC. Another issue that came up was that the new member states were rather focused on ensuring their own visibility and preferred to use standalone projects. Sida on the other hand preferred sector wide approaches and wanted to avoid small projects, both for administrative reasons and increased aid effectiveness. Since many of the new EU member states were not entirely aware of these processes, additional hands-on training had to be provided: for instance, when the Sida team in Kiev was approached for support by the Ministry of Finance of the Ukraine, Sida decided to try and include the Polish MFA as well, but they found that the ministry had capacity problems which made cooperation difficult.

Despite these difficulties and incompatibilities between the approaches of Sida and the ECE countries, a limited number of trilateral projects was eventually launched, which mainly meant Swedish resources and the participation of ECE experts in implementation. The need to ensure visibility, tying aid to procurement from national actors, lack of field capacities and resistance towards budget support all make coordination with other donors difficult, even in an ad hoc manner. There are sporadic similar examples of *ad hoc* coordination and joint work with other donors in all ECE countries, but perhaps the Czech Republic seems most keen on participating in such work. The Czech Development Agency for example regularly engages in trilateral work with the Austrian Development Agency, and has also signed memorandums of understanding with Sida, USAID and the Swiss Development Agency (SDC) for specific projects (Czech Development Agency 2014). The Czech Republic is also one of the two ECE countries to actively take part in the EU's Fast Track Initiative on the Division of Labour (FTI-DL), and acts as "supporting facilitator" in Moldova and Mongolia. The other country involved in the FTI-DL is Slovenia, which acts as lead facilitator in Macedonia (OECD 2011d).

4.4 Summary

The review of the practice of the five ECE donors along the ten benchmarks based on the Global and European Consensus on Foreign Aid is summed up in Table 4.7. A number of conclusions can be drawn from this review, which we group into three major clusters.

1   In general, the ECE new donors do not comply with most of the requirements of the Global Consensus on Foreign Aid and its European interpretation. Most spectacular shortfalls include the volume of their aid and their implementation of aid effectiveness measures like untying, using program based aid modalities like budget support and working together with other donors.

2   Despite this general non-compliance, the past ten years have not been totally wasted, as there has been significant progress in the ECE countries. They have mostly managed to create stable legal and strategic backgrounds for their international development policies, and have firmly placed development cooperation into the wider frameworks of their foreign policies. While their development programs are still in their "infancies" in terms of aid volume, and the economic crisis has made it difficult for them to increase the size of these programs, they may yet outgrow many of their current deficiencies once more funding is available. Membership of the OECD DAC for four of the countries is also likely to lead to changes in some areas in the medium term.

3   There are significant differences between the five countries. The Czech Republic seems to stand out among the countries, as it provides increasing amounts of aid to the poorest countries, has a well established legal and strategic framework, and has made clear efforts to concentrate its aid allocation. It is also the most transparent and is doing the most in terms of donor coordination. Slovenia also shows good performance in certain issues, it has the highest ODA/GNI share and has implemented some aid effectiveness measures. Hungary seems to be the biggest laggard, it is the only country that does not have any legal framework for development, has hardly made any efforts to implement reforms to increase effectiveness, and is the least transparent. Of course, one may argue that the differences between the five countries are not so significant, as they all have rather small aid programs which share many common characteristics. None the less, we argue that the trajectories of the countries are rather clear and there is a clear divergence between them, which will only make differences more visible in time. The "East Central European" face of donorship, if it ever existed, seems to be breaking up.

Why have the ECE countries not done more in implementing the elements of the Global and European Consensuses? They basically emerged as donors the same time as these Consensuses were formed, and had little expertise in

Table 4.7 Performance of the five donors along the 10 criteria

	Czech Republic	Hungary	Poland	Slovakia	Slovenia
Aid volume— 0.17/0.33 target reached or roadmap established	No	No	No	No	No
Aid law/ strategy exists and poverty reduction made a goal	Yes	Yes, but no law, and strategy only since 2014	Yes, but poverty reduction only indirect goal	Yes	Yes
Share of least developed countries and Sub-Saharan Africa in aid allocation	LDCs: high SSA: low (but upward trend)	LDCs: medium SSA: low	LDCs: low SSA: low	LDCs: medium SSA: medium	LDCs: low SSA: low
Tied aid	No data, but most likely a significant part of bilateral aid tied, and no trend of improvement is visible.				
Budget support	Not used, project aid is the only modality				
Country strategy papers	Yes	No	No	Partly	Partly
Transparency and predictability	Medium	Low	Low	Low	Medium
Number of Partners— reduction of official partners and decreasing fragmentation	Official partners reduced, and a decrease in fragmentation	No reduction in official partners, and increasing fragmentation	No reduction in official partners, and increasing fragmentation	Official partners reduced, but increasing fragmentation	No reduction in official partners, and increasing fragmentation
Number of Sectors— reduction of number of sectors with a view of maximum three per partner	Yes	Officially yes, but no data on practice	Partly	No	Partly
Usage of country systems and coordination with other donors	Partly	No	No	No	Partly

Note: See full text of the chapter for detailed elaborations.

development. Thus one could rightfully expect them to seek international best practices and recommendations as sources of inspiration on how to manage their new policies. Also, what are the reasons for the observed divergence between the five countries? Why has the Czech Republic (and to a lesser extent, Slovenia and Slovakia) done relatively better than Hungary or Poland? We turn to answering these questions in the following chapters.

Notes

1 Some elements of this section build upon Lightfoot 2010.
2 Interview with ECE MFA official C, October 2008.
3 Interview with ECE MFA official D, October 2008.
4 Interview with ECE MFA official E, May 2012.
5 Interview with ECE official F, October 2008.
6 Interview with ECE official G, April 2012.
7 Interview with EU-15 official A, October 2008.
8 Interview with ECE MFA official C, October 2008.
9 Interview with ECE MFA official D, October 2008.
10 Interview with ECE MFA official C, October 2008.
11 Interview with ECE MFA official F, October 2008.
12 Interview with ECE NGO representative B, October 2012.
13 Interview with ECE MFA official C, October 2008.
14 Interview with ECE MFA official H, March 2013.
15 Interview with EU-15 official B, April 2011.

5   The role of external actors

The ECE countries have expressed a desire to organize their aid policies along the lines of OECD DAC norms and thus implicitly to adopt the elements of the global consensus on aid. External actors play an important role in channelling the global consensus into the development policies of donors by putting various forms of pressure on them and attempting to socialize them. The EU was perhaps the single most important external actor, as creating international development policies was a prerequisite for membership for the ECE countries. However, the OECD and the UNDP also played a crucial role, as did many other established donors, which have helped the ECE donors in building their development policies through capacity-building assistance. Given the discussion in Chapter 4, it is clear that even if the ECE states thought they had a history of donor activity under Communism, the aid landscape these states were entering in the early 2000s was very different, and the ECE countries needed to re-learn doing international development. Thus, international organizations and other external actors took on the role of providers of assistance in this learning process. However, the knowledge that they sought to transfer cannot be seen only in normatively neutral technical terms, but also as a clear reflection of the global consensus on aid. This chapter looks at the way the EU, the OECD DAC and the UNDP have attempted to influence the emerging aid practices of the ECE countries during different stages of the journey. It examines what strategies (if any) they employed and then uses the conditions for effective socialization from Chapter 2 to determine how much influence these external actors may have had on shaping the preferences and policies of the ECE states.

5.1 External influence as a midwife

External actors seem to have had the most influence during the birth of international development policies in the ECE countries during the run-up to EU accession (Lightfoot 2008; Lightfoot 2010; Tulmets 2014). Clearly, this is the period during which the ECE countries might have been the most receptive to outside influence, as they began to undertake their mental re-orientation from a "receiver country" to a "donor country" (Rehbichler 2006). There was a concern that "these countries have no great tradition of development aid and no development cooperation policy in the modern sense" (Michaux 2002). Others argued that development cooperation had already existed in a lot of ECE states, "but in very different way."[1] Oprea (2012) identifies that a clear discourse of "unlearning" the previous, pre-1989 experience was present (especially in Romania), implying that the ECE countries were also eager to learn the new way of development from the established donors. An interviewee argued that at accession there was a "lot to explain, due to a huge lack of understanding," especially among officials in the national MFAs and various other line ministries.[2]

Two distinct elements can be identified in the pre-2004 forms of external influence: conditionality by the European Union, and a knowledge transfer and capacity-building process involving the UNDP and the Canadian International Development Agency, but also the EU to a more limited extent.

5.1.1 EU accession conditionality

Chapter 4 has discussed the role of the EU in the run-up to the accession process. While it is difficult to find any clear reference in the negotiation documents that the EU mandated the recreation of international development policies in the ECE countries, there seems to be a shared understanding in the ECE development communities that this was the case, and most interviewees also agreed on this. None the less, this raises questions about the clarity of conditionality, one of the key scope conditions of effective conditionality identified in Chapter 2. As elaborated in Chapter 4, the EU reviewed the state of international development policy in the accession countries in its annual progress reports, and while early reports concentrated on national adaptation of the *acquis* (mainly consisting of the Lomé/Cotonou conventions at the time), later reports also began evaluating the national institutional set-up for bilateral aid delivery, again signaling requirements to work on this issue. The existence of conditionality is therefore difficult to deny.

The second condition of effective conditionality is credibility. This is a complex issue, but evidence points to the fact that EU conditionality in terms of development policy was less than credible. There was a concern expressed during the initial phase of enlargement that "scant attention" was being paid to development co-operation policy. Baginski (2007) for example argues that neither the Polish side nor the European institutions, including DG Development, prioritized this aspect of the accession process. This was seen as significant because it reflected a view that enlargement would not fail due to development and that development had a low political priority within the EU, signaling the low credibility of conditionality (Lightfoot 2008). The fact that this policy area was really only discussed after 2002, when accession negotiations were far advanced, shows its status. Haughton argues that Commission officials lamented the "difficulty of maintaining pressure on accession states when almost all of the negotiating chapters had been closed" (2007: 240).

This produced a situation where, once members, some ECE governments were not clear about the EU's expectations regarding development policy (Grimm and Harmer 2005). This is reinforced by an interviewee from Slovenia who argued that Slovenia doesn't really have a history of development co-operation and the fact that the policy was not an issue on the agenda for accession was a "big mistake," leading to "surprises" after enlargement.[3]

Also, it is clear that the EU accession pressure worked mainly on the macro level, which also impacted on both the clarity and credibility of conditionality. The adherence to the *acquis* was judged according to whether accession states implemented the relevant parts of the *acquis*, mainly focusing on the hard law component, which was very little in case of development (see Chapter 3). EU conditionality in terms of creating bilateral development policies clearly went beyond the hard law *acquis*. The EU however did not have the capacity in this field to work with the accession states to operationalize their commitments. As one interviewee stated "The Commission was not ready,"[4] especially regarding development cooperation. DG Development's "late reaction was primarily due to lack of capacity."[5] Another interviewee highlighted that "development cooperation was low on the agenda for the Commission, which was apparent before and also after accession. There was a lack of internal will. Access to the Commission is also a problem, we would almost prefer to work with other MS or do it ourselves."[6] Another interviewee approached the issue based on the complexity of the accession negotiations: "the Commission did have development on the accession agenda. But you can't expect to spend that much attention on development as there are so many issues to be talked about. But the principles are there."[7]

The ECE countries clearly needed assistance.[8] Even the rather modest (and unclear) EU expectations were seen as "too high"[9] with institutional capacity being very small. As one interviewee highlighted in the early days "the entire development staff from all 8 ECE 2004 accession countries could fit into a small boardroom."[10] Overall, although there was some EU assistance given via the administrative capacity-building phase of the PHARE and other specific projects to help accession states develop capacities and expertise in the field of the development cooperation, but the pre-accession focus on trade and finance did not prepare the new member states for what is a wide ranging and complex policy area. The main vehicles were the Task Force for Accession Negotiations and the Twinning program. The task force focused on the capacity of the accession countries to apply the rules of the Cotonou Agreement (especially the preferential trade system) and to contribute to the European Development Fund starting in 2008 (Krichewsky 2003), which accession states most likely saw as a rather far-off commitment. The pressure to contribute to the EDF, which is outside of the EU's budgetary framework and can thus be seen as soft law, came from the Commission. Grimm and Harmer (2005: 12) highlighted the fact that during accession negotiations pressure was applied from Brussels to contribute to the EDF, resulting in the new member states finding out that "soft law was not so soft after all." This example again highlights the lack of clarity in how the EU's demands were articulated.

Other more general capacity development events included seminars organized by the European Commission on key policies and programs underpinning EC development cooperation for officials who would be working on these issues in the accession countries. There were also events organized in the ECE states, such as a seminar organized by the Czech authorities in Prague on "challenges for emerging donors" and a forum organized by the UK Department for International Development in Warsaw (Richelle 2002). Another example of assistance with capacity-building in the field of development policy was a task force of from the EC and member states (the main players were Germany, Austria, Belgium and Ireland) which offered advice to new member states on specific issues (Biesemans 2007). The member states were brought in because the task exceeded the human capacities of DG Development and DG EuropeAid. Indeed, Vencato (2007) argues that other actors such as the UNDP played a greater role than the EU in influencing both the institutional capacity of the state administrations and the institutional reconfiguration of development policy in the ECE countries. The task force met on three occasions and brought together civil servants and diplomats working in the area. Each meeting explored a different topic, such as implementation plans, efforts to raise public awareness, and coordination with non-EU partners. Twinning did occur, but in a much less systematic way than in other policy areas (Grabbe 2006: 85). Compared with the amount and extent of assistance given in other policy areas, especially regional policy and Justice and Home Affairs (JHA), the lack of importance given to the topic of development cooperation during accession becomes clear. The fact that the EU provided much less support for implementing the development *acquis* may have given signals to the member states that they need not take the issue seriously and make large efforts. This is crucial as research has highlighted that when the message on the *acquis* was opaque or signals were mixed, accession states chose the most domestically palatable options (Haughton 2007: 240).

Two further conditions on effective conditionality have been identified in Chapter 2: the temporal proximity of rewards, and the capacities of the international organization to monitor compliance. In terms of rewards, it is unclear if any were associated with the adoption of the development *acquis* per se. The accession states clearly saw little direct benefits in adopting it, and were skeptical about indirect ones, such as the ability of national actors to take part in development grant and contract tenders funded from the EU budget or the EDF, as these actors were seen as uncompetitive. These indirect rewards were thus likely seen as rather distant in time. The development *acquis* should be seen as a part of the wider accession process, and its adoption was just another hurdle in getting closer to the reward of membership. The capacity of the EU to monitor compliance was high, as evidenced by the annual progress reports (see Chapter 4). But, the sections on the development *acquis* in these reports ranged from one or two sentences to perhaps a paragraph, again signifying the low importance of the policy area.

The low level of clarity and credibility of EU accession conditionality in development policy, stemming from low political interest on both sides, lacking capacities, and the limited ability of the EU to provide capacity-building assistance, as well as the lack of any clear associated rewards and meaningful monitoring seems to have rendered the compliance of the ECE accession countries rather formal. This formal compliance and minimal efforts from the accession states meant that they created the formal structures and institutions for development policy, but allocated small staffs and budgets, and seemed to have no incentive to do anything more.

5.1.2   Learning from CIDA, the UNDP, and others

The second element of the pre-2004 forms of external influence was capacity-building and knowledge transfer provided to the new donors outside of the EU's framework. As discussed, this was especially important as the EU was unable to provide such assistance, and thus many donors stepped in to fill this gap, and even went beyond knowledge transfer by providing seed financing. As mentioned in Chapter 4, there were two major programs (along with several smaller ones, see Table 4.1 in Chapter 4) for sharing knowledge with the ECE new donors, the Canadian International Development Agency's Official Development Assistance in Central Europe (ODACE) program, and the UNDP's Emerging Donors Initiative (EDI).

Of the two, CIDA's program began earlier, already in 2001, and was more significant in financial terms. The program was seen as instrumental in providing the necessary expertise for restarting development policies in the region, so much so that in an event to celebrate 10 years of Slovak aid in 2013, an official from CIDA was even given an award for their role in creating Slovakia's aid policy. Canada was perceived as an "honest broker" by the ECE states, as opposed to the EU which was seen more in a role of policing whether the states had incorporated the *acquis* sufficiently into national law. The ECE countries had been eligible for CIDA assistance during the 1990s, but with their approaching EU accession, CIDA decided to graduate them. The ODACE program was seen as a form of "gracious graduation," which "helped these countries transform from recipients to donors" (Szent-Iványi and Tétényi 2012: 14).

The project included a total funding of USD 12 million for a seven year period between 2001 and 2008. Initially the project covered the four Visegrád countries (the Czech Republic, Hungary, Poland and Slovakia) and was later expanded to the three Baltic countries and Slovenia. An important aspect of the ODACE program was its "whole of country" approach, meaning that it did not only restrict assistance to MFAs, but was also instrumental in organizing national development NGO platforms, raising awareness on development issues among politicians, staff from other ministries, academics and also the wider public. It also aimed at fostering a longer term relationship between CIDA and the new donors, and thus represented an effort at donor harmonization and alignment as well.

The ODACE program had two main components. The first phase involved extensive capacity development assistance in the form of institutional and policy planning assistance (including drafting national institutional development plans and country strategies), specialized training sessions, study tours to Canada, internships for ECE staff at CIDA, mentoring, awareness-raising activities, etc. This phase ended in mid-2005. The second phase involved trilateral programming in order to operationalize the new capacities of the ECE countries, along with monitoring, evaluation and other assistance. Trilateral programming essentially meant funding programs in third countries on a matching basis by CIDA and the emerging ECE donor, and implemented by actors from the ECE countries.

CIDA did not carry out any formal end-of-project evaluation, but representatives of the agency interviewed agreed that the program was "by and large" productive and successful, and it managed to establish good relations with the new donors.[11] It was also crucial in building the institutional structures and giving initial training to staff, and trilateral programming was successful in creating more transparent, open project mechanisms. However, there is also evidence on the reluctance of the ECE donors to actually implement the advice and knowledge transferred by CIDA, and thus results fell short of expectations. ECE development policies progressed much slower than CIDA had anticipated, leading to delays in implementation. Much of CIDA's advice, stemming from expertise in its own operations, simply seemed unsuitable for implementation in the ECE countries due to the small size of the national aid programs. Coordinating the program in eight different countries with different legal, cultural and political contexts was also a huge challenge for CIDA, especially since it aimed to ensure flexibility and national ownership.

The UNDP created a regional center for Europe and the CIS region in Bratislava in 1997, and a number of country offices. The EDI program, started in 2003, had two main components:

> 1) support for the development of national capacities for development cooperation, in the form of policy advice, staff training, and public awareness raising; and 2) assistance in establishing development co-operation transfer mechanisms which conform to international standards in terms of transparency, accountability, and programmatical soundness.
>
> (UNDP 2012)

In practice, the program included much the same elements as CIDA's ODACE program did, such as policy work, strategy formulation, training sessions, assistance to development NGO platforms, awareness-raising, and curriculum development for universities. Indeed, an important element was assistance provided to universities in the region to start graduate level programs on development studies. As opposed to CIDA however, it had a small UNDP budget (about 300 000 USD) and relied mainly on co-financing from the ECE governments themselves. The CIDA and UNDP programs running in parallel not only caused some confusion,[12] but also raised the issue of coordination between the two agencies, which seems to have worked well (Szent-Iványi and Tétényi 2012: 23).

Different states responded to the EDI project in different ways. Estonia decided relatively early on in the project to stop working with the UNDP, as the country regarded itself as a donor which does not require any more capacity development assistance. The UNDP's focus was very highly skewed towards awareness-raising instead of government capacity-building in the cases of Poland and the Baltic countries. The UNDP signed agreements for the establishment of "Trust Funds" with the Czech Republic, Hungary, Slovakia and later Romania. These funds essentially meant development resources committed by the ECE countries themselves, but programmed and spent according to mutually agreed rules and UNDP guidance. The four Trust Funds mobilized a considerable amount of 22 million USD between 2004 and 2012, but they were implemented in very different ways in the four countries. The Czech Trust Fund focused on linking Czech experts into UNDP projects in developing countries, while the Slovak (which was by far the largest in financial terms) was used by the Slovak government as the main mechanism to finance projects of national NGOs. Indeed, UNDP seems to have had a major impact on forming institutional practices in Slovakia, where the Trust Fund's contracting office later turned into the Slovak Development Agency (see Chapter 7). The UNDP influence in Slovakia is very evident and perhaps the most important example of significant UNDP influence in the region, which may also come from the fact that there were frequent interactions between the UNDP and the Slovak authorities as the UNDP regional office was in Bratislava. In contrast to the Slovak authorities, Hungarian authorities were never comfortable with sharing control over their resources with the UNDP, and the Trust Fund remained rather marginal. The Romanian Trust Fund involved the transfer of Romanian funds to UNDP offices in Romania's priority partner countries in order to contribute to ongoing UNDP projects.

No formal evaluation has been carried out for the EDI program, but limited evidence points to similar mixed results as in the case of the ODACE program. The Trust Funds however were seen as good ways of ensuring and maintaining government commitment to international development. The advantage of CIDA and the UNDP was their presence on the ground and their focus on practical aspects. Thus their assistance should mainly be seen not in terms of its impact on policy, but in a more technical light: they helped fill the small national development policies that were created due to EU conditionality with some degree of technical expertise, but were not really significant in generating political will to take these policies further.

External actors clearly contributed to and facilitated the birth of international development policies in the ECE countries, but as the child began to grow, the influence of the midwife waned significantly. Even though the emerging policies were small and lacked the financing and sophistication of more established OECD DAC donors, most observers agree that they would not have existed (or only in an even more limited form) without the pressure of EU conditionality, and knowledge transfer and socialization by CIDA and the UNDP. After accession however, the external pressure seems to have disappeared, leading to a very different setting for external actors in terms of their possibilities for influence. The chapter proceeds by examining the influence the EU and the OECD DAC have had after 2004.

5.2 The European Union: post-accession social learning

As discussed, EU pressure was clearly vital in the pre-accession stage, but there seems to be a clear agreement among ECE development practitioners that after accession the "pressure was off,"[13] and there is "no one pushing from Brussels."[14] Haughton and Malova (2007: 74) talk about states being released from the accession straitjacket after 2004. This is true to some degree for most EU policies, but it is especially true for an area like international development, where most of the *acquis* is soft (Hartmann 2009). In cases of non-compliance with hard law, the EC has several tools to maintain pressure on member states even after accession, with the possibility of ultimately taking them to the European Court of Justice, or in case of the Stability and Growth Pact, even proposing financial sanctions (see Benczes 2013). In the case of soft law however, there is no such possibility, and the Commission must rely a persuasion and socialization strategies in order to ensure compliance among member states. As one interviewee highlighted, the EU should have been tougher in the pre-accession phase, as they cannot do much now.[15] The challenge in such strategies, as identified in a report for the European Parliament, is how to develop capacity in the new member states without the threat of conditionality, in order to allow the states to focus on priority countries where they have a distinct expertise, whilst at the same time "meeting their responsibilities to support development in less-developed countries" (PASOS 2007: 3).

Without the possibilities for conditionality which were present in the pre-accession phase, social learning remains the only mechanism through which the EU can influence the development policies of the ECE countries (Lightfoot and Szent-Iványi 2014). More than ten years have passed since EU membership, which may already be a long enough time frame to examine long-term processes of social learning, adaptation to different practices and the internalization of norms. As argued in Chapter 2, measuring socialization directly is very difficult, thus we identified four conditions which make socialization more likely. If these conditions are not present, it is reasonable to assume that processes of socialization are weak. The four conditions are the (1) perceived procedural and (2) substantive legitimacy of the *acquis*, (3) domestic policy resonance with the *acquis*, and (4) the presence of norm entrepreneurs. We continue by examining these four conditions.[16]

Procedural legitimacy of the acquis. The EU's development *acquis* includes a wide range of soft law recommendations for member states to implement in their national aid policies, which reflect a European version of the Global Consensus on aid. Procedural legitimacy mainly concerns how legitimate the member states perceive the process through which the *acquis* is made, which in turn may impact their willingness to engage in this process. The more legitimate they see it and accept it, the more likely they are to be socialized in terms of accepting the normative content of the rules. The soft law recommendations of the development *acquis* are proposed by the EC in the form of Commission Communications, which basically provide a draft text for the member states to discuss in the Council. The final outcomes are—with very few exceptions—in the form of Council Conclusions, and carry no explicit legal obligations for the member states to transpose them to their domestic legislation or base national policies on them. The wordings in the Council Conclusions clearly hint at this non-compulsory nature, with phrases like "Member States are *invited* to develop or review their own guidelines in the light of these Council Conclusions ..." (Council of the European Union 2012b: 4, emphasis added) being common. While it is the Council (i.e. Ministers of Foreign Affairs) that makes the final and formal decision on the EU's development *acquis*, it is the Council Working Group on Development (CODEV) which makes the actual decisions in the broad majority of the cases. CODEV is composed of specialized diplomats from the member state permanent representations in Brussels, and prepares the development-related agenda of the Committee of Permanent Representatives (COREPER) and thus ultimately the Council.[17] CODEV meets at least once a week, and many of the member state diplomats (especially in case of smaller states) also represent their countries in other Council working groups, thus interaction frequency between them is high. The work of CODEV spans a wide range of issues, from sexual reproductive rights to the developmental impact of trade, but only on the strategic level. CODEV was described as "rather informal," friendly, co-operative and consensus-driven group by member state diplomats and EU officials, although member states do have "red lines." CODEV is chaired by the rotating presidency, but much of its agenda is driven by the EC, and increasingly since the Lisbon Treaty, the European External Action Service. There is an informal goal to reach an agreement on the policy issues discussed, thus dossiers rarely go undecided to COREPER. Member states can be grouped into three, highly fluid groups in CODEV, depending on the issue. The first group is made up of states that have no interest at stake in the issue under discussion, or no expertise on it, and will mostly behave as passive observers. These states often only use the group as a platform for learning and getting information on the topic. The second group is just the opposite: states with a strong interest in the issue and significant expertise who will most likely drive the discussion. The third group is composed of states that do care for the issue and have some red lines, but will not drive the debate (Lightfoot and Szent-Iványi 2014).

When trying to evaluate the perceived procedural legitimacy of rule making in CODEV, an important question is how do the ECE member states perceive the group and how meaningfully are they involved in its work? During the interviews, six themes emerged that suggest less than full participation, which may have an impact on perceived legitimacy and thus openness to socialization (see Lightfoot and Szent-Iványi 2014).

First, ECE member states almost never drive the issues in CODEV, only sometimes falling into the third group of "carers" and in most cases are only passive observers. One ECE diplomat noted that the work of this group does not really concern them, but it is "interesting none the less."[18] Another argued that his country has little to contribute as they are not doing much in the issue area.[19] An official from the EEAS noted that the ECE states "tend to be on the quieter side, while representatives from the UK or France tend to talk a lot."[20] This issue was taken on by the 2008 Slovenian Presidency of the EU when it organized an informal meeting of the EU-12 on the issue to try and overcome the gap between the EU-15 and the EU-12 (Skok 2012). The Presidency stressed the need to listen to the new member states as "all the Member States should take the opportunity to play an active role in framing and implementing the European development policy" (Ster 2008).

The second theme has to do with the capacities of the ECE countries to participate fully in the work of CODEV. ECE representatives rarely receive detailed instructions from their capitals. Whilst this is not unusual in foreign policy (see Juncos and Pomorska 2011; Chelotti 2013), the ECE countries have additional problems in the field of development that exacerbate the problem. These include low policy staff numbers at MFAs, which means that they simply cannot react to all the issues discussed in CODEV and in many cases they think it is unnecessary to do so, as no national interest is at stake. Contrast this with CODEV representatives from established donors like Sweden, who receive detailed instructions on almost every issue discussed. Also, large EU-15 member states can often afford to have a separate diplomat for every Council working group, while the CODEV representative of smaller ECE countries like Slovenia or Slovakia typically has other tasks as well.

The third theme relates to the backgrounds of ECE CODEV representatives. While CODEV reps from the EU-15 generally have a strong development background, those from the ECE states are usually career diplomats. Critics highlight that the diplomatic practice of rotation gives them a shorter time perspective as they will only be in post three years (Horký 2012). In addition, much of their tenure in CODEV must be devoted to learning the ropes from scratch, thereby making them less effective. Evidence gained from the interviews suggests that some form of social learning is taking place in the build up of institutional memory within the ECE because, as one EU official noted that "every new [ECE] representative is a bit better than the previous one was when (s)he had been new,"[21] in a sense that they have better understandings of development issues and more knowledge on how development policy works. None the less examples such as this still exist: "I struggle getting feedback, and this has several factors: ... there is a lack of capacity, recently we have had a cut in personnel, the fact that I have to cover such a wide range of issues with no experience in this field and no one has done me a handover."[22]

Fourth, while the ECE countries seem to be novices, they rarely ask for advice from other (EU-15) member states or from the EC and the EEAS, even though asking for advice and conducting informal discussions on issues seem to be very much the norm in CODEV. One interviewee highlighted the "closed doors within ministries" when it came to learning from the EU.[23] Also, ECE diplomats make much lower use of networking opportunities and are not seen as often on EC organized events outside of CODEV as diplomats from the old member states are.

Fifth, the ECE countries seem to place a large emphasis on "transition experience" and the Eastern neighborhood (Czech Ministry of Foreign Affairs 2011; see also Chapter 4). This was seen to be an area where they have comparative advantages over other donors, although there was a feeling among EU officials that they do this at the expense of the myriad of other issues discussed in CODEV. One EU official actually called this an "obsession" with transition experience.[24] Most ECE diplomats interviewed argued that their transition experience is a true value added and the EU should make greater use of it, but there seems to be a feeling that old member states are not only not convinced by this argument, but are often irritated by how ECE diplomats always return to it like it's some mantra. Many EU-15 countries may see the emphasis on transferring transition experience as a potential threat to the poverty reduction agenda and ACP focus of the EU's development policy, and are thus not willing to support its integration on the EU level.

Sixth, while the work of CODEV is not heavily politicized, there are issues on which clear recurring political tensions exist between the ECE countries and the older members. Beyond transition experience, one such issue is the Eastern Neighborhood: while the ECE states would be keen on providing more support to the region, the older members, especially the UK and France, again see these efforts as threats to the EU's focus on Sub-Saharan Africa. ECE states have also been lobbying for preferential treatment in aid project implementation tenders for their national NGOs and companies, which the old members are again strongly against.

These six themes may have an impact on how the ECE countries perceive the procedural legitimacy of rulemaking in CODEV. They seem to have lower capacities and lower interest (aside from some specific niche issues like transition experience) to participate in the making of the development *acquis*, and there seems to be a feeling of being outsiders in this policy area and having little to contribute. This weakens potential socialization as the NMS do not perceive CODEV to be as receptive to their ideas as to those of larger and more established donors (see Lightfoot and Szent-Iványi 2014).

Substantive legitimacy of the acquis. The substantive legitimacy of the EUs development *acquis* can be seen as rather strong and difficult for any country to dispute, even the ECE countries. As discussed in Chapter 2, the recommendations of the development *acquis* are derived from the global consensus on aid, and thus the main goal of the development *acquis* is to increase the effectiveness of the EU's development efforts as a whole in terms of reducing global poverty through greater strategic guidance, coordination and joint initiatives. The fragmentation of donors and the lack of coordination among them increases the costs of foreign aid, places large administrative burdens on recipients and leads to wasteful parallel efforts. Although there are counter-arguments that donor pluralism has its merits (Frot and Santiso 2010), these are in a clear minority. The rules embodied in the EU's development *acquis* can therefore be seen as normatively consistent. Clearly, there is also a broader, "beyond-the-EU" consensus on much of the rules, as major parts of the development *acquis* can be seen as an EU-level translation of global initiatives. As discussed in Chapter 2, the fundamentals of the *acquis* are clearly linked to Millennium Development Goals. Quantitative aid targets are derived from the Monterrey Consensus (Orbie 2012). Many of the rules aimed at increasing aid effectiveness link in to the global aid effectiveness agenda, such as the Paris Declaration, the Accra Agenda and the Busan Partnership. While there are voices questioning whether the EU is the best possible forum for donor coordination as opposed to the OECD or even the UN (see Maxwell *et al.* 2010 for a full discussion), it cannot be disputed that the EU has done the most to put donor coordination into practice. Also, the EU can be seen as an authoritative actor which plays out these rules. The EC is one of the largest donors in the world, and has undergone a spectacular transformation in the past decades and became a rather effective aid agency (Carbone 2007). There is always room for improvements of course, like a report by the European Court of Auditors (2010) showed in the case of budget support, but the general direction of EU development practice is clearly towards improving the effectiveness of aid in reducing poverty. All these factors hint at the strong substantive legitimacy of the EU's development *acquis*, and in fact no ECE official interviewed disputed this substantive legitimacy. Rather they questioned the *acquis*' appropriateness for their national policy contexts. This however has more to do with domestic resonance, an issue we turn to next (see also Lightfoot and Szent-Iványi 2014).

Resonance. Once a Council Conclusion is released, how does it enter national policy-making? The general impression emerging is that the ECE countries rarely make use of these documents. According to one diplomat interviewed, "there is nothing to implement on Council Conclusions, as they are not law."[25] Other statements are also telling: "the Conclusions are used as a source of inspiration"[26] or help "fine tune" national policy documents. According to a Polish official, the EU *acquis* has forced the government to "think about development cooperation in a systematic way,"[27] but nothing more. In general however, the following quote from an EC official sums it up nicely: "[the ECE countries] tend to forget the European dimension."[28]

The ECE countries may see little need to channel Council Conclusions into national policies due to low policy resonance stemming from prior, ingrained beliefs on development policy. These beliefs run against many of the norms set out in the various EU documents. Almost all MFA representatives voiced concerns as to how relevant the EU recommendations are for their contexts, or even argued outright that they are unsuitable for the realities in the ECE countries. Budget support was one of the most frequently mentioned examples. The EU pushes for increased usage of this modality based on the grounds that it is more effective (Council of the European Union 2012b). The ECE states however resist using budget support claiming that it would lead to decreasing visibility of their efforts and that they would have little influence on how the money is actually spent. Another example is joint programming, an issue which the EU promotes as the main tool for donor coordination and reducing donor fragmentation (Council of the European Union 2011a). ECE diplomats argue that their countries have little capacities in the field, and as they could only contribute relatively small resources to joint programs, they would have little influence on how the programs are designed and implemented. A pilot initiative for joint actions in Moldova, organized by the EC in 2011–12, provides an example of this reluctance for working together. Some ECE countries, such as Hungary abstained from it totally, while the involvement of others was characterized as unenthusiastic and low-key (see Lightfoot and Szent-Iványi 2014).

While resistance to implementing the *acquis* in the issues above may stem from material interests, often the lack of money, these arguments have also become strong ingrained narratives which no ministry official was willing to question. Material interests alone cannot explain why these beliefs were uniformly strong in all five ECE countries NMS, even when some of them, like the Czech Republic or Slovenia, have significantly higher per capita spending on aid than others. Material interests also cannot explain why in light of the financial crisis aid spending remained relatively constant. There is thus only limited evidence of resonance with most of the EU rules, highlighting that socialization may be difficult in face of such strong ingrained beliefs.

Norm entrepreneurs. National NGDOs form an important group of norm entrepreneurs that can play a role in gradually changing these beliefs by lobbying governments and also pressing for the implementation of EU rules. We discuss their role in detail in Chapter 6, here we just mention one issue: NGDOs act as watchdogs, but are also beneficiaries of government funds as implementers of development projects. This fact makes their advocacy work Janus-faced: while in principle they lobby governments to increase development effectiveness, they rarely mention issues which could harm their access to government funding, such as budget support. Hungarian NGDOs for example talk rather vaguely about increasing aid quality, without going into details on exactly how (Kiss 2011). Czech NGDOs mainly focus on rather technical issues when discussing aid quality like publishing tender forecasts (FoRS 2012). NGDOs do however seem highly committed to increasing bilateral aid, and refer to the 0.33 percent target of the *acquis* frequently. This "selectiveness" in which aspects of the *acquis* to promote and which not can make one question just how much NGDOs can be conceptualized as credible and consistent norm entrepreneurs as opposed to self-interested agents.

The Commission itself can also be thought of as a potential norm entrepreneur. As an initiator of many of the *acquis*, it could be logical to assume that it would promote actual implementation as well. Indeed, the EC has developed some tools to assist the ECE countries in implementation and through this also provide additional channels for socialization. There is a weekly breakfast meeting between ECE CODEV representatives and EC officials, and the EC has also been running several "capacity-building" schemes for the ECE states, which focus mostly on technical training, but the 2011–12 round attempted a more practical approach with the joint actions in Moldova mentioned above.[29] Capacity-building however has more or less been phased out post-2014. Opinions on what role the EC should play greatly diverged. Some ECE diplomats complained that the EC is not doing enough to help them, and does not show an understanding of their problems.[30] Others argued that the capacity-building offered is very "light" and a more hands on approaches would be needed.[31] It was also mentioned that assistance from the EU has been rather marginal compared to capacity-building initiatives from other donors like the UNDP.[32] EC officials on the other hand argued that the EC cannot force things, and it is ultimately the responsibility of the member states to implement what they have agreed to. The Commission "presents examples but it is entirely flexible; countries can choose their own path."[33] Whatever the merits of the argument, the EC does not have any explicit strategy to socialize the ECE countries, and seems unwilling to engage in one, which reflects the soft nature of the *acquis* in this sensitive policy area.

Table 5.1 sums up the arguments of the strength of EU influence in the post-accession phase, and also includes the insights on the pre-accession

Table 5.1 A summary of the determinants EU influence on ECE development policies

Pre-accession: Conditionality		*Post-accession: Socialization*	
Clarity	Weak – not mentioned explicitly in negotiation documents, but development policy regularly reviewed in progress reports	Procedural legitimacy of the *acquis*	Weak – ECE countries feel as outsiders and do not participate fully in the making of the development acquis.
Credibility	Weak – development policy not seen as a crucial area, and much of the *acquis* is only soft law. Formal compliance was seen as satisfactory.	Substantive legitimacy of the *acquis*	Strong – the development *acquis* is based on the Global Consensus on Foreign Aid.
Temporal proximity of rewards	Weak – no direct rewards associated with development policy *per se*. Indirect rewards seen as distant and unsure.	Resonance	Weak – ingrained national beliefs on development policy seem to be strong.
EU capacities to monitor compliance	High, development policy reviewed regularly in annual progress reports.	Norm entrepreneurs	Weak – Inconsistent or lacking clear socialization strategies.

Source: Authors.

phase from section 5.1.1 for the sake of completeness. It is rather clear from the arguments above that the post-accession socialization potential of the EU, and thus its ability to influence development policies in the ECE countries is rather low due to the low procedural legitimacy of the rule making process, weak resonance, and the inconsistent activities of norm entrepreneurs. Even though the normative (substantive) legitimacy of the development *acquis* is strong, this does not resonate with ingrained national beliefs in the ECE countries. We argued that the effects of EU conditionality in the pre-accession phase had limited success in re-starting ECE development policies, but did not heavily influence their content and scope. The possibility for post-accession influence, with the disappearance of conditionality (already problematic and ineffective), appears even more limited.

5.3 The OECD DAC: a return to conditionality?

The OECD's DAC has served as the main body for coordinating the foreign aid policies of the "Western" donors since its inception in 1960 (OECD 2006). It has played a key role in the formulation of the international development system: Ruckert (2008) notes the role played by the OECD DAC in the formation of codes of best practice in the implementation of development assistance and international development targets, which subsequently formed the core of what has become known as the United Nations' Millennium Development Goals (Sumner and Mallett 2013). It has also been instrumental in the launch of the processes which led to the Paris Declaration and its follow-up documents. The OECD DAC is also in charge of collecting and publishing statistics on ODA, as well as defining what expenses of members actually count as ODA.

A core activity of the OECD, and thus also the DAC, is the generation of innovative policy ideas and solutions (Marcussen 2004). The nature of the OECD DAC is similar to that of the EU in terms of international development policy, in sense that it also creates recommendations and soft rules on how members should formulate their policies. As shown by the examples of the MDGs and the global aid effectiveness agenda, these recommendations can transcend the OECD's boundaries and evolve into global norms. The OECD DAC is clearly in the same vein as other elements of the OECD in that it is a fora where discussions tend to be framed by experts. Jacobsson suggests, in fact, that it is from such "meditative fora that hard regulations frequently emerge, and from which the standards or 'benchmarks' that constitute the stuff of inquisition are derived" (2006: 208). These benchmarks permit cross-national comparison and ranking. These "league tables" clearly show each country's relative performance and thus puts pressure on the "laggards" to improve (Mahon and McBride 2008: 8). The OECD DAC itself has a special mechanism to make such pressure even more visible, its system of peer reviews (Liverani and Lundgren 2007). Each year, the OECD DAC carries out in-depth reviews of about 4–5 member states' international development policies, reviewing each member every five years. Each review is organized and technically supported by the OECD DAC's secretariat, but carried out by experts from two different member states (peers of the country under review). The basis for the review is the self-evaluation of the country under review, mainly focusing on how it has acted on the recommendations of the previous review. The evaluators also visit the country to conduct a number of interviews, as well as two key partner countries of the donor. The draft review is discussed with the donor, and the resulting reviews are publically available.[34] Although the peer reviews have been criticized for being too diplomatic, they are seen as rather accurate in identifying the main areas where the given country should carry out reforms (Mahon and McBride 2009). The focus of the peer reviews is of course reforms aimed at the domestic implementation of the global consensus on foreign aid, but they also go beyond that as they tend to give advice to countries on how to reform institutional structures and division of labor on the national level (one recurring theme is the reduction of national level institutional fragmentation), change aid delivery processes, etc.

The OECD plays a significant but under-studied role in global governance (see Mahon and McBride 2009). There is evidence that the OECD's system of policy surveillance based on peer pressure, with a focus on the OECD DAC's peer reviews, has been able to achieve some results in forming the development policies of members. Mosley (1985) highlights the impact of the OECD DAC and peer pressure in maintaining aid levels. He argues that the increase in Japanese aid in the 1970s could be attributed to international pressure from the donor community (Mosley 1985: 378). Round and Odedokun (2004) argue that peer pressure can have positive effects: what is assumed here is that the aid effort of a donor is a positive function of the aid effort of other donors. There are a number of reasons for this. First, contributions to multilateral institutions (including the UN's development agencies and multilateral development banks) are often decided jointly, through some form of consensus among OECD DAC member countries. Ordinarily, each OECD DAC member strives to honor such collective decisions. Second, the OECD DAC itself sometimes establishes certain aid targets and as certain members honor these targets, aid efforts of each donor tend to move in unison with those of its peers. Third, ordinarily, each donor is inclined to raise its aid effort to match the perceived efforts of other OECD DAC members, regardless of DAC targets or other forms of formal collective decisions. The converse applies when aid efforts of other donors are declining. Lim (2014) argues that compliance with OECD DAC rules and policy change depends on domestic institutional structures. She argues that taking domestic variables into account, one can explain why some countries have done better in implementing the Paris Declaration than others. The fragmented institutional structure in South Korea's foreign aid policy for example has not allowed much compliance. The role of institutions in the ECE states is something we return to in Chapter 7.

The OECD DAC's channels of impact on the ECE countries can be seen as a mixture of conditionality and social learning. The peer pressure system, by its nature, should only be thought to have an effect on countries which are already members of the OECD DAC. As discussed in Chapter 4, many ECE countries joined the OECD in the mid-1990s, but they did not join the DAC. However, the OECD DAC should still have been able to have a form of impact on the ECE countries: if their desire for accession to the OECD DAC was strong, the DAC could impose accession conditionality; and it could also involve countries in its work by granting them observer status, and thus allowing some social learning to take place. We return to the issue of accession conditionality below.

Accession to the DAC is not automatic for OECD members, and in fact there are several OECD member states beyond the ECE countries as well, which are not full members of the committee (such as Turkey, Mexico or Chile). The OECD DAC has formulated a number of conditions that accession countries must meet in order to accede to the Committee. According to the OECD DAC's website (OECD n.d.a):

> Candidate countries are assessed in terms of the following criteria: the existence of appropriate strategies, policies and institutional frameworks that ensure capacity to deliver a development co-operation programme; an accepted measure of effort; and the existence of a system of performance monitoring and evaluation.

The "accepted measure of effort" means that the ODA of any country wishing to join must reach 0.2 percent of its GNI, or at least 100 million dollars. The policy and institutional framework criteria is rather vague and open to interpretation. In practice, this means that the OECD DAC will conduct an accession review of the country's development policy and assess its readiness to join the committee. It is however not clear what qualitative criteria an accession country must conform to.

One can look at OECD DAC accession conditionality in the light of the four variables which determine the strength of conditionality outlined in Chapter 2 (clarity, credibility, proximity of rewards and capacity to monitor), as well as the potential costs and benefits of membership. Concerning the clarity of conditionality, the quantitative criteria are rather clear, but the qualitative are not. While it is clear what a country needs to strive to implement (i.e. the elements of the global consensus on aid), Chapter 3 has discussed that very few countries have actually done so, and many existing OECD DAC members also fall short. Thus, what is the "acceptable minimum effort" from accession countries? The OECD DAC has not disclosed any general *ex ante* benchmarks on this, and most likely decides on a case by case basis. This however means that a significant portion of accession conditionality is far from being clear. Interviewees in ECE foreign ministries often downplayed or were not even aware of the qualitative aspects of the OECD DAC accession criteria. A high ranking Hungarian official for example knew all the details about the quantitative benchmark, and saw the rest as "a formality of going through a Special Review."[35]

The first country to undertake the Special Review process was the Czech Republic in 2007. Czech officials were always rather consistent in attributing the restart of their foreign aid policies to OECD membership in 1995 (as opposed to EU accession almost a decade later). The review of the Czech Republic (OECD 2007) was special in a sense that the Czech government played a much stronger role in it than the country under review usually does. The resulting review is also much shorter than the "normal" peer reviews. The main recommendations of the review are along the lines of the global consensus on foreign aid, such as creating a roadmap for increasing the volume of aid, or implementing the Paris principles, but they also focus heavily on institutional reform, and how the Czech Republic should change its relevant institutional structure with a view of increasing aid effectiveness and efficiency. The Czech Special Review was followed by one on Poland (2010), Slovakia and finally Slovenia (both in 2011). Their contents showed a rather high degree of similarity with the Czech report, which indicates that these countries faced rather similar challenges, but there are also a number of country-specific issues.

The recommendations in the four peer reviews can be seen as rather clear. What is not clear however is what the countries need to actually implement from these reviews for the OECD DAC to accept it as a member. The Czech Republic has implemented much of the institutional reform recommendations from the peer review (see Chapter 7), but suggestions on increasing aid levels, increasing aid effectiveness by employing the principles of the Paris Declaration, reducing the geographic fragmentation of aid allocation went largely ignored. Slovakia and Slovenia also acted on (or in coherence with) some of the institutional recommendations (Hanusová 2012; Hulényi 2012). The Slovak government hosted a high profile conference in 2012 in Bratislava one year after the country's review was published in order to present its answers to the review: while they agree with the identified problems, the emerging feeling was that they had done little to address them. Poland on the other hand seems to have been rather "angry" at the OECD for a review they perceived to be rather negative compared to what they had anticipated,[36] and not much action was taken other than what was already planned before the review (mainly passing the law on international development). None the less, as they all gained accession to the OECD DAC, their compliance was most likely seen by the OECD DAC as satisfactory, which leads to the issue of credibility.

As the case of the ECE countries has clearly shown, OECD DAC conditionality is declining in importance. The fact that the past decade has seen the rise of many major non-DAC donors like China, India, Brazil, Russia, Turkey and the Arab countries has definitely decreased the relevance of the DAC, which is now struggling to show that it is still a useful organization, like the OECD in general (Eyben 2013), and not just an obsolete "club" of the Western donors. Thus, circumstances have changed and the OECD DAC needed to show its ongoing legitimacy in a changing world, something it could do by accession: the fact that non-members want to join it or work with it, signals that it is still perceived by outsiders as relevant. More than 10 years after its last enlargement (Greece in 1999), the OECD DAC admitted South Korea in 2010, followed by Iceland and four of the ECE countries in 2013.[37] In three years more countries joined the OECD DAC than in the previous 20! The OECD DAC has also expressed openness for cooperating with emerging donors which are not members of the OECD (Smith *et al.* 2010), and initiated possibilities for these countries to take part in its work: non-OECD countries can become associates or partners of the Committee, which basically allows full participation in "all non-confidential meetings of the OECD DAC, including its High-Level and Senior-Level Meetings and the meetings of its technical sub-committees" (OECD n.d.b), without participation in formal decision-making.

This expansion fever however comes at a price, namely relaxing the strict membership conditions. The Czech Republic and Poland have fulfilled the quantitative accession criteria (219 and 421 million dollars spent on ODA respectively in 2012), and Special Reviews have been carried out in both cases (OECD 2007, 2010). Slovakia (80 million and 0.09 percent) and Slovenia (59 million and 0.13 percent) on the other hand did not fulfill the quantitative target, but were none the less admitted. While Hungary fulfills the quantitative criteria (118 million), it has up to mid-2014 not applied for membership and thus there is no Special Review on the country's international development policy either. Except for the Czech Republic, none of the ECE countries had strong systems of performance monitoring and evaluation in place either. To show the lack of credibility of OECD DAC conditionality, the OECD DAC has even informally hinted to Hungarian officials that it would allow the country's accession without the Special Review, which the Hungarian government has been reluctant to undertake thus far.[38] Civil society critics interpret the government's reluctance as "it must have something to hide."[39] Many had hoped during the mid-2000s that accession to the OECD DAC would be an important instigator of reform and change in the ECE countries, relaxing the admission criteria however seems to have caused severe disappointment.

Concerning rewards and their temporal proximity, it may be more instructive to think more generally about the costs and benefits of OECD DAC membership. The main benefit is non-material, as it means an increase in international prestige and an acknowledgement that the country is on its way to becoming a full-fledged donor (or graduating from the "emerging donor" label). Benefits may also accrue to certain actors within the country: the Czech MFA for example was able to use the promise of OECD DAC membership to greatly raise the profile of development cooperation in the country (see Chapter 7). Concerning the cost side, one may argue that as accession conditionality is only partially clear and not even credible, adaptation costs in terms of policy reform can be minimized. DAC membership has no additional financial costs for a country towards the OECD, but it does have some minor costs as the acceding country must be ready to report its ODA statistics according to standards of the DAC's Creditor Reporting System (CRS), and must also be ready to engage in the work of the Committee through both a permanent specialized diplomat at the country's representation to the OECD in Paris, and also frequent travels for specialists from the capital. There are also political costs, as membership means a tighter scrutiny of the country's foreign aid policy and practice, including the obligation to report highly detailed data on international development activities. The OECD DAC will now be able to carry out regular peer reviews on the country, which would include much more detailed criticism and recommendations as opposed to the special (accession) review. Governments may be wary of public criticism on their policies, and these criticisms also will mean increased pressures on decision makers to spend more on aid and also increase aid effectiveness, in line with the global consensus. Still, there will be no legal obligations. Countries like Greece or Italy, which have been members of the OECD DAC for decades, have still to reform their aid systems. The exact balance of costs and benefits will depend on what weight individual governments place on them. Also the temporal proximity of benefits (increased international prestige) is rather immediate after accession, but increased scrutiny can be rather distant, as peer reviews on a country are only carried out every five years.

In light of the above, capacities of the OECD DAC to monitor compliance may not matter. If accession conditionality is not enforced, then there is not much to monitor. The OECD DAC only has capacities to carry out the peer reviews, but not to engage in continuous monitoring of accession states' development policies.

Despite the fact that OECD DAC accession conditionality seems to have been doomed to ineffectiveness due to the political interests of the OECD DAC to show its legitimacy and relevance, the Committee could still have had an impact on the ECE countries through social learning prior to accession. The ECE states all expressed their goal to eventually accede to the OECD DAC early on.[40] Kragelund (2008) and Dreher *et al.* (2013) highlight that interaction with the OECD DAC is what differentiates these donors from other non-DAC donors, and that they all argue that OECD DAC standards and allocation criteria are relevant for them. None the less, without full OECD DAC membership, possibilities for social learning were rather limited for the ECE countries, despite their observer status. Countries with only observer status have no role in formal decision-making. Observer status would allow participation in the work of the OECD DAC's technical sub-committees, but the ECE countries have had little capacities to take part in these meaningfully. Some OECD DAC driven processes however have gone beyond the member states, such as the Paris aid effectiveness process. The ECE countries did not originally participate in drafting the Paris Declaration, but have only joined the process later. In general, the ECE countries have taken little part in OECD DAC rule making and beyond, which means that the procedural legitimacy of these rules can be seen as low.

We have discussed the substantive legitimacy of the rules of the Global Consensus in section 5.2., and government receptiveness is an issue which will be addressed in Chapter 7. Thus, the main determinant of social learning remains the effectiveness of the OECD DAC itself as a norm entrepreneur. One way the OECD DAC could act as such would be through using more hands-on approaches in training the ECE donors, i.e. providing them with capacity-building assistance. The OECD DAC however is not a funding organization, thus its resources for providing such assistance for countries in meeting recommendations such as those embodied in the Special Reviews are limited. It did not have a formal capacity development program towards the ECE new donors, although it did assist them with a series of *ad hoc* efforts, mainly through providing advice on the reporting of ODA statistics. The ECE countries, before their accession, have had much less interactions with the OECD DAC than they have had with the EU, which also means fewer possibilities for social learning.

5.4 Summary

External actors like the EU, the OECD DAC and others have had much interaction with the ECE donors since the turn of the Millennium. International influence, mainly EU accession conditionality was clearly crucial in ensuring that the ECE states restart their international development policies along the norms of the EU's development *acquis* and the OECD DAC, and even more broadly the global consensus on foreign aid. ECE states were in the "unique situation of being recipients of aid from the EU while simultaneously preparing to become donors" (Carbone 2004: 245). However, due to the low salience of development, the EU did not have a large impact on what actual forms the new ECE policies took, and indeed all countries opted for rather minimal international development policies. It is clear that EU pressure was more crucial during the accession process. In the period up to the closing of the negotiation chapter on external relations, the EU had the upper hand. Once the chapter was closed, EU influence declined. Post membership formal EU influence, especially in a legal sense, is reduced as the policy area is mainly characterized by soft law, leaving only possibilities for social learning. The variables which determine the strength of social learning however processes seem to have been rather weak, thus limiting the post-accession impact of the EU. This chapter has shown that in a policy area like development cooperation where the EU shares competence with the member states and the policy area is peripheral to the functioning of the internal market, Europeanization has tended to be shallow. This conclusion supports the finding that EU power over the accession states varied according to the phase of the accession process and also according to how salient the policy area was to the EU (Haughton 2007: 235; Sedelmeier 2012).

The EU can have difficulties in shaping the precise nature of a member state's foreign aid policy on the ground, and it has only marginally attempted to play this role. In many ways this is consistent with the nature of the EU, and it would be surprising if this changed for a policy area that touches on aspects of foreign and security policy. The "on the ground" role was played in the early days by the UNDP and some OECD DAC members. The UNDP's and CIDA's role was a systematic attempt to shape policy developments. This was successful in those states which engaged with the process and allowed the ECE states to meet the basic requirements of the *acquis* and global aid norms. The role of these external actors decreased once the ECE states became member states. Advice from other OECD DAC members appeared to occur in an ad-hoc manner, although it should be noted that whilst ECE officials expressed a desire for more advice it is not clear how actively they searched out the information. Very few officials admitted to seeking advice from EU bureaucrats and even sharing experiences within say the Visegrád grouping was periodic and informal.

The OECD DAC could have had significant influence on the policies of the ECE countries, but it has failed due to do so. It relaxed much of its accession criteria for the sake of its own expansion. The four Special Reviews conducted to date did have some impact on institutional reforms, especially in the Czech case. An important conclusion emerges from this, which will be discussed in more detail in Chapter 7: when the reforms promoted by external actors coincide with the interest of *some* governmental actors (i.e. there is domestic resonance), the governmental actor may use the external actor as an ally to increase its own bargaining position domestically. However, socialization processes may become more pronounced for those states that have joined the OECD DAC, as their density of interactions with the organization increases and they become more involved in its policy-making and coordination work.

One more issue must be noted. Distinguishing influence from different international sources can be difficult. The EU and the OECD DAC, as well as the various actors which provided capacity-building assistance broadly recommended similar reforms to the ECE countries. As stated by Horký (2010a: 8): "the EU and its member states operate in a multilevel environment and form a multilevel policy network themselves; this complicates attribution." While external pressure was uniformly weak on all countries, it did have more of an impact in some countries as opposed to others. The main reason relates to domestic mediation of these pressures and resonance with the interests and beliefs of various actors. We examine these differences in Chapter 7, but first Chapter 6 discusses the influence of domestic actors, which also varies among the five countries.

Notes

1 Interview with EU-15 official A, October 2008.
2 Interview with EU official A, October 2008.

3 Interview with ECE MFA official F, October 2008.
4 Interview with EU-15 official A, October 2008.
5 Interview with EU-15 official C, October 2008.
6 Interview with ECE MFA official C, October 2008.
7 Interview with EU-15 official C, October 2008.
8 This section develops and expands work in Lightfoot 2010.
9 Interview with ECE MFA official I, November 2009.
10 Interview with CIDA official, November 2013.
11 Joint interview with three CIDA officials, March 2012.
12 One interviewee (ECE MFA official J, March 2012) was not even aware that the ODACE and EDI were separate programmes, and talked about joint CIDA/ UNDP assistance.
13 Interview with ECE NGO representative A, July 2010.
14 Interview with ECE MFA official I, November 2009.
15 Interview with ECE MFA official K, April 2011.
16 The following analysis is based on and expands upon Lightfoot and Szent-Iványi (2014).
17 For more on EU rule making procedures in the Council, see Naurin and Wallace (2010).
18 Interview with ECE MFA official L, February 2013.
19 Interview with ECE MFA official M, January 2013.
20 Interview with EU official B, January 2013.
21 Interview with EU official B, January 2013.
22 Interview with ECE MFA official D, October 2008.
23 Interview with EU-15 official B, April 2011.
24 Interview with EU official B, January 2013.
25 Interview with ECE MFA official M, January 2013.
26 Interview with ECE MFA official N, January 2013.
27 Interview with ECE NGO representative A, July 2010.
28 Interview with EU official B, January 2013.
29 Interview with EU official C, January 2013.
30 Interview with ECE MFA official N, January 2013.
31 Interview with ECE MFA official M, January 2013.
32 Interview with ECE MFA official J, March 2012.
33 Interview with EU official A, October 2008.
34 See OECD (2013) for the methods and process of a DAC peer review. See also Pagani (2002) for a critical evaluation.
35 Interview with ECE MFA official O, June 2013.
36 Interview with ECE NGO representative C, July 2010.
37 Jon Lomoy, executive director of the DAC secretariat even labelled 2013 as an "exceptional year for the DAC" (Lomoy 2013). Parts of this statement are revealing: "To some observers, the DAC remains an exclusive club of large, generous donors. However, 2013 proved that the DAC is a heterogeneous group that welcomes different development actors ...."
38 Interview with ECE MFA official O, June 2013.
39 Interview with ECE NGO representative D, June 2014.
40 Interview with ECE MFA officials C, D and F, October 2008.

6 Non-governmental organizations

Non-governmental organizations play a key role in foreign aid policies of donor countries (Ahmed and Potter 2006; Riddell 2007; Lister and Carbone 2006). Their activities are usually characterized along four roles. First, they are the main providers of awareness raising on global development issues. This includes high profile campaigning, informal development education through organizing workshops and seminars, and also in some countries they even play a role in the formal education system. Second, they attempt to influence government foreign aid policies and have clear activities in terms of advocacy. Usually, they can be conceptualized of as advocators of the global South's interests in the North, and as such they mainly lobby for more and better aid to developing countries. Third, they serve as watchdogs of government aid policies and monitor whether governments actually keep their promises on aid. Fourth, they implement foreign aid projects in developing countries, which they can either finance from grassroots contributions from the donor countries or grants from either bilateral donors or international agencies. NGOs are thought to possess certain comparative advantages in terms of project implementation as opposed to official actors or other non-state actors like private businesses. NGOs are often seen to be more flexible, more willing to take risks and work in insecure environments and through their contacts with Southern NGOs, they may have a much better understanding of what is happening in the field.

NGOs are especially important in the ECE countries. Since the mid-1990s development NGO communities have emerged in all ECE countries, a phenomenon which has received very little scholarly attention. Having their roots mainly in faith-based humanitarian organizations, these NGOs are often characterized as relatively small and weak, but have none the less carved themselves an important role in ECE aid policies. Their role as implementers of aid projects is especially pronounced when compared to the more established donors. Profit-oriented private sectors in the ECE countries have yet to be engaged in foreign aid, although this trend is (slowly) changing in some countries, most notably the Czech Republic.[1] The presence of businesses is none the less still highly limited in the implementation of aid projects abroad, and this vacuum has been filled by NGOs. As awareness in ECE on global development issues is low, or rather discussions on these issues do not figure highly in public debates, NGOs also have a larger than usual role in educating the public and drawing attention to these issues.

This chapter looks at the role non-governmental development organizations (NGDOs) play in the foreign aid policies of the ECE countries in terms of their advocacy and watchdog work. NGDO communities have emerged in all ECE countries as partners of the MFA and have put forward clear agendas on what shape they would like their countries' international development policies to take. They have engaged their countries' MFAs on several levels, but it is also clear that influence differs among countries. The main goal of this chapter is to provide some insights on just how influential NGDOs have been in the five countries. In doing so, it discusses the history of these organizations, the interests they articulate, and analyzes their influence along the five variables identified in Chapter 2.

6.1 Civil society in ECE: historical legacies and EU accession

During Communism, independent civil society in ECE was heavily discouraged (see Ost 1993; Palubinskas 2003; Wallace *et al.* 2012). Communist governments saw civil society initiatives as potential forums from which political opposition can emerge and organize itself. The official argument was that the dual, but also interwoven structure of the state and the Communist party was enough to channel social aspirations. While NGOs relating to special interests and hobbies were allowed with state/party supervision, those with more political agendas were heavily curtailed, banned, or driven by the state/party. One such example of the latter are trade unions, whose main role was reduced to expressing how satisfied workers are with the system, as opposed to representing their interests towards employers and the state. Another example is the various peace movements, which were actually organized by the state and used as forms of anti-imperialist propaganda. Churches were also restricted in their activities and very little humanitarian work was allowed for them, especially as the official standpoint argued that there is no need for such work as there was no poverty or unemployment in the Eastern bloc. Due to this heavy state influence, most people retreated to their private lives, and a culture emerged in which civil activity was not seen as worthwhile. Due to its close association with the state, people regarded "civil" activism with outright suspicion.

After the fall of Communism, a clear surge in civil society activity began in East Central Europe (Smolar 1996). The legacy of the past 40 years however could not be washed away, and the new civil society organizations emerging have generally been described as weak, disintegrated, and ineffective, at least compared to the idealistic hopes of 1989–1990 (Howard 2002, but see also Rikmann and Keedus 2013 for a critique of the "weakness" argument). Citizens in the ECE countries seem to have lower levels of organizational membership, less aptitude for volunteer work, and are generally still mostly invested in their private lives (Howard 2002). This apparent apathy towards greater public involvement has been explained by factors like low levels of interpersonal trust, suspicion, envy and a perception predominant in the region that ordinary people can do little to change politics (Crawford and Lijphart 1995). Low levels of participation meant that emerging NGOs were typically elite organizations detached from their grassroots, which had impacts not only on their perceived legitimacy, but also on their possibilities to raise funds and mobilize masses for their cause. Western donors rushed to support fledging NGOs in the early 1990s, and while this has allowed a large number of organizations to do meaningful work in a wide range of fields, it also caused severe distortions in the sector by relieving the need for the organizations to strengthen ties with their grassroots and also made them more receptive to donor needs than to needs at home (Fagan 2005; Fink-Hafner *et al.* 2014). None the less, civil society organizations in the region have gone through a process of professionalization: while having weak grassroots and low capacities for mobilization, they do seem to have developed relatively stronger capacities for interactions with the governments and also each other, and thus have been able to exert some level of influence (Petrova and Tarrow 2007).

NGOs in the ECE countries were heavily impacted by accession to the EU, both directly and indirectly (see Roth 2007; Nielsen *et al.* 2009; Börzel 2010; Jacobsson and Saxonberg 2013; Cox and Gallai 2013). The direct impacts relate to the fact that EU membership opened up new possibilities for NGOs on the European level. For one, they became eligible to apply directly to the EU institutions for project-based grant financing. Second, it also opened possibilities for them to join EU-wide transnational advocacy groups and epistemic communities and become more involved in their work. This exposed ECE NGOs to a wide range of formal and informal learning dynamics and allowed them not only to acquire new skills and techniques in fields like campaigning, advocacy or fund-raising, but also opened up possibilities for socialization and contributed to raising their domestic profile (Börzel 2010: 3; Kutter and Trappmann 2010). Third, NGOs were now given the possibility to "circumvent their national governments in the policy process" (Börzel and Buzogány 2010: 708) and lobby the EU institutions directly.

NGOs have also experienced indirect impacts from EU accession, which relate mainly to the fact that EU membership and the adaptation of the *acquis* changed national legislation and policy-making processes. This clearly transformed the context in which NGOs work. For example, in many policy areas, such as environmental issues, the EU has clearly mandated member states to involve civil society in policy-making processes, which not only means making these processes more transparent and open, but also the institution of regular consultations with key NGOs in the issue areas. This has led to process of learning and professionalization, making NGOs more professional in dealing with the state (Petrova and Tarrow 2007). In some areas, adopting the

EU's rules also meant giving direct tasks and responsibilities to civil society in policy implementation or monitoring, such as the case of the EU's regional funds (Batory and Cartwright 2011). NGOs now also have stronger possibilities for legal and other action in case of non-compliance by the state (Börzel and Buzogány 2010), as they can turn to European forums to force the state to comply.

These direct and indirect impacts of EU accession have put pressures on ECE NGOs to "become more European." In order to access financing from the EU institutions, NGOs must propose projects that fit the EU's policy agendas. These EU grants are often rather large and require co-applications from several member states, thus forcing smaller national NGOs to apply as members of international consortia. This is highly conducive to building Pan-European networks and deeper relations with counterparts in other European countries. The increased frequency of international interactions has also increased the sensitivity of ECE NGOs to the European dimension of their issue area.

However, it is difficult to deny that EU integration also had negative effects on ECE NGOs, and the net balance of these effects is not clear (Fagan 2005; Kutter and Trappmann 2010; Batory and Cartwright 2011). States often had to adopt the EU's *acquis* in rather short timeframes, and this left little room for meaningfully involving civil society. This process not only sent mixed signals to NGOs, but also maintained a lack of trust between them and the state and made subsequent dialogues difficult as well (Grosse 2010). Despite the positive impacts of EU accession, NGOs in most ECE countries have remained weak and underfunded, lacking the necessary capacities to engage with the state in policy-making. Mobilization and invoking rights also remains difficult (Börzel and Buzogány 2010; Gąsior-Niemiec 2010). Most of the funds for the ECE NGO sectors comes not from grassroots donations, but from sources like the EU and other international agencies. This fact provides incentives for NGOs to strive to meet the expectations of funders, as opposed to the expectations of the societies they are supposed to represent (Fagan 2005; Kerényi and Szabó 2006). This reliance on external funding also distorted the skills development of NGOs, as project proposal writing skills remained key, as opposed to wider fundraising and grassroots networking.

6.2 The emergence of development NGOs

In general, NGDOs emerged in the ECE countries more or less in parallel with the emergence of international development policies after the turn of the Millennium (see Brubacher 2003; Miszlivetz and Ertsey 1998; Chimiak 2014; Szent-Iványi and Lightfoot 2015). However, a number of NGDOs in the region actually predated official development policies. During the early 1990s (and in some cases even earlier, such as the Hungarian Maltese Charity Service in the mid-1980s), with the renewed autonomy of churches, a number of faith-based domestic social care and relief NGOs emerged, with served as a root for NGDOs. The focus of these organizations was mainly on the domestic alleviation of poverty, which had been aggravated by the economic and social crisis caused by transition process. It was during the mid-1990s that these faith-based NGOs, and also some other, new initiatives started to venture abroad, mainly by providing *ad hoc* humanitarian aid to victims of various armed conflicts, such as the wars in Yugoslavia and Chechnya. Providing assistance to these people also prompted the emergence of secular NGOs, the most notable among them being Polish Humanitarian Action (PAH) and People in Need from the Czech Republic (Drążkiewicz-Grodzicka 2013: 68). These humanitarian activities provided several learning opportunities for these NGOs, and together with the faith-based ones, they soon began to see the need to engage in post-conflict rehabilitation and longer term development projects.[2]

Beyond these faith-based and secular humanitarian NGDOs, a smaller group also emerged with a highly different background. Many NGOs in the ECE countries were created during the early 1990s to promote and monitor the development of human rights and democracy in their home countries. Some of them received rather significant amounts of US funding. After EU accession and acknowledgement of their countries as functioning democracies, these NGOs, such as the Stefan Batory Foundation in Poland, DemNet Foundation in Hungary or Pontis Foundation in Slovakia, were forced to seek new mandates in order to ensure their survival. Providing democracy assistance to countries in the neighborhood, especially the former Soviet Union and the Western Balkans seemed like a viable option, thus turning these NGOs into NGDOs as well (Szent-Iványi and Lightfoot 2015).

The creation of official foreign aid policies in the ECE countries, closely followed by accession to the EU, had profound effects on the small NGDO communities by opening up a whole range of new possibilities for them. Representatives from ECE NGOs interviewed all agreed that EU accession had extremely positive effects on their work, and some even credited the EU for their very existence. The main indirect effect of EU accession was of course the recreation of national foreign aid policies, as documented in Chapter 4. Due to the ten year hiatus in official foreign aid, governments had lost much of their expertise in the area, and had to turn to NGDOs, which were active in the field since the mid-1990s. NGDOs clearly possessed expertise in the implementation of development projects that the government did not, and nor did any private businesses. Thus NGDOs were seen as a source to complement the scarce capacities of governments.

In order to engage the government effectively, the NGDO communities began organizing themselves due to the need to communicate with the government with a single voice. NGDOs created their national advocacy platforms between 2002 and 2005 in almost all ECE countries, and the governments acknowledged these as official partners in policy-making processes. The CIDA and UNDP capacity-building projects, detailed in Chapter 5, played a key role in this process, and CIDA even funded the new platforms in the first couple of years, which meant that they could engage in policy work towards the governments and the MFAs in particular. The European Commission began funding a project called the Trialog Information Service. Based in Vienna, it aims to facilitate the flow of information between NGDOs and their platforms in the ECE countries and also organizes trainings on issues like advocacy and fund-raising. The NGDO platforms in the ECE countries are detailed in Table 6.1.

EU membership also had a number of direct effects on NGDOs. Most importantly perhaps, national NGDOs gained access to development project grants administered by the European Commission. National platforms became members of CONCORD, the pan-European "platform of platforms," which exposed them to EU level advocacy and ties with NGDOs from other countries. After extensive lobbying through CONCORD, the EU even "ringfenced" a certain amount of its budgetary development funds for ECE NGDOs, which they could use for awareness-raising and development education projects. CONCORD also included the new members in its AidWatch initiative, an EU-wide program to monitor national aid policies. Most national platforms now produce more or less regular national versions of these AidWatch Reports, which are perhaps their most visible policy documents that detail the interests and wishes of the NGDO community. Many NGDO experts stated that membership in CONCORD has had profound effects on how they work, as CONCORD provided numerous training sessions to them on advocacy techniques, fundraising, and preparation of EU grant proposals. CONCORD has also been influential in guiding the ECE platforms on what to focus their advocacy work on, bringing their rhetoric more in line with NGDOs from other EU countries. Issues like policy coherence for development for example were not traditionally addressed by ECE NGDOs, and it was CONCORD which drew their attention to this. Thus, the advocacy work of NGDOs was clearly given a stronger European dimension.

Table 6.1 NGDO platforms in the ECE countries

Acronym	Full Name	Established	Members + observers (2013)
HAND	Hungarian Association of NGOs for Development and Humanitarian Aid	2003	16
FoRS	Czech Forum for Development Cooperation	2002	30 + 15
MVRO	Slovak Non-Governmental Development Organizations Platform	2003	25 + 8
SLOGA	Slovenian Global Action	2005	35
Grupa Zagranica	Uses Grupa Zagranica as full name in English	2004	61

Source: NGDO platform websites.

Ten years after accession, it is clear that the NGDO communities in the ECE countries remain underdeveloped, despite the obvious benefits from EU accession and the creation of national development policies. This state of affairs obviously reflects the fact that there is less financing available, both in terms of grants and procurement from the state, and also in terms of private donations. As a result, most NGDOs in the region are rather small affairs with only a few permanent staff members. Low capacities and funds also mean that most NGDOs do not actually do development projects in developing countries, but rather focus on development education and awareness-raising domestically, which is seen as less costly. The work they in developing country contexts mainly consists of small scale standalone projects, like building a village school, clinic or children's center, or sending volunteers (and more recently "voluntourists").

There are of course organizations that have managed to grow rather large, although they are still relatively small compared to large globalized Western NGDOs like Oxfam or Save the Children. These larger ECE NGDOs usually have significant permanent staff, are capable of long term operation in foreign countries and thus implementing more complex projects. They have diversified sources of financing and stronger capacities to raise donations. An important characteristic is that these large NGDOs are often the large domestic social care NGOs, which have gained a good reputation and contacts with their national governments primarily through their domestic activities (such as People in Need or Hungarian Interchurch Aid). Many of them also have strong humanitarian programs and often lead the national responses to high profile international humanitarian catastrophes.

Therefore, ECE NGDO sectors represent an interesting duality. On the one hand, there are a few rather large, internationally competitive (in terms of securing EU grants) organizations, with diversified financing and activities, who are capable of engaging in long term development and humanitarian aid projects abroad. On the other hand, the majority of NGDOs are rather small, mainly focused on policy work, education and campaigning, which often survive from one grant to the next.

6.3 NGDO interests

There seems to be a consensus in all ECE countries that advocacy work and engagement with the state is generally done by the platform, while individual NGDOs concentrate on their own operational tasks like global education, awareness-raising or development fieldwork. Due to the heterogeneous nature of NGDO communities outlined above, it can be difficult for platforms to speak with a single voice, although there are large differences between the countries and it is not easy to generalize. None the less, in many cases what the platforms advocate should be seen as the lowest common denominator among the national NGDO communities, and if some member organization would want to go beyond that, or are working in a niche area, it will engage in advocacy outside of the platform.[3] The tension between faith based and non-faith based groups is a major issue in many countries. For example, in Slovenia the largest NGDO is not part of the platform because of differing views around crucial issues such as reproductive rights.[4]

The annual AidWatch Reports, both the European one by CONCORD with individual country pages supplied by the national platforms, as well as the longer reports of the national platforms represent ideal starting points when attempting to collect the interests of NGDOs, as well as the reforms they would like to see implemented on the level of their respective country's aid policy. A word of caution is however in order with these. The AidWatch Reports are always read by the relevant ministry officials, and thus could be seen as toned down critiques of the actions of the government, although the platforms do still criticize government action when appropriate. Most platform representatives interviewed stated that they often feel the need to strike a balance in their criticisms of government practices in order to maintain a constructive relationship with the government. An expert working at a Czech NGDO argued that Czech NGDOs have become "politically savvy" and know when to criticize and when to step back.[5] Also, while platforms themselves usually receive little direct government funding (with the exception of MVRO, the Slovakian NGDO platform), their member organizations often heavily rely on this source of income. Thus, members are also seen as to put pressure on the platforms to be more moderate. This mostly translates into forms of self-censorship. FoRS in the Czech Republic has experimented with stronger criticism: their 2011 report used much stronger language than previous versions, something that the MFA clearly did not appreciate and expressed its perplexity towards the reasons for what they saw as FoRS's sudden hostility.[6] MFA officials also noted that FoRS brought up many issues in the published report which it did not mention in consultations with the MFA. In the 2012 report FoRS duly returned to a more toned down voiced, and also carried out a more intensive consultation process with the MFA while preparing the report.[7] Thus, the question emerges how much the contents of the AidWatch Reports should be taken to represent the actual interests of the NGDO communities. Private discussions and interviews with NGDO platform representatives reveal that they are often much more critical with the international development policies pursued by their governments then what they say in the reports, and often representatives voiced strong frustrations and even disillusionment. None the less, even if this frustration is missing from the way the reports are voiced, it is safe to assume that they include the most important reform needs. AidWatch Reports are also the only source of NGDO interests which are comparable for all five countries.

Table 6.2 summarizes the main recommendations by NGDO platforms from the 2012 and 2013 CONCORD AidWatch Reports. There are many similarities in the issues that the national platforms criticize their governments on and the reforms they lobby for. Most NGDO platforms call for an increase in aid, often referring to the international commitments made by

Table 6.2 Main NGDO recommendations towards national governments, 2012 and 2013

Platform	Main recommendations and reform demands
FoRS (Czech Republic)	• Increase effectiveness (vague) • Continue increasing transparency, sign up to the IATI • Continue monitoring and evaluation • Support Czech NGOs in winning EU grants • Create stronger field presence for the Czech Development Agency • Keep the elimination of poverty the core goal of development policy • Strive to find political support for increasing ODA • Introduce a plan for the implementation of Busan, Accra and Paris • Increase the in-depth understanding of the needs and situations of partners and coordination with other donors
HAND (Hungary)	• Prepare a strategic and legislative framework for ODA • Decrease the number of partner countries • Introduce monitoring and evaluation • Improve ODA statistics and increase transparency, sign up to IATI • Transform the development cooperation system to improve effectiveness • Create and adopt a roadmap for increasing Hungary's ODA • When finalizing the list of priority countries, focus on LDCs
Grupa Zagranica (Poland)	• Significantly increase the amount of ODA. • Increase ODA for Sub Saharan Africa. • Introduce monitoring and evaluation • Increase the ownership of partners • Prepare programs for partner countries • Include clear goals, targets and tools for evaluation • Implement the Busan declaration, join the DAC and IATI • Introduce legal provisions on policy coherence for development • Make recognizing poverty reduction as the primary objective of Polish assistance • Increase the transparency of grant calls for CSOs • Introduce long-term financing of development cooperation
MVRO (Slovakia)	• Increase aid quantity and aid quality • Sign up to the IATI • Effectively implement the National Global Education strategy • Realize common projects with other Visegrád countries and participate in EU joint programming • Engage in the policy coherence for development agenda • Reconsider ways of involving the private sector in development cooperation • Prepare the country strategy papers
SLOGA (Slovenia)	• Increase bilateral aid and focus it on reducing poverty • Prevent any further ODA cuts • Improve transparency • Improve the consultation process with civil society • Define the role of the private sector in development • Implement the Busan commitments • Build a framework that will ensure increased levels of policy coherence for development

Source: Compiled by the authors based on CONCORD (2012, 2013).

their governments. Almost all platforms put an emphasis on ensuring greater transparency and urge their governments to publish more and better data, as well as join the International Aid Transparency Initiative (IATI). In terms of aid quality, monitoring and evaluation of aid projects seems to be an important issue, as so far only the Czech Republic has the appropriate mechanisms in place. There are other references to aid quality, but these are usually either rather vague, or simply call on the government to implement the Paris/Accra/Busan commitments.

Beyond the similarities however between the five countries, the differences and country-specific issues are also striking.[8] In case of the *Czech Republic*, the difference in wording as compared to the other platforms is interesting. Looking at Table 6.2, FoRS talks about "continuing" to increase transparency, "continuing" the current monitoring and evaluation practices, or "keeping" the elimination of poverty as the core goal of development policy. This implies that FoRS does not want major changes, but is in general satisfied with the way the Czech government manages foreign aid. Beyond the CONCORD report, FoRS also published an annual AidWatch Reports of its own, and these also give the impression that they are generally satisfied with the system, with the exception of the 2011 report (FoRS) mentioned above. The 2012 report (FoRS 2012a) praises the increasing transparency and effectiveness of the system, welcomes many initiatives of the MFA like launching a systematic evaluation program, and mainly calls for fine-tuning. For example, it recommends that the Czech Development Agency (CzDA) publish indicative lists of future calls for proposals, an issue that the agency has since promised to do.[9] FoRS also pushes for expanding Czech field presence in partner countries—something the CzDA is lobbying for as well.

FoRS's criticisms have been seen to have been toned down since the 2007–2011 transformation of the Czech development cooperation system (Chapter 7), implying that the transformation has addressed many of their previous concerns. Czech development cooperation underwent major restructuring between 2007 and 2011, which strengthened the MFA and centralized all implementing tasks to the CZDA, a new MFA agency. The law regulating the policy area (Act 151 of 10 April 2010) made poverty reduction, with a reference to the Millennium Development Goals a key priority. The law explicitly mentions NGDOs as important partners. A key strategic document called "The Development Cooperation Strategy of the Czech Republic 2010–2017" operationalizes the law and guides official policy. Since the transformation and the new law, FoRS's AidWatch Reports tend focus on more minor technical issues as opposed to criticizing the system on the policy level.

Looking at *Hungary*, HAND points towards rather significant institutional shortcomings, like the lack of legislation on international development and a highly fragmented implementation system. Beyond what's in the CONCORD AidWatch Reports, the reports published by HAND also strongly critical of Hungary's foreign aid practice. These reports formulate a large number of demands towards the MFA, and call for both policy-related and technical changes. The first HAND AidWatch Report in 2007 (Kiss 2007) grouped these requests into twelve points. The most important of these followed more or less what is in the CONCORD reports, but also emphasized the creation of a roadmap towards the 0.17/0.33 percent ODA/GNI targets and a greater focus on poor countries and sectors that would most strongly promote the achievement of the MDGs, as well as vague references to aid effectiveness. These twelve points were later complemented with an additional request, the reduction of partner countries (Kiss 2011). The 2012 report (Hódosi 2012) reiterated these issues noting that there has hardly been progress on any of them. The only significant change came in 2014, when the MFA drafted the country's first strategy on international development, which was greeted by the NGDO community.

Polish NGDOs advocate very similar demands as their Hungarian counterparts. They also place an emphasis on increasing transparency and the introduction of project evaluations. They repeatedly called on the Polish government to significantly increase foreign aid, with a special emphasis on giving more to the Sub-Saharan African countries (CONCORD 2012: 58). In its own AidWatch Reports, Grupa Zagranica (2011a: 2) also emphasizes the need for a clear, long term strategic vision on aid. This issue was coupled with the request to create a legal framework for foreign aid and also a move to multiannual financing. The priority countries of Poland have been shifting throughout the years, but a common problem mentioned by Grupa Zagranica is that these countries often do not receive the bulk of bilateral aid. Bilateral aid must therefore be refocused. The Polish government seems slightly more receptive to criticisms from Grupa Zagranica as the Hungarian government is to those of HAND. In 2011, the Parliament passed a law on development cooperation, which was not received well by NGDOs who have voiced substantial criticism towards its contents and have called for its amendment (Grupa Zagranica 2011b). The MFA drafted a Multiannual development program in 2011, and introduced clear moves towards multiannual financing. Transparency in reporting has also greatly improved and Grupa Zagranica seem satisfied with the issue, and there is also evidence of increased involvement of NGDOs in policy-making (Grupa Zagranica 2011a: 2). Many issues however have remained contentious: foreign aid volumes have been stagnating for years and despite the new law NGDOs still argue that there is no coherent vision behind Polish aid.

Slovak NGDOs do not seem particularly vocal in the CONCORD AidWatch, or at least they do not voice serious institutional concerns like the Polish and Hungarian platforms, implying, that like the Czech platform, they are to some extent satisfied with the institutional setup in Slovakia. Indeed, there are no serious institutional shortcomings, as there is both a law on development cooperation, and regularly published medium-term strategies on how Slovakia spends its aid. In 2007, the government created an implementing agency, SlovakAid, as an administrative and contracting unit for bilateral programming. In 2010, MVRO signed a memorandum of understanding with the MFA, which elevated it to the status of official partner, granting it consultation rights on all official strategic and policy documents. MVRO even gets an annual grant from the MFA, but it is not an institutional block grant, but rather MVRO has to apply each year and its form changes from year to year. Thus, MVRO does not see this financing as secure and argues that it does not allow long term planning and stability. None the less, MVRO is the only platform among the five ECE NGDO platforms that receives such financing, making it perhaps even more prone to self censorship in its dealings with the government.

MVRO acknowledges that progress has been made in Slovak development cooperation, and the main issue is the low amounts spent on aid, especially on programmable bilateral aid.[10] These low amounts are the main issue discussed in the annual AidWatch Reports published by as well (MVRO 2011, 2012), and the platform calls the MFA each year to make good on its commitments and take specific action towards reaching the 0.33 percent target. Other issues mentioned include the creation of country strategies with specific sectoral priorities. Interestingly, the justification behind this is not so much increasing recipient country ownership of Slovak aid projects, but rather to allow Slovak entities (NGDOs) to better plan their capacities. MVRO also calls for greater engagement in PCD, and the development of specific institutional solutions, something other NGDO communities do not place so high on their agenda. The fact that MVRO does put an emphasis on PCD may signify that there are no other long term, unsolved contentious issues, at least not ones which they would publicly like to voice. Another issue that MVRO raises, and is also unique in doing so, is that the government should place more attention on engaging Slovak businesses in development cooperation. MVRO is also the only platform to call for greater cooperation among the Visegrád countries in development aid, and also for increased coordination with the EU.

Last but not least, a particularly striking issue in *Slovenia* is that NGDOs still perceive that their consultation processes with the MFA are inadequate, and call for consultation to be made "more meaningful and structured." SLOGA would like the MFA to make a compact acknowledging it as an official partner (like in the case of Slovakia, see Bučar 2012: 89), but the MFA argues that it has no legal ground to do so due to the Slovenian legislation on NGOs.[11] The Slovenian law on development cooperation from 2006 does mention vaguely dialogue with NGDOs, but mainly sees them as project implementers, not as organizations that should be deeply involved as stakeholders in policy design. The Slovenian development cooperation system also builds on several state-sponsored "centres of excellence," which focus on project implementation in strategic issues, and have been created by the government and receive bloc grants from it (Bučar 2012: 88–89, see also Chapter 7). These centres are seen by the NGDOs as rivals and competitors for government financing, and a perception in SLOGA is that the MFA was to some extent against the creation of the NGDO platform as it already had its own network of project implementers.[12] Besides the issue of formalizing SLOGA's consultative role, the platform raises few institutional concerns.

Further issues voiced are more or less in-line with those raised by other platforms, with a few exceptions, like the integration of human rights into development policy (SLOGA 2011: 11), PCD, and the definition of the role of the private sector in development, the latter two are similar to the requests of the Slovak NGDO community.

Three conclusions emerge from this overview of the recommendations and calls for reform voiced by the national NGDO communities in the five ECE countries. First, ECE NGDOs, just like their counterparts in the more established donors, put a strong emphasis on increasing aid levels and making aid work better for the countries of the global South. All platforms call for increases in aid, and they also call for better aid. All platforms wish to see governments make commitments on aid that are focused on poverty reduction. Second, they do not promote the interests of global South from a totally altruistic point of view, as issues related to their own survival and access to increasing government financing is also clearly present. Increased bilateral aid levels may not only be better for developing countries, but they also provide more opportunities for NGDOs to serve as project implementers. Also, they seem to be rather selective in the aid quality issues that they lobby for. Few platforms mention for example aid effectiveness enhancing reforms which would harm their member's access to government financing, such as increased usage of the budget support modality, or untying aid from national procurement. References to the global aid effectiveness agenda are usually rather vague. Third, the severity of criticism voiced by NGDOs towards official aid policies, as well as the specific issues raised by them varies between countries. This indicates on the one hand the fact that ECE development policies are rather heterogeneous in their levels of development, and on the other hand that there are varying degrees of satisfaction among the NGDO platforms with what their national governments have achieved. The criticisms made by Czech NGDOs have been becoming milder and milder throughout the years, with recent publications focusing on rather technical issues, telling the government to keep up the good work, or asking the MFA to do things that it wants to do anyway, but probably has troubles getting through the wider government. All these may imply that Czech NGDOs are either relatively satisfied with the system, or refrain from strong criticism for some other reasons. Slovenian and Slovak NGDOs are also rather mild, and they even voice issues like PCD or private sector involvement which are not typical. Hungarian NGDOs on the other hand have remained highly critical throughout the years, which implies that not much of their recommendations have been heard by the government. Polish NGDOs also voice serious concerns.

Why are some NGDO platforms more satisfied with their country's international development policy than others? This satisfaction, or to be more precise, refraining from serious criticism can imply many things on how much impact NGDOs have had in shaping the system, or what relationship the platform has with the government. Before we turn to explaining the varying degrees of influence using the framework from Chapter 2, it is worthwhile to investigate public opinion on international development as the societal context in which NGDOs work in.

6.4 Public opinion and aid

Even if NGDOs in the ECE countries are seen as elite organizations with little grassroots support, their capacities, as well as the legitimacy of their demands towards the government can still be influenced by underlying public opinion. In his 2004 study, Schmidt argued that it would not be easy to integrate the EU-10 into EU's development policy because there was little public awareness of development cooperation as an issue. The historical context outlined in Chapter 4 created a situation where there was low public awareness about development cooperation: to many citizens development cooperation is either "political assistance or humanitarian aid."

One way to investigate the attitudes of the ECE public towards development aid is via the Eurobarometer surveys that have been carried out on the subject. These are the most comprehensive surveys, and the only ones that produce data that are comparable between the new member states, and to some degree even comparable over time. We acknowledge some of the issues associated with the Eurobarometer surveys (see Nissen 2014), such as the fact that the questions relate mainly to EU level development policy and that Eurobarometer surveys are said to serve a political purpose in a sense that the questions are often biased to show high support from citizens for Community level action. However, they provide a useful tool to highlight attitudes to aid over the time period under study. The series of Eurobarometer surveys show that in many ECE states, there is a relative lack of knowledge about development aid compared to EU-15 states. The 2005 special Eurobarometer report on Attitudes towards Development Aid found a noticeable disparity between the views of the EU-15 group and those of the new member states. It found that in Estonia, Hungary, the Czech Republic, Latvia and Slovakia, respondents were more reluctant to take a strong stance on the question that it is important to help people in poor countries as compared to some EU-15 states, although the overall proportion believing that this is "fairly" important remains very high (Eurobarometer 2005: 26). The report concluded that there appeared to be a lack of knowledge in many of the new members concerning development issues. The study also showed that there was a strong belief that poverty within each ECE state needed resolving and that EU funds should be used for this purpose. The disparity between EU-15 and the ECE states was still evident in the Special Eurobarometer survey Europeans and Development Aid (Eurobarometer 2007), with citizens in the EU-12 states taking a less strong line on the importance of development assistance. By 2009 though, it did appear that the gap was narrowing (see Eurobarometer 2009), although in part this was driven by a fall in support for development assistance in EU-15 states affected by austerity measures, in particular in Portugal and Greece, rather than solely an increase in the ECE states (Eurobarometer 2012). When considering the future of the MDGs, respondents from the ECE countries were more likely to emphasize employment, health, economic growth and food and agriculture as areas of focus for development policy, whereas EU-15 respondents tended to emphasize education, democracy and human rights, and water and sanitation (Eurobarometer 2013).

The issue of public opinion also needs further unpacking. When asked about support for human rights and democracy promotion, the Eurobarometer reports highlight a strong level of public support in the ECE countries. Given their historical experiences of authoritarianism this is unsurprising, but it shows that the picture is more nuanced than some surveys suggest. It also chimes with the general foreign policy directions of the countries. Baun and Marek (2013: 211) highlight the importance of human rights and democracy in the foreign policies of the Czech and Slovak Republics and the Baltic states. Making sure the "right" questions are asked is therefore crucial.

The 2013 Eurobarometer also highlights some divergence within the ECE states. Poland showed a very high level of agreement with the statement: "It is very important to help people in developing countries," the Czech Republic was mid table, whilst Slovakia, Slovenia and Hungary all had high levels of respondents arguing that it was not important to help people in these countries (Eurobarometer 2013). Slovenia has seen a decline in support for aid spending since accession to the EU.[13] In Hungary only 51 percent of respondents stated that it was very important or important to help people in developing countries. This Eurobarometer is especially interesting given the links between support for aid and relative economic prosperity. As Longhurst (2013: 367) argues: "Poland has seemingly escaped much of the fallout from the global economic crises of recent years and has emerged, as some have argued, as 'Central Europe's Power House'." In contrast, Hungary has been very badly affected by the crisis and this may help explain the relatively low figures. These differences may have an impact on the influence of NGDOs.

Public opinion on foreign aid in the ECE states shows some similar traits to those in older EU states in a sense that a large proportion of the public support giving aid (Paxton and Knack 2012; Milner and Tingley 2013), even if this proportion is smaller than in more established donors. The drivers behind this concern are a mixture of moral, religious and social issues, with the added component of being recent recipients of aid (see Paragi 2010). People in the ECE states have an understanding of how aid can raise living standards through their own experience of the EU's PHARE program and pre-accession assistance Aid spending is also seen to be a sign that a certain level of economic development had been reached. Whilst it would be hard to say that all ECE states were "rich," there was a sense amongst sections of the population that their increased standards of living obliged them to help others. This obligation has two faces. The title of a report by the Romanian NGDO platform, FOND, sums up the positive view perfectly: "It's our turn to help" (FOND 2009). In contrast, development aid may be seen as an obligation forced upon ECE states—they give aid "because we have to."[14]

Radu (2013) shows that the ECE public is less post-materialistic than those in Western Europe, none the less surveys in Romania (2009) and Poland (2010) highlight aspects such as "moral duty" and a "clear conscience." In some ECE states, especially Poland, religious belief is rather strong and the charity element is important. The "enforced" voluntary contributions under Communism did have a legacy effect on how aid was perceived in ECE states. In Slovenia the legacy of the past meant that the public did not see development as a "noble business."[15] The Eurobarometer surveys do seem to show that the gap between older and newer member states in this area is narrowing and other factors apart are increasingly playing a role, such as the impact of the financial crisis. However, it is clear that more work is needed to raise awareness among the population on development issues and the necessity of this is a recurring issue in the annual AidWatch Reports.

National opinion polls beyond the Eurobarometers are rather hard to come by, and they are by no means comparable. One recent representative poll in Hungary carried out by DemNet Foundation in 2013 (Bördős and Gregor 2014) shows rather different conclusions than those of the Eurobarometers. According to this survey, about two thirds of Hungarians think that Hungary is in need of aid, and only 10 percent thinks that Hungary is developed enough to provide aid. Only 41 percent of the population are aware that Hungary provides development aid, and only 14 percent support increasing the amounts. These stark differences compared to the Eurobarometer surveys are probably a result of how the DemNet poll's questions were phrased, which placed the issue much more strongly into the Hungarian context, as opposed to the often rather abstract questions that are asked in the Eurobarometers. Research conducted by Glopolis in the Czech Republic suggests that politicians in the country pay little attention to global issues and to their relation to development in poor countries. Meislová (2010) supports this conclusion by showing that development issues played a marginal role in the election manifestos of the main parties. Glopolis suggests that one reason given is that there is a "lack of demand from typical Czech voters" (Glopolis 2010).

Due to the problems with the Eurobarometers and the lack of comparable cross-country public opinion surveys, it is difficult to draw strong conclusions. One thing is clear however: even if the gap is shrinking, public support for foreign aid has been smaller in all ECE countries than in the EU-15, which clearly has impacts on NGDOs in terms of their fund-raising possibilities and the legitimacy of their demands. While there is some evidence of differences between countries, especially since the economic crisis, the data do not allow any strong conclusions and thus this topic merits further research. With this social context in mind, we now turn to examining the determinants of NGDO influence.

6.5 Engaging with the state and effectiveness[16]

Formal relations between NGDOs and the MFA exist in all countries. However, the precise formulation of this relationship varies. The MFAs circulate draft policy documents among the NGDO community for comments, and formal meetings are also regular. MFA officials interviewed stated that they operate open door policies and the platforms are welcome to state their issues any time. The official acknowledgement of their consultative status clearly empowers NGDOs and makes development policy-making more open. However, nothing obliges the government to take the recommendations of the platforms into account when doing strategic planning, programming or implementing aid projects.

As elaborated in Chapter 2, the influence of NGDOs on national foreign aid policies will depend on five variables: (1) the composition of and power relations among the development NGOs; (2) organizational capacities of the NGOs; (3) their abilities to mobilize international allies for specific causes; (4) foreign donor assistance in the form of financing and knowledge transfer; and (5) attitudes and administrative capacities of state actors. We proceed by examining these in the five countries

6.5.1 Structure and power relations within the NGDO community

NGDOs should not be thought of as natural allies of each other. They work in different areas, have different perspectives and interests, and compete with each other for funding from the state, which is rather scarce in the ECE context. There is also a problem of collective action: engaging actively in the advocacy work of the platform will have costs, while all NGDOs will enjoy the benefits in terms of more favorable government foreign aid policies, thus encouraging free riding. Whether NGDO communities manage to overcome these two problems of rivalry and collective action is an important determinant of their influence.

Hungary can be seen as a rather extreme case of fragmentation within the NGDO community and warrants a more detailed study. One thing that is striking in Table 6.1 is that the Hungarian NGDO platform HAND has much fewer members than the size of the country and the amount of Hungarian aid relative to the other four ECE countries would imply. The Slovenian platform for example has more than twice as many members as HAND, and while Slovenia is a richer country than Hungary, its population is about a fifth of Hungary's. The fact that HAND has relatively few members can hint to weaknesses in the Hungarian NGDO community, thus it is worthwhile to examine the Hungarian scene in a bit more detail.

In fact, looking into details, it is not just the number of members in HAND, but also the composition of membership that is striking. For one, neither of the two largest and most significant Hungarian NGDOs, Hungarian Interchurch Aid (HIA) and Hungarian Baptist Aid (HBA) are members of HAND (see Krichewsky 2003, Szent-Iványi and Lightfoot 2015). HBA left the platform soon after its creation, and while HIA was a main driver behind its activities for several years, it also left in 2010.[17] The third member of the "big three" of Hungarian faith-based NGDOs, the Hungarian Maltese

Charity Service (HMCS), is actually the only large NGDO which still remains as a member of HAND. HMCS is by far the largest domestic relief and social care NGO in the country with a wide charity network across Hungary, but has much less significant international development activities than either HIA or HBA. While HAND is the officially acknowledged representative of the NGDO sector by the MFA, it does seem that the two large non-HAND member NGDOs also have some sort of "special relationship" with the ministry. The MFA regularly asks for their opinions,[18] and they are often directly requested to implement (mainly humanitarian) projects without any open tenders on short term notice. The MFA argues that HIA and HBA are the only organizations having the necessary capacities for such urgent tasks, which is most likely true. It is not clear however if HIA and HBA engage in policy advocacy. The issues that HAND lobbies for are rather clear and transparent due to the AidWatch Reports, but the views of HIA and HBA are not known. The MFA maintains that the two organizations are not involved in policy related advocacy, rather only consult on specific issues, e.g. how Hungary could react to various humanitarian catastrophes.[19] According to HIA, the main reason why they left HAND was that they felt that they are not getting enough for their membership fees and that they could be more effective engaging the MFA themselves.[20]

The fact that two influential actors are not members of the Hungarian NGDO platform is telling about the existence of rivalries. Problems of collective action are also evident: a recent mapping exercise carried out on the Hungarian NGDO sector (Selmeczi 2013) revealed that there are around 60 organizations in total doing some form of international development-related work. Why are only a fraction of these organizations a member of the platform? Many of these NGDOs are relatively small "on again, off again" affairs with few or no paid employees, thus they may find it difficult to pay membership fees. Whatever the reason, their absence, as well as the absence of HIA and HBA, make HAND unrepresentative of the NGDO sector, something the MFA may also be aware of. To make things even more complicated, there is a second, more specialized NGDO platform besides HAND, created in 2008, the Hungarian Africa Platform, with slightly overlapping membership, but with little visible activities.

There are no signs of such strong fragmentation in any of the other four countries. This is not to say that internal differences do not exist in the national NGDO communities, but they are less visible and do not hinder the working of the NGDO community to such an extent as they most likely do in Hungary. Some rivalries and differences are apparent in Poland, with development NGOs split along two groups, which is not surprising given the different origins of NGDOs discussed in section 6.2. One group of organizations seems to favor poverty reduction and focus on the global South (such as PAH or the Institute of Global Responsibility), while the other group advocates for democracy promotion and the focus on the Eastern neighbors of Poland (such as the Stefan Batory Foundation or the Polish-American Freedom

Foundation).[21] Both these groups are strongly represented in Grupa Zagranica, with all major NGDOs being members. Due to this diversity, Grupa Zagranica openly acknowledges the fact that the platform cannot represent all interests equally, and its members often have their own advocacy agendas.[22] The positions published and issues advocated by Grupa Zagranica seem to reflect the opinions of the pro-South NGDO group more strongly (see Grupa Zagranica 2011b).

The Czech NGDO sector for example can be seen as rather strong and active. FoRS does not face similar problems as HAND, as it includes both big and small organizations,[23] most importantly PiN, the Adventist Agency for Relief and Development (ADRA) and Caritas, the three biggest NGDOs in the Czech Republic. This membership structure clearly increases the legitimacy of the platform, because FoRS is used as the single advocacy body for the sector, and large NGDOs have made it clear that they will not bypass it.[24] Interviews suggest that the fact that FoRS has effectively lobbied the MFA with demonstrable results has increased its acceptance amongst the NGDO community.[25] Representatives of the Slovak NGDO platform claim that they are able to speak with one voice as their organization again represents all the large NGDOs, and perhaps are even dominated by them, as board members of MVRO are usually from larger organizations. None the less, they have established a good system of communicating with each other and finding common ground.[26] Similar findings emerged for Slovenia, although some minor tensions were seen to be present in the platform between secular and faith-based NGDOs. Thus, NGDO sectors in the Czech Republic, Slovakia and Slovenia can be seen as rather unified, the one in Poland shows some internal tensions, and that of Hungary can be seen as highly disintegrated.

6.5.2 Organizational capacities of the NGDO community

The composition of the NGDO platforms described above not only impacts their ability to speak with one voice and articulate clear demands, but also their capacities. While usually not a significant source of their income, all NGDO platforms charge membership fees, which are often proportional to the size of the member organization. Thus more and larger members mean more resources. Resources determine the ability of the platform to retain staff who can engage in policy/advocacy work, provide information services to members, and also seek out other sources of funding for the platform. If financing is not stable and predictable, then staff at the platform may be diverted away from their other activities and concentrate excessively on fundraising for the platform. Financial data on the platforms is not readily available, thus we look at other factors, such as number of permanent staff members, to gain insight into their capacities.

During the early days of the re-emergence of international development policies in the ECE states, the capacity development programs by CIDA and the UNDP (Chapter 5), also addressed the issue of NGDO platforms (Szent-Iványi and Tétényi 2013). In fact, CIDA was instrumental in helping the creation and initial capacity-building of HAND, FoRS and MVRO, while playing a lesser role in Poland and Slovenia. CIDA provided not only technical assistance in the creation of the platforms, but also seed financing, which enabled the platforms to engage in policy work early on. As this financing ran out however, the platforms needed to find alternative sources.

FoRS has a relatively large number of fee-paying members, including the largest NGDOs. In recent years, it has been able to maintain a permanent staff of five people, which includes a full time policy officer. The policy officer's main duty is to engage with the MFA on policy issues, and support such efforts of the FoRS's chairman and board members by preparing background materials. The composition of its membership predetermines HAND to weak capacities, as the platform mainly comprises small NGDOs. For much of its existence, HAND has worked with a single or at most two permanent staff members, and only being able to expand this number if it was able to secure a larger, multiyear grant (mainly from the EU), or during Hungary's EU presidency. This situation has been exacerbated by the post-2008 crisis, with many members facing increasing difficulties paying their membership fees.[27] HAND relies mainly on international project grants to stay alive, but it is difficult to cover regular operating expenses from these. HAND therefore has little capacities to support the advocacy work of its board members.

Grupa Zagranica should be the largest platform in the region based on its membership, but it does not stand out based on its capacities. It works with a staff of 3–4 people. Grupa Zagranica has an active system of thematic working groups which focus on advocacy in their respective areas (such as Africa, Belarus, development education, etc.). Each working group has dedicated administrative support from the permanent staff members. The group's financing is based on grants from the EU and other international sources. MVRO is in a special situation, as it is the only NGDO platform in the region which receives regular annual funding from the MFA. This is welcome by MVRO, but it is not without problems. Due to legal reasons, the MFA is unable to direct provide bloc financing for the operating expenditures of MVRO, but rather there is an annual call for proposals, and the platform has to submit a proposal each year with a specific project that the MFA will finance. The call is different each year in terms of conditions, so applying for this funding means considerable work for the platform, and they also have to "make up" a project each year for this call.[28] The fact that MVRO is relatively stable in its financing and capacities is shown by the fact that it has four permanent staff members. SLOGA has five staff members including a policy officer, which hint at strong capacities as compared to other platforms (which should represent much larger NGDO sectors than SLOGA). Most of its financing is also from EU grants and relatively small contributions from the MFA. SLOGA has a policy of not-applying for grant calls which are designed to implement specific actions in areas in which its member organizations are active, which may limit its financing options. Bučar (2012: 89) argues that: "SLOGA has also matured and established clearer policy dialogue within itself (the internal membership scheme, assembly voting on key policies, decision-making procedures, etc.) and can act with more self-confidence as a true representative of the NGDOs in Slovenia." SLOGA has also managed to professionalize its services. "SLOGA's Policy Working Group is preparing, on a regular basis, various policy proposals and/or amendments on topics such as aid effectiveness and institutional framework of Slovenian development cooperation."

Neither platform is able to raise significant contributions from donations, and this is true for the ECE NGDO sectors more broadly as well. NGDOs usually blame low levels of public awareness for their inabilities to raise funds from donations, although Czech NGDOs have noted that the private donations they receive, while still not substantial, are increasing.[29] Large NGDOs, as-well-as quasi NGOs like the national Red Cross Committees, have also been able to raise large amounts of donations for humanitarian issues, especially in case of high profile catastrophes covered extensively in the media like the 2005 South East Asian Tsunami or the 2010 Haiti Earthquake. There is little evidence however of NGDOs in any of the countries ever initiating visible fund-raising campaigns for development issues.

6.5.3 *Access to foreign financing and learning*

As mentioned, EU accession has opened the possibility for ECE NGDOs to apply for grants from the EU to finance specific projects. As mentioned, the EC "ring fenced" some EU funds for ECE NGDOs after 2007 for domestic awareness-raising and development education projects. Grants given by the EC typically require some degree of co-financing, and are usually above 100,000 euros in value, with the minimum project value for the 2014 call being 1 million euros. This puts smaller NGDOs at a disadvantage, many of which are only able to apply as members of consortia, and only the largest NGDOs from the region are able to lead such applications (see OECD 2007; Najslová 2013). The relatively low number of large NGDOs in the region implies low participation in EC grants, which is confirmed by the data for all five countries, but again one can observe differences. The data on grant winners provided by the EC is not sufficient to allow for a thorough analysis, as there is no data on how many applications are submitted from each country, nor is there information on how many NGDOs apply as partners in consortia. The EC's Grant Beneficiaries Database[30] only reveals the identity of the lead partner in successful grant applications, which is undoubtedly an imperfect proxy for ECE NGDO participation.

The database however does provide some telling figures, and these can be compared to participation of NGDOs from other EU members and partner countries. Between 2007 and 2011, 95 grants were approved for NGDOs from the five NMS (see Figure 6.1), as opposed to the total number of 11,135

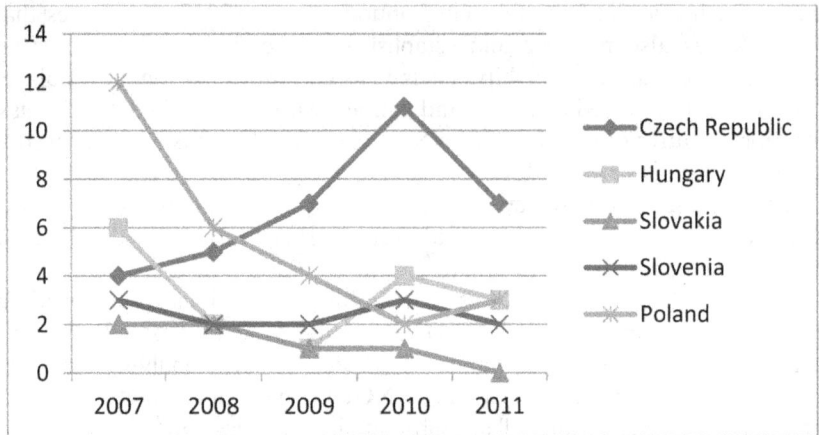

Figure 6.1 Number of EU-financed external assistance grants won by NGDO lead
partners from the five ECE countries
Source: EC Grant Beneficiaries Database and Zázvorkova (2011).

grants approved during the five year period. This is a relatively small number,
Belgian NGOs for example have won more than 400 grants during the same
period. Out of the 95 grants, 34 were won by Czech NGDOs, 27 by Polish
ones, 16 by Hungarians, 12 by Slovenians and 6 by Slovakians. If one scales
this based on the size of the countries, Slovenia is by far the most successful
with almost 6 grants per million inhabitants, followed by the Czech Republic
(3.2), Hungary (1.6), Slovakia (1.1) and Poland (0.7).

While the EC is the most important international source of financing for
NGDOs in the two countries, other sources, such as the UN system, the
European Economic Area grants, or the Visegrád Fund may also play a role.
However, it has not been possible to obtain comparable data on all five countries
on NGDO participation from these sources.

International sources of financing are important, but many interviewees
acknowledged that international networks like CONCORD, the DEEEP
project (on development awareness-raising) or Eurodiaconia (for faith-based
NGDOs) provide very important sources of learning which can also be vital.
CONCORD for example has pointed out many topics on which the platforms should engage the government and has provided opportunities to share
expertise on how to do effective advocacy, as well as capacity-building and
financing for the national AidWatch Reports. Through CONCORD, ECE
NGDOs learned that their responsibility is not only to be partners of governments in project implementation, but they must also act as watchdogs of
government activities.[31] These and other international forums can clearly have
indirect results on NGDO empowerment, but it is difficult to see any differences between the NGDOs in the five countries. Platforms and NGDOs
interviewed in all countries emphasized how actively they take part in these

and other specialist networks and how much they have learned from these contexts.

6.5.4 *Ability to mobilize foreign support*

The ability to mobilize foreign support for specific issues seems to be marginal in all five countries. As discussed, all five platforms are members of CONCORD, and they provide information for the one-page sections on their respective countries for CONCORD's annual AidWatch Report (see for example CONCORD 2012). This gives their concerns with national aid policies an international dimension. CONCORD itself however does not lobby national governments directly, only the EU institutions. National platforms can use CONCORD's reports in their advocacy towards their national governments, and try to emphasize the additional legitimacy that being parts of a network like CONCORD gives to their demands. Beyond the annual CONCORD AidWatch exercise, there have been no visible examples in any of the countries of the national platforms relying on other networks or international organizations to lobby the government. There is also little evidence of any platform lobbying Brussels directly. None of them have offices in Brussels, and they state they do any such lobbying through CONCORD (see Pleines 2011). A positive example of lobbying the EU through CONCORD was that the NMS platforms managed to achieve a certain level of positive discrimination towards NMS NGDOs in EU grant calls, but this did not have any effect towards national governments.[32]

6.5.5 *Government attitudes and capacities*

Government attitudes towards the platforms and the NGDO sectors more broadly were perhaps the most interesting thing to study. All MFA representatives argued that they have excellent relationships with the national platforms and "how greatly they appreciate the AidWatch Reports"[33] and any other policy inputs of the NGDO community. It however emerged during the interviews, that NGDOs on the other hand, while in general also acknowledge that the relationship is good, add several things to this general statement which at least nuances the governments' attitudes. We highlight some of more interesting findings from the five countries.

The relations between FoRS and the MFA were described as cooperative by both sides. NGDOs evaluated it as "good and stable," with the MFA being open to discuss all issues,[34] while MFA officials maintained that they take the views of the sector seriously and value it.[35] FoRS is an observer in the Czech Council on International Development Cooperation, which is an inter-ministerial body mainly charged with strategic decision-making. Real decisions however are made in the MFA, and FoRS is regularly invited to comment on draft policies. According to MFA officials, FoRS is very vocal, but generally supportive of the MFA.[36] The MFA seems to have developed a close partnership with FoRS, something acknowledged by the OECD DAC special peer review in 2007 (OECD 2007), and instead of viewing consultation with the platform as burdensome, it uses FoRS to enhance its own legitimacy. There seems to be recognition that FoRS is a natural ally of the MFA as opposed to other branches of government, an issue which was clearly shown during the 2007–2011 institutional transformation of Czech development policy, elaborated in Chapter 7. The Czech MFA and the wider government have many practices that the NGDO community seems highly satisfied with. While the government was forced to introduce many austerity measures in the wake of the economic crisis, spending on international development has actually increased modestly between 2008 and 2012. There are regular calls for proposals for NGDOs, and the MFA runs a special scheme to help NGDOs raise the necessary co-financing for EU grants, which may in part explain the relatively higher success rate of Czech NGDOs. As discussed in section 6.3, the legal and strategy framework is seen as strong and appropriate by the NGDO sector.

In Hungary, the attitude and capacities of the government seem more problematic. HAND perceives its relationship with the MFA as "normal," and values the MFA's open door policy,[37] and MFA diplomats have also talked about a good relationship.[38] However, there have been several instances of tension between the MFA and HAND in the past years, which point to a less rosy picture. One recurring theme is related to the publication of the Aid-Watch Reports, with the main issue being access to data. Hungarian foreign aid is one of the least transparent in the world (Publish What You Fund 2013), and according to HAND, getting data from the MFA for the reports is always difficult. In 2007, HAND turned to the Ombudsman for Data Protection to force the MFA to provide necessary data for the report.[39] There were severe delays in publishing the 2011 report, with HAND blaming the MFA for not providing the data on time, and the MFA maintaining that they did provide all data and HAND was unable to analyze it in time. The 2011 report even notes it in its text that the MFA did not provide data (Kiss 2011: 6). All these issues point to a less than fully cooperative relationship, although, to be fair, HAND officials have noted that the MFA itself is facing difficulties in getting data from the other line ministries. The Hungarian NGDO community has also noted that they feel the MFA is getting more cooperative, which is in part due to the influx of young people to the ministry, and even former NGDO experts "changing hats."

In Poland, the attitudes of the MFA have changed in recent years towards NGDOs and their requests for the better. The MFA seems rather open, and Grupa Zagranica has been granted easy and regular access to the Undersecretary of State. This was not always so: before 2010 there were often cases of animosity between the MFA and the platform, and the MFA was not really receptive to the requests of the NGDO community. The animosity now seems to be a thing of the past.[40] Experts in the NGDO community attribute this to several factors: pressure from the EU on the MFA, change in the composition of MFA staff, with younger people becoming dominant, the formulation of written rules and procedures for NGDO inclusion (e.g. Grupa Zagranica has a role now in monitoring how MFA grants are allocated). Also, as there is little political attention to development policy, Grupa Zagranica feels that it can step in with ideas and fill this vacuum.[41] This changing attitude is reflected in the practice of the MFA, as there is some evidence of actual NGDO influence. In 2012, the MFA published its first grant call to support NGDO co-financing for EU grants, something Grupa Zagranica had lobbied for. It remains to be seen whether the current good relationship between the NGDOs and the MFA will translate into further NGDO requests being met.

The Slovak MFA has concluded a written memorandum of understanding with the platform and the fact that it provides direct financing to the platform hints at favorable government attitudes. However, MVRO experts interviewed stated that "it's nice to have a good relationship on paper, but what does it mean in practice?"[42] There seems to be a feeling in MVRO that the MFA does not take them seriously, and in fact, as opposed to the Czech Republic where in general the Development Department is a close ally of FoRS, in Slovakia it does not seem to stand firmly by the platform. The main reason why the MFA's statements of a good relationship can be questioned is that the way the MFA works is unpredictable. Grant calls are published without any clear schedule, and there are no tender forecasts. The platform was an observer in the grant decision committee of the MFA, but the MFA recently removed them without any justification. While there were important reforms in Slovak aid policy up to 2007 with the acceptance of the law and the creation of Slovak Aid, MVRO feels that the MFA, and the Development Department especially thinks that things are now "finished" and there is nothing to fight for. Thus, the MFA is rather passive and unreceptive.

The Slovenian case, similar to Hungary and Poland, also shows signs of improving MFA receptiveness. Bučar (2012: 89) argues that "it is clear that the cooperation between the government and NGDOs has intensified during the last six years." The reform of the institutional structure for international development has helped in this. As Bister noted in 2005: "because of an ODA system which is divided among several ministries, NGOs find it hard to cooperate with the government." The lack of transparency and of clear responsibilities on the governmental side, made it difficult for NGOs to lobby their interests. The MFA noted that they had "good links" with SLOGA,[43] although SLOGA believes it can still ask "nasty questions from the government" and in 2011 they went as far as to abolish cooperation with the MFA during the annual development days. However, it is clear that the MFA is open to ideas from SLOGA and thus SLOGA is able to "influence" directorate thinking (Zrinski and Bučar forthcoming). The MFA relies on SLOGA as it can provide an institutional memory for the MFA in light of the staff rotation policy.[44] As shown by Bučar (2012: 95), cooperative activities between the government and NGDOs are increasing, which is a sign both of a more receptive government and greater NGDO capacities. The OECD DAC peer review (OECD 2011c: 11) noted that the government should develop an NGO strategy to "help clarify how and when the MFA and NGOs would co-operate." In 2012, new strategic documents were developed, including guidelines on cooperation between the MFA and NGOs.

6.6 Summing up

The NGDO sectors in the five ECE countries have come a long way since the 1990s, and have undergone a process of professionalization. Legacies of the past however are strong, and civic activism still has low levels in the ECE states, and the political culture of consulting with civil society also shows problems in some countries. EU accession has given a huge boost to the NGDO sectors in terms of access to financing and learning opportunities, but has also alleviated any needs they might have faced to engage in grassroots fundraising. However, many NGDOs rely on the MFA for financial support, mainly in the form of aid project implementation tenders, which weakens their watchdog role. Diversifying income streams, mainly towards the public, is a key task.

NGDOs have created advocacy platforms in all five countries, and have formulated rather clear demands towards their governments. The analysis shows that some NGDO communities have been more successful in getting their requests heard than others. Four of the five variables which have an impact on the influence of NGDOs (with the exception of the ability to mobilize foreign support) seem to vary between the five countries and can thus give us insights as to how influential NGDOs can be. In the Czech Republic, one can see a unified platform that is able to speak with a single voice and has strong capacities, NGDOs which are relatively successful in securing external funding, and an MFA which is highly receptive and sees the NGDO community as its allies. NGDOs are thus likely to be influential. In Hungary, the NGDO sector is disintegrated and lacks capacities. NGDOs are only moderately successful in securing EU funding, and relations with the government have been tense, although there are clear signs of improvement. Poland's NGDO sector also shows some signs of internal conflicts, but is more unified than Hungary's. Capacities of the platform however are relatively small compared to the size of the country, and organizations do poorly in securing EU grants. The government is becoming increasingly receptive, and has initiated some favorable changes for the sector. The Slovak platform seems able to speak with a single voice, but NGDOs do poorly in securing EU funding. The platform, despite getting direct funding from the MFA feels that they are not taken seriously. Slovenian NGDOs have relatively strong capacities, do well in winning EU grants, and have greatly improved their relations with the government, thus also seem well posed to influence their governments' decisions in international development policy. NGDOs in the Czech Republic and Slovenia thus seem the most influential, while the ones in Hungary the least. Polish and Slovakian NGDOs should be seen as somewhere between these two extremes.

The platforms have clearly decided that the sections of the MFA with responsibility for development are better as allies, with Hungary being a potential exception. As a result, the platforms tend to pick their battles more carefully and in a more targeted fashion. The tension between various groups does undermine the unity of some platforms, although the general sense that the platform is the recognized voice (both by the MFA and by the NGO community) is no longer contentious, unlike say in Lithuania where two national platforms exist. On the whole, government attitudes towards the NGDO platforms have softened with officials in the MFA appreciating the institutional memory role the platforms can play, the ability of NGOs to undertake projects that the MFA or the Agency (where one exists) does not have the capacity to undertake itself, and the in-country experience often associated with NGOs. This change can also be linked to the fact that one can witness a higher level of professionalization with regard to the organizational capacities of the NGO community across the board.

Notes

1 Interview with ECE MFA official Q, August 2014.
2 Interview with ECE NGO representative E, February 2013.
3 For example, BOCS Foundation in Hungary is championing family planning and contraceptive rights of women, something the Hungarian NGDO platform has not put on its agenda, thus BOCS is heavily engaged in advocacy work itself.
4 Interview with ECE NGO representative F, January 2013.
5 Interview with ECE NGDO board member A, March 2013.
6 Interview with ECE MFA official H, March 2013.
7 Interview with ECE NGO representative G, March 2013.
8 See also Szent-Iványi and Lightfoot 2015 for a more detailed examination of the Czech and Hungarian cases.
9 Interview with ECE MFA official L, February 2013.
10 Interview with ECE NGO representative H, April 2013.
11 Group interview with ECE NGO representatives, January 2013
12 Group interview with ECE NGO representatives, January 2013.
13 Interview with ECE NGO representative F, January 2013.
14 Interview with ECE NGO representative I, February 2012.
15 Interview with ECE NGO representative J, January 2012.
16 Analysis in this section expands upon Szent-Iványi and Lightfoot (2015).
17 Interview with ECE NGO representative E, February 2013.
18 Interview with ECE NGO representative E, February 2013.
19 Interview with ECE MFA official R, April 2013.
20 Interview with ECE NGO representative E, February 2013.
21 Interview with an ECE expert on development policy, May 2013.
22 Interview with ECE NGO representative K, July 2013.
23 Interview with ECE NGO representative E, February 2013.
24 Interviews with ECE NGO representative E and G, 2013.
25 Interview with ECE NGO representative G, March 2013.
26 Interview with an ECE NGO platform board member, April 2013.
27 Interview with ECE NGO representative E, February 2013.
28 Interviews with an ECE NGO representative and board member, April 2013.
29 Interview with ECE NGO representative G, March 2013.

30 The database can be accessed at: http://ec.europa.eu/europeaid/work/funding/bene ficiaries/index.cfm?lang=en.
31 Interview with ECE NGO representative E, February 2013.
32 Interviews with ECE NGO representatives F and E, 2013.
33 Interview with ECE MFA official R, April 2013.
34 Interview with an ECE NGO platform board member, March 2013.
35 Interview with ECE MFA official H, March 2013.
36 Interview with ECE MFA representative H, March 2013.
37 Interview with ECE NGO representative L, February 2013.
38 Interview with ECE MFA official R, April 2013.
39 Interview with ECE NGO representative L, February 2013.
40 Interview with ECE MFA official O, June 2013.
41 Interview with ECE NGO representative K, July 2013.
42 Interviews with ECE NGO representative and platform board member, April 2013.
43 Interview with ECE NGO representative F, January 2013.
44 Group interview with ECE NGO representatives, January 2013.

7 The domestic politics of aid

Aid policy outcomes, including institutional and legal structures, aid volume and aid allocation, are shaped by the domestic politics of aid, which we conceptualized as a bargaining process between government agencies in Chapter 2. Having discussed the external sources of influence on this process in Chapters 5 and 6, Chapter 7 focuses on explaining changes in the foreign aid policies of the Czech Republic, Hungary, Poland, Slovakia and Slovenia between their creations around the turn of the Millennium and 2014. The chapter is structured into five country case studies, preceded by a short overview of government agencies and institutions in the ECE region. Each case study first describes the initial policy and institutional setting in the country at the time of the (re)creation of international development policy before EU accession (the 't = 0' state), which is followed by a discussion of the main subsequent policy changes. The explanatory part of each case study then uses the three sets of variables identified in Chapter 2 (*institutions* which distribute power, actor *capacities* and the ability of actors to form *coalitions*) to explain why policy change happened (or failed to happen) in the given case.

7.1 Government agencies and institutions in ECE

The most visible element of any reform in international development policy will be related to institutional and legal structures, and such reforms can be the most contentious as well. Institutional reforms are likely to have an impact on all actors involved in the policy area, as they may change "how the cake is distributed" among the governmental actors involved. Thus, all actors are likely to exhibit strong preferences. We focus primarily on explaining such institutional and legal reforms in this chapter, but also reforms which bring the given country's international development policy closer to the global consensus on foreign aid.

There are several institutional models for organizing a country's international development policy. Development policy, as a tool of a country's foreign policy, comes under Ministries of Foreign Affairs to some degree in all OECD DAC member countries. According to the OECD DAC, there are four main organizational models (OECD 2009a; Lundsgaarde 2013b: 3):

1   Development policy is fully integrated into the MFA, both in terms of policy and implementation (e.g. Denmark and Norway).
2   A specialized development cooperation directorate or agency within the MFA leads and is responsible for policy and implementation (such as Finland, Ireland, Italy or the Netherlands).
3   The MFA has overall responsibility for policy and a separate executing agency is responsible for implementation (France and Sweden).
4   A ministry or agency other than the MFA is responsible for both policy and implementation (UK).

Even though the MFA may be responsible overall for foreign aid, several other line ministries may be involved, and often aid resources may be fragmented along these agencies. We can draw conclusions on the relative weight a government places on foreign aid policy from where it is located within government. Lancaster (2006: 19) argues that aid fragmentation in government equals weak development purpose in government aid programs. The OECD DAC has acknowledged this and is encouraging donors to "rationalize aid administrations by placing all development-oriented work across government departments under a common strategic umbrella and increasing the coherence of country-level oversight of aid programmes" (Lundsgaarde 2013b: 3). As we discuss in the five case studies, the fragmentation of international development policy is a common theme in ECE countries.

As argued in Chapter 2, in order to avoid circular reasoning in our model, we take the initial foreign aid policy setup in the ECE countries as exogenously given. These initial institutions already distribute some degree of advantages and disadvantages to various players. All five ECE countries began their new aid policies with highly fragmented institutional setups, with the MFA having overall responsibility for policy and strategy, and implementation being fragmented among several line ministries. Initially, none of them created official executing agencies, although some "hybrid" solutions for this did emerge. There was no legislation on international development, all countries started off with rather crude policy statements outlining their motivations and priorities, as well as government resolutions which more or less laid down the division of labor between government bureaucracies.

Since then, the institutional structures in the ECE states have undergone some revision in the 10–15 years since they were created. Reviewing the work by Dauderstädt (2002), Krichewsky (2003) Bučar *et al.* (2007), Szent-Iványi (2012b), and the OECD DAC Special Reviews gives a sense of the changes undertaken in specific states: some countries have managed to accomplish rather spectacular reform up until 2014, which in some cases included a radical overhaul of the institutional framework and the creation of a stable legislative and strategic background, which reflects at least certain elements of the global consensus on foreign aid. Others have managed to do much less. The remainder of this chapter examines these reforms along five country case studies.

7.2 The Czech Republic—a radical transformation

Officially, the Czech Republic was the first ECE country to reboot its international development policy, although on a very low scale level, in 1996, just a year after the country's OECD accession. The country's first aid strategy was accepted in 2002 (Czech Government 2002), which declared poverty reduction as the central goal of Czech development assistance, advocated partnership and introduced several principles to increase the transparency and efficiency of Czech aid. In 2005 the Czech government was already characterized as having the strongest policy and institutional set-up in the region, in part because of its longer tradition of official and private aid-giving (Grimm and Harmer 2005: 13). This structure however underwent significant reform between 2007 and 2011, making the Czech institutional set-up the most centralized among the ECE countries. The main goal of the reform was to introduce a stronger strategic focus and increase the effectiveness of Czech development cooperation, and thus the Czech Republic is a clear case of radically changing policy and administrative structures.

Two distinct phases can be identified in post-transition Czech development policy. Until 2010, the situation was one of institutional fragmentation. According to the Competences Act (Act No. 2/1969, as amended in March 1995), the Ministry of Foreign Affairs was the Czech Republic's central public administration authority in the field of foreign policy; as such, it was responsible for creating the concept of and coordinating development cooperation and external economic relations. The MFA formulated the principles and strategies of Czech development policy and gave opinions on development aspects of other government policies. However, line ministries were responsible for developing and implementing international development policies in their relevant field, and had rather extensive powers (Adamcová *et al.* 2006: 12; Tulmets 2014)—in total, nine of them were involved in development cooperation. Indeed the Special OECD DAC Review in 2007 highlighted the fragmentation and weak role for the MFA as an issue that needed to be addressed (OECD 2007). As an interviewee highlighted:

> Foreign Affairs is the coordinator of development cooperation in our government, but they are not fully in charge. We have a decentralised structure: 9–10 ministries are involved in developing the line policies. This is not very good. We are now trying to centralise development cooperation policies more, developing a more central role for Foreign Affairs.[1]

As development cooperation was split between so many actors, the budget was also fragmented, with the MFA only disposing over a relatively small share of 25 percent in 2006 (Adamcová *et al.* 2006: 75). Duplication of projects and administrative structures clearly led to inefficiencies and gave little scope for a unified and strategically driven Czech foreign aid policy (Czech Ministry of Foreign Affairs 2007). Policy documents mainly related to foreign aid implemented by the MFA, and had little impact on activities of the other ministries. As an additional actor in the system, the Institute of International Relations, a government-owned think tank affiliated with the MFA created the Development Centre, with the goal of providing scientific advice on Czech foreign aid policy, and also assisting in selecting projects, evaluation and monitoring (Adamcová *et al.* 2006). While some reforms were carried out between 2002 and 2007, they basically left the fragmented system intact (Czech Ministry of Foreign Affairs 2007; Waisová 2011; Tulmets 2014).

According to both Sládková (2011) and Waisová (2011), it was the OECD DAC Special Review in 2007 which prompted change and a gradual shift to the second phase, as the review clearly spelt out what the Czech Republic needs to do in terms of creating a strong policy and institutional structure. Government Resolution No 1070/2007 initiated the transformation process, and spelt out the main tasks for the following years. These included a gradual shift of new projects to the MFA, while line ministries gradually phased out their existing projects; and a unification of the official development assistance budget under the MFA. A major step in the reform process was the acceptance of the Act on Development Cooperation and Humanitarian Aid in 2010 (Act No. 151/2010), which centralized the decision-making for development cooperation within the MFA, although full responsibility for foreign aid decisions is shared with the Ministry of Finance. Development objectives are contained in the Development Cooperation Strategy of the Czech Republic 2010–2017. The length of this strategic period has been praised as it allows for long term planning (Végh 2013). The centralization of Czech development policy is clearly a move towards institutional models found in countries like Sweden, even though some line ministries still retain international development related implementation capacities and budgets, such as the Ministry of Education (scholarships to students from developing countries, is a "permanent exception"), or the Ministry of Interior (migration). The Ministry of Finance also seems to have retained an important role, as it is in charge of a program which aims at sharing Czech experience on transition and EU integration with partner countries, in the field of public finance. The Ministry of Interior's and Finance's role is seen as a "temporary exception," and these responsibilities should also be transferred to the MFA in the future (Czech Ministry of Foreign Affairs 2007).

A further important element of the reform transformed the Development Centre into the Czech Development Agency (CzDA) in 2008, "responsible for identification of potential areas for cooperation, formulation of procurements and calls for proposals, contract management and monitoring of the overall implementation" (Sládková 2011: 3). The CzDA actively participates in the creation of development cooperation programs between the Czech Republic and priority countries as well as on the other stages of the project cycle management. The agency reports to the MFA, although its day to day independence from the ministry is seen to be important (Végh 2013). With the creation of the agency, the MFA could focus its resources on strategy formulation, policy work, and programming.

As a final important element of the reform, the Act on Development Cooperation and Humanitarian Aid also created the Czech Council on International Development Cooperation, which is an inter-ministerial advisory body for the MFA, with the main role of ensuring coherence with other policy areas. Thus, the line ministries continue to be involved in development cooperation, even though they generally no longer implement projects. The Council has several thematic working groups, and three non-governmental platforms act as observers (FoRS, the Platform of Private Entities Working in Development Cooperation and Union of Towns and Municipalities of the Czech Republic).

One can argue that the Czech reform between 2007 and 2011 followed the spirit and the letter of the Special OECD DAC Review. No further institutional reforms are foreseen, although fine tuning is necessary on the policy level.[2] The Czech government has also reacted to some other recommendations of the OECD DAC, leading to further changes in the Czech development system, although clearly not as spectacular as the overhaul of the institutional and policy structure, but perhaps going beyond fine-tuning. These include the following:

- The adoption of a project cycle manual in the identification, formulation and management of development projects.
- The creation of an evaluation strategy at the MFA based on OECD DAC guidelines, with all evaluation reports being uploaded to the MFA website. About six evaluations are contracted each year, carried out by external experts. However, as these evaluations refer only to the project level, and the projects are often not planned with future evaluation in mind, problems with indicators, baseline data, and constructing a counterfactual scenario limit the usefulness of these (Špánik 2012). However, they have been judged valuable in strengthening the culture of evaluation at the MFA.
- A slow and gradual decrease in the number of partner countries.

7.2.1 Explaining the Czech case

The degree of transformation which happened in the Czech case is clearly rather spectacular among the five ECE donors. It is not hard to imagine how difficult pushing such a reform through must have been: many line ministries had their foreign aid budgets taken away and centralized to the MFA, creating a large number of losers of the reform, who thus most likely also opposed the change, or had to be compensated some way for their losses. While some concessions were undoubtedly made, as a few ministries managed to retain some of their international development budgets, the fact remains that such thorough reform is impossible without political leadership and guidance. Also, when looking at the pre-transformation system in terms of capacities and institutions, it is not much different than that found in other ECE donors. Thus, what was present in the Czech Republic that allowed such radical change to happen, but was missing in the other four countries?

There are several reasons why the transformation happened in Czech development policy, and these reasons fit a coherent story. The MFA, having a central but weak role in the pre-transformation system, clearly wanted change which would increase its resources and prestige. But, the MFA itself was too weak to push any reform through, and thus engaged in building outside support for its case by getting the OECD DAC to carry out a Special Review on Czech development cooperation, and allying itself with the NGDO sector, who were among the strongest in the ECE region due to a unified platform, high capacities, and success in securing international financing (Chapter 6). These two allies played a crucial role in building political support for the reform, which the MFA and the department responsible for international development within it could not have secured otherwise. We detail this story by looking at the three sets of variables which influence the outcome of the governmental decision-making game: institutions, capacities and coalitions.

Institutions. After its re-creation, international development policy in the Czech Republic did not stand out among the other ECE countries in terms of institutional structures and capacities. Broader government foreign policy strategies did not give any strong role to development policy. A document entitled "Conceptual Basis of the Foreign Policy of the Czech Republic for the 2003–2006" period (Czech Government 2003) can be seen to characterize foreign policy in the early era of Czech development policy well. In this document, international development is not among the priorities of Czech foreign policy—indeed the document mainly focuses on EU integration, security issues, and bilateral relations. The strategy includes two rather vague paragraphs on foreign aid, which mainly emphasize how the Czech Republic will remain committed to providing aid. There is however no mention of any scaling up or reform. This does not give any strong legitimacy for international development policy within the MFA, or the MFA within the government. While the MFA was officially the "chief coordinator" (Adamcová *et al.* 2006: 3) of the country's foreign aid policy, it had little scope to influence how the other line ministries actually spent their resources allocated to international development activities.[3]

Capacities. There is evidence that the Czech MFA did have some capacities which made it stronger than its peers in the other ECE countries, although it is not clear how significant these differences are. Most importantly, as the Czech Republic was the first to restart its international development policy in 1996, four-five years earlier than the other countries, thus it clearly had more time to accumulate expertise. While staff rotation was mentioned to be an issue,[4] there also seems to be some level of continuity as well, as many key development staff members have remained in development throughout the years. There is also evidence of movement from the NGDO sector to the MFA, which has also contributed to developing a better understanding of foreign aid in the ministry (Végh 2013). In comparison with other MFA development departments, the Czech one seems to have had a relatively higher number of staff (CRPE 2013).

Coalitions. One can argue that outside pressures, coming from the NGDO sector and internationally, mainly from the OECD, have not only had a clear impact in formulating the preferences on the government level, but the MFA was able to use these strategically and build coalitions with these actors. It was the MFA which turned to the OECD DAC Secretariat in May 2006 and requested the OECD to carry out an evaluation of its development cooperation policy. The intention behind this was to use the resulting conclusions as a basis to advocate for reform towards the broader government. This was unprecedented, as the OECD DAC had never carried out a review of a non-member, but they agreed to tailor the methodology of the peer reviews to what was a named a "Special Review," and features a much stronger consultative element than the peer reviews generally do (OECD 2007: 5). According to the review, the main objective was to inform and offer advice "to the Czech authorities' internal dialogue on the reform of the country's ODA system" (OECD 2007: 5), thus reinforcing the argument that the MFA mainly aimed to use the report to generate political will for reform. The Special Review's results were discussed by government and other stakeholders, as well as OECD DAC experts in April 2007, which led to the final published report. Thus, the review process already had an important role in building consensus on the reform process. In 2013, Deputy Foreign Minister Jiří Schneider stated that "the recommendations from the first Special Review conducted by the Development Assistance Committee of the OECD in 2007 triggered a crucial transformation of the Czech ODA system" (Czech Ministry of Foreign Affairs 2013). Other sources (Waisová 2011; Hlavičková 2012) and inter-viewees[5] also confirmed the central importance of the review in initiating reforms.

However, in order for international pressure to have an impact, there must be a certain willingness domestically to engage in reform. A second ally of the Czech MFA was the relatively strong development NGO sector, with good political contacts. As discussed in Chapter 6, Czech NGDOs can be seen as having the relatively strong advocacy capacities in the region due to a well organized and well endowed platform, as well as successful participation in EU and other international grants. Also, Czech NGDOs have been lobbying for reforms along the lines of the 2007–2011 transformation, and have wel-comed the process.[6] But, the key to their effective advocacy was most likely the fact that they managed to forge an alliance with the MFA's development department, and also foster high level political support for development cooperation. There was a clear perception among the line ministries that the NGDO sector and the MFA are allies.[7] This alliance was then able to present a strong case to higher level politics on the necessity of the reform.

The role of specific people in creating this alliance must also be taken into consideration (see Breuning 2013). Interviewees credited a strong push towards the transformation in the Czech development system to this coalition-building, and have often mentioned one person, Šimon Pánek.[8] Pánek was a student activist during the Velvet Revolution, and in 1992 he was the co-founder of People in Need (PiN), which has since grown to be the largest development and humanitarian NGO in Central and Eastern Europe. He also worked in the presidential administration of Václav Havel, who was known to be a supporter of PiN's work (Thoolen 2014). In 2004, he became the chairman of FoRS, and he had an important role in behind-the-scenes advocacy for the transformation. Due to his background as a student activist during Czechoslovakia's transition, he knew and had easy access to most Czech politicians, as many of his student activist peers chose a political career (Vaughan 2006). According to an interviewee, Pánek, who's a household name in the Czech Republic, was not only instrumental in building high level political support for the transformation of development policy through his political contacts, but the work of PiN, often receiving high publicity contributed to sensitizing Czech politicians and the wider public to humanitarian and development issues.[9]

Access to high level decision makers was therefore given, and it seems politics was attentive. The Czech Republic has often been described as the ECE country where politicians have seen the value of international development cooperation, not only in decreasing poverty or reacting to wishes of the Czech people, but also as a tool to gain markets and to increase the international prestige of the country through projecting an image of a responsible donor. This sense of international identity is a strong one within Czech foreign policy and the position on foreign aid can be linked to other aspects of foreign policy, notably human rights (Zemanová 2013). Besides the work of PiN, the strong humanitarian beliefs of President Havel were key in building political attention. The Czech Republic was the first to restart its international development policy in 1996, quite a few years before any other ECE donor did. A government document in 2001 already stated that the "the mere fact that the Czech Republic provides foreign aid is not enough and it is necessary to strengthen the efficiency and transparency of the system" (Czech Ministry of Foreign Affairs 2007). Statements by politicians are revealing. In a speech to the chiefs of Czech diplomatic missions, Prime Minister Mirek Topolánek said the following in 2006 (Topolánek 2006):

> In the future, the importance of development assistance will undoubtedly increase ... This is one of the tools of foreign policy, which allows, among other things, building markets outside the EU common market. The effectiveness of development assistance, as one of the supporting pillars of future Czech foreign policy, however, is significantly damaged by its administrative fragmentation across multiple departments. Currently, the projects of Czech development policy are implemented by nine

departments. This situation is untenable. It is necessary to create a clear institutional structure of Czech development assistance policy. ... The possible emergence of a new institution must not mean an increase in the number of officials, or growth in administrative costs.

Gaining the support, or at least dampening the opposition of the line ministries was also an important issue. It seems that the Ministry of Finance was a crucial player to get on board the reform, and this could only be done by sacrificing part of the reform, by giving the ministry a role in transition programs, and also allowing it a key role in financial decisions. While having a rather different understanding of foreign aid, especially in terms of its goals,[10] in general, the MoF was not against some elements of the reform, such as the creation of a centralized, professional aid bureaucracy which could manage implementation related tasks (Hořejš 2008). There was a strong rhetorical commitment to keep the other ministries involved in development cooperation, but on a different level: ministries should actually become involved in development on a much deeper level than previously through policy coherence. Thus, the creation of the Czech Council on International Development Cooperation can be seen as an effort to console the line ministries and give them the perception that they still have an influence over the policy area and how the money is spent. The transformation was also planned as a gradual process at the request of the line ministries "to allow for adaptation of all actors and maintain the expertise of other departments, without compromising the continuous implementation of ODA projects" (Czech Ministry of Foreign Affairs 2007).

Summing up the Czech case, we see an initial state of a fragmented and inefficient institutional and policy structure, in which all actors were basically free to pursue their own agendas, despite the coordinating role of the MFA, which underwent significant transformation between 2007 and 2011 and emerged as a highly centralized, poverty-focused system which hopefully increases efficiency significantly by reducing duplication and allowing strategic planning and implementation. The MFA was able to strategically harness the support of external actors like the OECD DAC and the NGDO sector, and use this to foster political will for reform. While compromises were still necessary to decrease opposition to the reform, it has been judged highly successful. The MFA clearly emerged as a winner, but only time will tell whether the other line ministries will remain committed to development (through work on policy coherence, for example) now that they have lost their budgets.

7.3 Hungary—stagnation, but some signs of (late and partial) reform

The initial institutional structure in Hungary can also be characterized as highly fragmented, with only small changes between 2003 and 2013, and some of these changes have actually been rather regressive. This fragmented structure has its roots in a 2001 concept paper. This document created a system of development aid where implementation responsibility is with line ministries, which dispose the bulk of the development budget, with the MFA acting as a coordinator. "According to the Concept Paper of the International Development, the MFA takes a role of the interdepartmental coordinator and is responsible for drawing up the annual plan of the development activities" (Bučar *et al.* 2007: 4). Each line ministry had its own budget for "international cooperation," and could decide relatively freely how to allocate that. The MFA administered about 20 percent of the country's contribution to international development in 2006 (Hungarian Ministry of Foreign Affairs 2006).

The concept paper also created the Development Cooperation Governmental Committee, a high level inter-ministerial forum, chaired by the Minister for Foreign Affairs, to serve as the main forum for coordination between the ministries and to determine the main priorities of development policy. This committee was supported by an expert level inter-ministerial working group. The MFA's responsibilities and competences in terms of foreign aid were set down in the Government Decree 82/2003, but this decree does not give the MFA any power to influence the decisions of the line ministries on how to allocate their aid budgets. The MFA's position in Hungary was also weakened by the fact that as of early 2014, there was still no law on international development policy which could have given it a stronger mandate. The MFA also had the responsibility to inform the Foreign Affairs and Budget Committee of the Parliament about the international development activities.

Furthermore, to develop links with civil society, politicians and academia, as well as to raise public awareness, a Civil Advisory Board for International Development Co-operation was established in 2003. It is composed of the representatives of political parties in Parliament, public and professional organizations, academics, the MFA and development NGOs. The goal of creating the body was to establish a forum for discussing foreign aid policy with society, and to channel public opinion into government policy-making. The body met twice a year, and its first chairman was Árpád Göncz, the respected first president of the republic after the fall of Communism.

Within the MFA, the International Development Co-operation (IDC) Department was established in October 2002, and an interdepartmental working group has also been created in March 2003 to allow MFA-wide coordination of development policy with other departments which may play a role (such as multilateral diplomacy, EU coordination, regional and country desks). According to the original intentions, the role of IDC Department would focus on the policy level, and a separate agency would be charged with implementation tasks. Accordingly, in 2003 the MFA contracted an independent not-for-profit company, HUN-IDA to serve as an implementing agency. According to an interviewee, contracting an independent, privately owned company as opposed to creating a government agency was something unprecedented among donors.[11] HUN-IDA's tasks were rather limited, as tendering actually remained the task of the MFA and the agency's job mainly focused on contracting and monitoring implementation, as well as organizing the

MFA's technical assistance projects and taking part in capacity-building activities (see Paragi 2010). This meant that as an aid agency it had very limited responsibilities and was only involved in reviewing and assessing project proposals from a technical and financial point of view. The main reason for using HUN-IDA was most likely an attempt by the MFA to get around the constraints they faced on staff numbers, and outsourcing certain activities seemed as an option. HUN-IDA was also seen as a way of increasing flexibility, and as a non-governmental organization it provided opportunities to overcome certain legal constraints, for example ones state organs face in terms of providing payments to foreign organizations.

HUN-IDA did not take on any implementation responsibilities towards the international development budget of the other line ministries (as does SlovakAid, for example), and thus its presence did not contribute to reducing the fragmentation of the Hungarian aid system. Interestingly, HUN-IDA was not a newcomer to the field of international development, but was an affiliate of TESCO (not to be confused with the British retailer). TESCO was the state-owned company in charge of technical assistance to the South during the Communist regime, but had been privatized during the 1990s. Thus, it was in a position to claim that it was the main "repository" of past Hungarian development expertise.

Not much significant change happened in the Hungarian international development system in the decade after its inception. The fragmented structure has remained, as have the channels and institutions for governmental coordination. Despite several attempts, no law on international development has been presented to Parliament, making Hungary the only such country among the five case studies. While a relatively high profile project involving academics and NGOs to prepare background studies for an eventual law did happen between 2006 and 2008, and at least two different drafts of the law were circulated, these never entered the Parliamentary approval process. The Hungarian government is the only one among the five countries which has so far not requested an OECD DAC Special Review. Officials were reluctant to provide reasons for this other than the associated costs of OECD DAC membership.[12]

Some smaller changes did happen which had impacts on the institutional and legal environment. One of these changes is related to the status of HUN-IDA as implementing agency. In 2006, the MFA launched a public procurement tender for the position of implementing agency for the duration of three years, which HUN-IDA won, despite criticisms it had received for its previous activity in terms of being too expensive and lacking in transparency.[13] This new contract expired in 2009, and the MFA decided not to renew it, leaving the Hungarian international development system without a separate implementing agency (see Szent-Iványi and Tétényi 2013). The decision behind this was most likely the fact that successive government austerity measures had shrunk the international development budget of the MFA, which no longer warranted a separate agency. A second change is related to the policy level, the formulation of the country's first international development strategy (valid for 2014–2020, see Hungarian Ministry of Foreign Affairs 2014), which was presented by MFA for consultation in mid-2013, and accepted by Parliament in early 2014. It is striking that Hungary only managed to accept its first strategy in 2014, as opposed to, for example, Slovakia which already presented one in 2003. While the strategy does refer to all important principles of the Global Consensus on Foreign Aid, and its annex includes a timetable for increasing aid expenditure, it does not say much on how these will be implemented in Hungarian foreign aid practice, nor does it draw up any ambitious plans to reform the ineffective institutional structures aside from mentioning the need to create an implementing agency. Rather it simply describes and acknowledges the current situation. None the less, the creation of the strategy was welcomed by both civil society and academia, and is seen as a major achievement in light of the past decade.[14] The new strategy also restarted talks about the need for a law on development cooperation.

7.3.1 Explaining the Hungarian case

The fact that there has been relatively little change and even some regression due to shrinking funds in Hungary's international development system stands in stark contrast not only with the Czech case, but all the other case studies as well. As discussed in Chapter 5, the influence of external actors has been weak in all five ECE new donors, and interview data point to especially weak socialization in the case of Hungary. For example, Hungary is the only country among the five ECE case studies which has not requested a special peer review from the OECD DAC. Chapter 6 has shown that Hungarian NDGOs are unlikely to be too influential due to lack of capacities, as well as coherence and unity in the sector. They have generally been unable to speak with a single voice towards the MFA, which may have allowed the MFA to neglect their inputs. However, they did play an important role in the process of formulating the 2014–2020 strategy, which is discussed below. The general weakness of outside influence on international development policy-making, both external and domestic, points to the fact that policy outcomes should mainly be explained in terms of bureaucratic politics within the MFA and within the government.

Institutions. Initial institutional structures made the MFA the central coordinator of foreign aid policy, and the minister her/himself chaired the governmental committee on development policy issues. The MFA was given a rather strong organizational mandate by a government decree, but it had little authority to actually influence the decisions made by the other ministries on their own aid budgets. In practice, the only thing the MFA could do is to *ex-post* acknowledge the way other ministries had spent their budgets. There are several instances in which the MFA has had difficulties even in gaining access to data and information on what the other ministries did in terms of foreign aid, and in this context coordination seemed next to impossible.

Broader government foreign policy strategies may have empowered the MFA to a certain degree, especially in terms of the process of formulating the 2014–2020 strategy. The socialist-led government presented a foreign policy strategy in 2008 (Hungarian Government 2008), meant to be valid for a 12 year period, and which followed long preparatory work involving about 100 experts (Szent-Iványi 2012). Interestingly, this strategy gave foreign aid a relatively important role, as it discussed the issue in three paragraphs. In these paragraphs, a reference was made to Millennium Development Goals, a commitment to increase aid and reach the 0.17 and 0.33 percent ODA/GNI targets set by the EU Council, as well as discussing wide geographical priorities (with an emphasis on maintaining a close relationship with Southern and Eastern Europe). Resolution 1/2008 of the International Development Cooperation (IDC) Governmental Committee, approved by the Government in spring 2008, acknowledged the fact that IDC is identified as one of the important activities in Hungary's External Relations Strategy. The 2008 foreign policy strategy can therefore be seen as strengthening the MFA and the IDC Department within it by giving it a point of reference. However, less than two years after its acceptance, the new government led by the right-wing Fidesz party scrapped the strategy, and presented its version in 2011 (Hungarian Ministry of Foreign Affairs 2011). This new strategy did not talk explicitly about international development policy, but it emphasized the need for Hungary's foreign policy to "open globally," especially towards developing countries (Tarrósy and Morenth 2013), without truly specifying what this opening means. "Global opening" clearly had a strong economic dimension, with the need to diversify foreign trade by increasing trade with non-EU partners (MTI 2014), but some have argued that it is a means of increasing Hungary's prestige in the global East and South, which certain actions of the Fidesz-government have heavily eroded in the West (Népszava 2013). Global opening became a catchphrase of the Fidesz-era's Hungarian foreign policy, and international development was clearly seen as one of the tools.[15] Thus, the Fidesz-led government's foreign policy strategy, while not talking explicitly about development, actually did more to empower the IDC Department and the MFA than the previous foreign policy strategy. This is reflected in a statement by Péter Wintermantal, deputy foreign minister: "development policy can only win with the global opening" (Asiaport 2014).

Capacities. The number of people working at the IDC department has fluctuated between 8 and 13 during the last decade, which is more or less proportional with the number of people working in the departments of the other case study countries. The main issue on capacities is not necessarily related to the number of people (although all IDC department members interviewed complained of being understaffed as compared to the tasks they have), but rather to expertise. Only a small minority of the people working in the IDC department in the past decade have been development professionals. Most of them were career diplomats who started to learn the profession from scratch, but they had no strong incentives to put much effort into this learning process, as they saw their position in the department as temporary before they were rotated to a different department or a foreign posting. Young graduates hired by the department usually did not stay there for long either. Development cooperation clearly had a low prestige within the Hungarian MFA. Typically, a person would not stay longer at the department than three years, and there is only one person who has been at the department throughout the decade after its creation. In the Czech case, there seem to have been much stronger efforts to maintain continuity and build up institutional memory.

Coalitions. The main variation between the Czech and Hungarian cases relates to coalitions and the ability to mobilize external allies: while the Czech MFA used this strategically, the Hungarian MFA seems to have been rather reluctant in building wider support for international development. Together with the other two groups of variables, this reluctance can explain why Hungary has not done much reform in its international development policy up to 2014.

It is difficult to find evidence of the MFA attempting to build coalitions with other Ministries or with the NGDO sector. In fact, the relationship between the MFA and the NGDO community, and especially the umbrella organization HAND has been outright confrontational in some cases. While HAND interviewees acknowledged that the position of the IDC department within the MFA may be rather weak[16] and this can be a reason why their recommendations go unheard, there are several instances of evidence that the IDC department itself has not been acting in a fair manner with HAND. HAND representatives have complained that the IDC department usually gives them very short deadlines for commenting policy drafts. There have also been cases of the department not granting HAND access to data which should be public (Kiss 2011), and in one case HAND even decided to turn to the ombudsman for data protection which ruled in their favor. It is difficult to understand why the IDC department has not seen the opportunities that building an alliance with the civil sector could provide it.

Among other government agencies and potentials for coalitions, one must mention the ministry responsible for external economic affairs (its names and exact structure has changed rather frequently between 2003 and 2013 due to governments reshuffling their portfolios: Ministry of Economy and Transport 2002–2008; Ministry of National Development and Economy 2008–2010; Ministry of National Economy 2010–2014. After 2014, external economic affairs have been moved to the MFA, which was renamed the Ministry of Foreign Affairs and Trade). The ministry is responsible for trade development, export credits and a practice which the Hungarian system has labeled "tied aid credits," essentially investment projects abroad financed by a concessional government loan and implemented by Hungarian actors. The Hungarian Investment and Trade Agency, a government agency affiliated at times with both the MFA and the Ministry of National Economy for example talks about international development cooperation as an "opportunity for Hungarian businesses."[17] Clearly, officials working in this field have a very different understanding of foreign aid, and think of it mainly as a tool for export promotion.

It is a highly telling example of the Ministry of National Economy's influence that a clear reference to Hungarian business interests made it into the final version of the 2014–2020 aid strategy, which was missing from the first draft prepared by the MFA's IDC department. But, it is also interesting how these perceptions on the need to promote business interests have influenced the position of the MFA itself, as some interviewees there have also talked about the need to use aid to support Hungarian businesses, or the need to "win back our money" that Hungary contributes to the European Development Fund or the International Development Association of the World Bank.[18] A senior official at the MFA's IDC Department argued that "development policy and trade policy, helping Hungarian companies gain a foothold on foreign markets are not contradictory, but highly compatible goals" (Asiaport 2014). Supporting Hungarian businesses clearly has a much stronger resonance with the government than development and poverty reduction, especially in the absence of any pro-development public opinion and weak NGOs (Chapter 6). If the MFA itself sees that promotion of business interests is part of its mandate, then it is no wonder that it does not build coalitions with the NGDO platform HAND, which would prefer more poverty focused aid.

These differences in interests and perceptions between the MFA and NGDOs can explain why not much reform has happened between 2003 and 2013. However, something must have changed in order to allow the birth of the 2014–2020 strategy, which can be seen as an important achievement compared to the previous ten years of muddling. We argue that there are two reasons for this: first, as discussed in the section on institutions, the Fidesz government's wider foreign policy of global opening provided a more favorable environment for foreign aid. Second, NGDOs changed their strategy in terms of advocacy and began to engage in coalition-building with actors other than the MFA, most importantly Members of Parliament, focusing on the Parliament's Foreign Affairs Committee. Despite the inherent weaknesses of the Hungarian NGDO community discussed in Chapter 6, this strategy seems to have been successful. Various NGOs have had several projects aimed at sensitizing these MPs to international development issues, which included organizing study tours for them to developing countries. For example, in 2010, in the framework of a EuropeAid financed project, the NGO DemNet Foundation organized a study trip to Kenya for three MPs, who visited Hungarian and other ECE development projects (DemNet 2010). These sensitization activities seem to have paid off, as these MPs were instrumental in pushing a Parliamentary resolution through in early 2013 which mandated the MFA to create an international development assistance strategy (which eventually became the 2014–2020 strategy). The NGO sector clearly sees the creation of the strategy as its own success,[19] and circumventing the MFA seemed to have worked in this case.

Summing up the Hungarian case, one can see an ineffective institutional structure and a practice which is far from being aligned with the Global and

European Consensus on foreign aid. Since the creation of this system, very little has changed. This can be explained by the weak position and capacities of IDC Department within the MFA, and its unwillingness to build coalitions with NGOs due to past confrontations. Also, the MFA, and the IDC Department within it, seem to align themselves with more general government rhetoric, as the example of business interests clearly shows, and thus cannot be thought of as a champion of development goals. However, a change in the government's wider foreign policy strategy involving a global opening and a new advocacy strategy by NGOs targeting MPs seems to have born some fruit. The real question is however whether the 2014–2020 strategy will actually be implemented and whether it can generate momentum for institutional and legal reform.

7.4 Poland—reform but still not punching to its weight?

While Poland's modern aid program dates back to 1998 (Drozd 2007), it was a 2003 strategy paper which outlined the goals, tasks, principles and mechanisms of Poland's aid program (Polish Ministry of Foreign Affairs 2003, see Bučar *et al.* 2007). Initially, the aid program was coordinated by the Department of the United Nations System and Global Affairs of the MFA (Baginski 2002), and it was only in 2005 that a new, dedicated focal point, the Development Cooperation Department of the MFA (DCD) was created to take on policy leadership within the national system. As with the other ECE countries, Poland's initial institutional set-up was also characterized by the heavy participation of line ministries.[20] The institutional framework was complicated with bilateral assistance delivered through three main mechanisms: development assistance managed by the MFA (projects, humanitarian and multilateral aid through international organizations); financial aid managed by the Ministry of Finance (preferential credits, foreign debt relief, etc.); and educational aid managed the Ministry of Education (scholarships for students coming from developing countries). According to the 2003 strategy paper, the role of the leading national coordinator of development activities was played by the MFA. The DCD however only managed about 10 percent of Poland's aid. Line ministries had to report to MFA *ex-post*, and all activities were coordinated through the Development Cooperation Policy Board. As with other ECE countries, it is questionable just how much the MFA was able to influence the allocation decisions of the other ministries. A 2008 report even went as far as to argue that "it is difficult to speak about a single development assistance strategy. It is rather a sequence of activities undertaken by particular institutions" (Iłowiecka-Tanska and Pejda 2008: 7). The 2003 strategy paper did not provide a legal basis for Polish aid and so for many years the aid policy of Poland was based upon existing collections of legal rules, scattered throughout many other legal ordinances (Krichewsky 2003; Tulmets 2014).

Reforms in Poland following EU accession have not been as ambitious as in the Czech Republic or Slovakia, but seem to have achieved two clear (and interrelated) results: (1) a legal basis for development cooperation has been created in 2011, which has helped in putting Polish development cooperation on sound strategic and programmatic grounds; and (2) a clear vision has emerged on the main goal of Polish development policy: perhaps Poland has gone the farthest in specializing its policy on democracy promotion and the transfer of Polish democratization experience, which cannot be separated from the strong Eastern focus of Polish foreign policy.

In terms of legal and strategic reforms, the Polish Government approved the Act on Development Co-operation in February 2011, which was subsequently approved by the Parliament later in the year. This became the first overarching legal act on international development policy in Poland (Végh 2013). The DCD came under the National Coordinator for Development Cooperation, who has the position of Under Secretary of State, which aims to highlight the importance of the policy area. The law mandated the creation of multiannual plans (to be approved by the Council of Ministers), at least four years in length, on which the development cooperation program would be based. The first such medium-term document was the Multiannual Development Cooperation Programme 2012–2015. However, the document with the strongest impact on the actual implementation of Polish aid is the Annual Plan, prepared on a yearly basis by the MFA, as it includes financial allocations and defines thematic and regional fields for Polish foreign involvement. In practice this is translated into the annual call for project proposals announced by the MFA, for which only Polish NGOs are eligible. Subsequently, only the projects which correspond with the call (hence with the Annual Plan) will get funding. There is also a bulk of activities that are part of Polish Aid, mainly managed by the other line ministries, which are not part of this call, and as such do not necessarily align in their objectives with the strategic goals laid out in the annual and medium term programming documents, or the Act on Development Co-operation. Also, even though planning has become multi-year, the OECD DAC Special Review highlights perceived constraints to multi-year budgeting (OECD 2010a: 24), even though the Public Finance Law would allow it (Chapter 4).

In terms of vision, the 2011 law made "promoting and supporting the development of democracy and civil society" the primary goal of Polish aid (Pospieszna 2014), making it rather unique in the ECE context (Chapter 4). This goal was given high visibility by the creation of a new institution. According to the Multiannual Development Cooperation Programme 2012–2015, the delivery of Polish aid is organized in three main forms: (1) bilateral channels, (2) multilateral cooperation and (3) the Solidarity Fund. This latter is a dedicated democracy support agency, functioning as a "quasi-governmental" NGO. The Fund was created in 2001 as the Polish Know-How Fund, but suspended its activities in 2005. In 2011, in order to make Polish democracy support more visible in the spirit of the Act on Development Cooperation, it was decided to reconstruct the foundation. It now finances all of Poland's external democratization projects as a re-granting agency where NGOs can apply with their project proposals. The fund is institutionally independent from the MFA, although it distributes public funds. While Polish development policy was always characterized by an Eastern trajectory and the issue of democracy promotion, over time policy makers learned to spell it out better, and it got more crystallized and more focused (see Pomorska 2011), as evidenced by the 2011 Act and the creation of the Solidarity Fund.

Even though Poland is the largest donor among the five ECE countries, it does not have a separate implementing agency (unless one considers the Solidarity Fund to be such, although it only focuses on democracy promotion projects). For a brief time before the 2011 Act, there were two departments in the MFA dealing with development policy—the directorate for programming and one for the implementation of foreign aid (Zajączkowski 2012), but this was seen a short lived experiment that "went wrong"[21] due to emerging rivalries between the two departments. Even though all activities are under one department now, the tasks are divided among several units within—one being in charge of planning and two in charge of implementation. The division is between the countries of the Eastern Partnership and everything else, showing well the geographic priority (Végh 2013: 9). Reforms have not done anything to address the issue of fragmentation: in 2013 there were 16 government agencies involved in foreign aid, with the MFA managing 21 percent of total aid disbursement (Kugiel 2014: 2).

Thus, even though Poland was not able to reform its inefficient institutional structure, a clearly articulated vision has emerged on how the country should engage in international development, which is in-line with the country's wider foreign policy.

7.4.1 Explaining the Polish case

Institutions. Initial institutional structures made the MFA the coordinator, as in all other countries, but gave it little actual power to do this task. The fragmentation and the lack of MFA influence seems to have been so strong that at one stage the MFA and the Ministry of Finance even had different lists of priority countries (see Lightfoot 2008). The creation of the Solidarity Fund seems to have complicated things even more by adding an additional institutional actor to the system. As noted, this organization funds democratization projects conducted by civil society organizations in a set of countries defined specifically by the Fund. Végh (2013) highlights the lack of any formal division of labor between the Fund and the MFA. She highlights that "the very same non-governmental organizations can apply both to the MFA and to the [Solidarity Fund] to conduct development projects in the same countries." The added-value of the Fund is that it can support opposition groups in authoritarian countries without the Polish government's direct involvement. Given the focus of activity in Belarus for example, this arms length approach is important (see Pospieszna 2014).

Broader foreign policy strategies of Poland however show that there is an increasing resonance between the country's foreign policy goals and heavily democracy-promotion based approach to foreign aid, thus giving support to aid policy. Of the countries under study in this book, Poland has the largest foreign policy reach. In recent years it appears to have been achieving greater consistency in its foreign policy. Two key factors are at work here. The first relates to greater consistency in foreign policy goals, which is linked to domestic stability (Baun and Marek 2013). During interviews with officials in 2008 one said with regard to priorities "we are waiting for the new government."[22] This is clearly an issue for all officials as governments change, but the swings in Polish politics have been dramatic. There was a sense in 2008 that "already a lot of programmes are in place and society seems in favour of development. Problem seems to lie with the politicians, not with the citizens."[23]

The fact that the Polish government was re-elected in 2011 has given some consistency to Polish foreign policy goals after a period characterized by sharp swings in preferences (Baun and Marek 2013: 219; Longhurst 2013). The Tusk government is seen as more pragmatic, especially in terms of building alliances internationally. For example, around the issue of the Eastern Partnership, Poland built a strong alliance with Sweden, a country seen as an effective EU player (Kaminska 2013: 31). The second is the role of EU membership. EU membership was seen as crucial as it forced Polish government to "think about development cooperation in a systematic way."[24] Kaminska (2013: 26) shows how participation in EU external relations increased the MFA's budget.

The foreign policy priorities of the Tusk government for 2012–2016 include a clear and strong reference to development policy, and frame it mainly in terms of democracy promotion (Polish Government 2012):

> Increasing the role of development cooperation in Poland's foreign policy so that this international activity could also contribute to Poland's security and the stability of its neighbours and partners in development cooperation; supporting measures for the dissemination of human rights, the rule of law and democracy, in particular, in order to create a friendly international environment and to prevent conflicts.

Key tasks according to this policy paper are to develop the activities of the Solidarity Fund and to increase the share of the Eastern neighborhood in Polish aid allocation. While developing countries and poverty reduction are also mentioned, they are clearly only marginal considerations in Poland's foreign policy, which seems to see the spread of democracy in its Eastern neighbors, especially Belarus and Ukraine, as a key to its own security and economic prosperity. Poland can be a more credible supporter of democracy than the other ECE countries due to its much larger size, higher volumes of aid, and significantly larger weight in the EU. Thus, it can afford to use democracy promotion to a much larger degree than the other ECE states and expect these tools to meaningfully contribute to its own security. Clearly, the government has realized that using foreign aid primarily as a tool of democracy promotion can serve its interests well, even if this goes against the Global Consensus on foreign aid which emphasizes poverty reduction.

Placing democracy promotion in the center of foreign aid policy and also giving it a prominent role among broader foreign policy goals is most likely a reflection of general public attitudes and nostalgic sentiments related to the Solidarity movement. Many Poles see themselves as freedom fighters and supporters of democracy, and through the country's historical experience feel a need to help others in their struggles (Drążkiewicz-Grodzicka 2013: 70). Using aid for these goals clearly resonates more with public opinion than reducing poverty in the global South (see Chapter 6). The level of political discourse around development issues as distinct from issues of democratization and human rights has tended to be low.

Resonance with foreign policy goals can also provide an explanation as to why no political will has emerged to make the Polish aid system more effective through centralization and the creation of an aid agency. A separate agency has been created for democracy aid, which was seen as politically important, while the effectiveness of the "rest" of the aid provided by country may not have emerged as a political issue.

Capacities. As the largest country among the ECE states, Poland has always had the highest number of staff in development cooperation in absolute terms. The capacities of the DCD were further enhanced in 2009 when it was merged with the Department of the European Integration Committee, which almost doubled the Ministry's capacity for development cooperation. Not only staff numbers, but also the level of expertise increased, as new staff were familiar with aid, having worked on development programs of foreign donors in Poland previously (Drążkiewicz-Grodzicka 2013: 69). Accordingly, the number of staff dealing with development cooperation at the ministry has increased from less than 40 people to more than 60. Subsequently, special posts for development cooperation experts have been created in some Polish embassies (Kugiel 2011). However, in relative terms, these numbers are not all that high: the Czech Republic (a country with about a fourth of Poland's population) has more than 30 people working in development (in the MFA and the CzDA together, see CRPE 2013: 12).

Drążkiewicz-Grodzicka (2013: 66) claimed that the DCD is among the least prestigious departments in MFA. This fits a general view that international develop is not part of career aspirations in the MFA because it is perceived to be a risky area of policy and it can be more difficult to get embassy positions from there. However, the previous and current Deputy Ministers are seen to be "into development," which helped raise the profile within the MFA.[25]

Coalitions. Inter-ministerial rivalries seem to be strong in Poland and have limited the possibility for coalitions within the government. The most significant rivalry can be observed between the positions of the Ministry of Finance and the MFA regarding the establishment of an implementing agency favored by the MFA (Zajaczkowski 2012). The OECD DAC peer review seemed to be steering Poland in the direction of an agency (OECD 2010a). In part, the logic is that "20 people in an agency are more effective than 50 people in MFA who rotate" and given the staff numbers in Poland an agency could be easily staffed.[26] However, the MFA seems to have been unable to use these arguments, or to ally itself with the OECD DAC to push for reform as was evident in the Czech case.

The strong institutional rivalries can be an explanatory factor in why no significant centralization has happened thus far: each ministry was highly keen on protecting its own turf. The Ministry of Finance can be seen as a veto player (Janulewicz, 2014). Line ministries are traditionally strong actors in aid policy, but they have to report to the MFA and all activities are coordinated through the Development Cooperation Policy Board. Although at the time of writing this remains just an advisory and consultative body, evidence is coming through that the MFA is using this board to gain support from other ministries for its position vis-a-vis the MoF. It is clear that the MFA is engaged in coalition-building against the MoF.[27] This may have an impact on future policy-making.

The MFA has so far failed to build international coalitions as well. It did not use the OECD DAC Special Review to push for reform as Czech MFA did, but rather there was a sense that the review was not well received in Warsaw. The MFA was expecting to get much praise from the OECD DAC and primarily use the review to show towards the government how well they perform, but instead they got a review which was rather critical and highlighted several potential needs for reform. The UNDP, even though it had a small office in Poland and supported a public campaign called "Millennium Development Goals: time to help others!" in 2004, which was the first UN-driven campaign in ECE in support of the MDGs (Harmer and Cotterell 2005), played a much smaller role in Poland than in the other ECE countries, as it never established a Trust Fund with the Polish government.

The OECD DAC Special Review (OECD 2010a: 28, italics added) highlighted that "Poland's development NGOs are dynamic and well informed partners and *could be* useful allies for MFA in advocating for increased support for development and shaping new policy." It does seem that relations between the MFA and the NGDO platform Grupa Zagranica could be better and the model of cooperation in the Czech Republic is one that is looked on with admiration. Some reforms have occurred; NGDOs for example have been included on the Coordination Board. The NGDOs were "happy to be there" and this was seen as a "gain for them."[28] It is also noted that at a more technical level NGOs have the leading role, but their influence on policy seems to have been small. This was evidenced with the 2011 Act, where NGDOs unsuccessfully lobbied for stronger references to poverty reduction and the MDGs. As discussed in Chapter 6, there seem to be tensions within Grupa Zagranica between organizations that favor democracy promotion in the East, and ones that promote poverty reduction in the South. This division may not have allowed Grupa Zagranica to emerge as an ally of the DCD on poverty reduction. Democracy promotion NGDOs on the other hand have tended to support the government's wider foreign policy and the creation of the Solidarity Fund as a dedicated re-granting agency.

Summing up the Polish case, we see an institutional structure with strong fragmentation and rivalries between agencies. The biggest unresolved "fuzziness" is between the MFA and other ministries within the government, but even tensions within the MFA have been evident. This system has not been reformed, despite the fact that Polish aid got a clear legal and strategic framework, and a rather unique vision has emerged that democracy promotion must be the main goal of Polish aid. This has been emphasized by the creation of the Solidarity Fund. The main reason for this constellation is the high resonance of democracy aid with broader government foreign policy goals, the self image of Poles, and support from a number of democracy promotion NGDOs. The fragmented foreign aid system however has not been reformed as the MFA has been unable to muster support for centralization.

7.5 Slovakia—stepping up to the plate

As we have shown Czechoslovakia was an important player within the CMEA aid system (Waisová 2011). Slovakia thus potentially had a history to build upon, but like the other cases under study in the book, choose to re-build its aid policy more or less from scratch. In many ways this was linked to building a national identity via foreign policy (Bátora 2013). Zolcerová (2006) highlights that since gaining independence in 1993, Slovakia has gone through three periods of providing development assistance: inertial (up to 1998), transformational (between 1999 and 2002) and growth (after 2003).[29] Up until 1998, Slovak aid policy was little more than scholarships, contributions to international organizations and humanitarian aid. Beňáková (2010) shows that between 1999 and 2002 a variety of basic documents, including the "Strategy of Development Aid" and the "Charter of Active Development Aid and Cooperation" (1999) and the "Mechanism of Providing Governmental Development Aid of the Slovak Republic" (2001) were adopted. In these documents, and in particular the 2003 "Medium-Term Strategy for Official Development Assistance," Slovakia officially undertook a commitment to participate in alleviating poverty and hunger in developing countries (see Szép 2004).

As with all the other case study countries, the initial institutional set-up involved all line ministries as agents of aid delivery with the MFA acting as coordinator. The system was coordinated via the Coordination Committee for Slovak Official Development Assistance, which met twice a year and was chaired by a senior representative of the MFA, and also included representatives from the NGDO Platform (OECD 2011b). The Committee was responsible only for Slovakia's bilateral development cooperation and was established in order to ensure the active participation of the line ministries in the Slovak foreign aid policy (Hanšpach 2004). Because it worked on the high level, the Committee was complemented with a Project Committee for operational decision-making. This committee was an internal body of the MFA, although some Ministries, especially the Ministry of Finance, would have liked it to include representatives from other ministries (OECD 2011b: 27).

The growth period saw the legislative framework coming into place with the Act on Official Development Assistance in 2007 (No. 617/2007) and the Budget Law, which set down allocations for foreign aid. The Act provided a long-term framework, particularly for the bilateral component of foreign aid, including defining basic principles, tools, goals and forms of realising development assistance, specifying further the status and competencies of the relevant ministries and of the development agency (Slovak Government 2007b). This was complemented by the Mid-term Strategy of Development Aid (2009–2013) which set out the overall planning of development aid and the project countries (see Vittek and Lightfoot 2009). Based on this mid-term strategy, the government approved a National ODA program annually (CRPE 2013).

The creation of the Slovak Agency for International Development Cooperation (SlovakAid) in 2007 was also an important part of the transformation of Slovakia from a recipient to a donor (Beňáková 2010: 5), as it made Slovakia the first ECE state to establish its own development agency. It is perhaps interesting to note that the Slovak aid budget is much smaller than that of Poland, but Slovakia argues that having an implementation agency is cost effective, while Polish officials argue the opposite (Végh 2013). The division of labor is that the MFA coordinates Slovak aid, while the Agency is in charge of implementation. SlovakAid's core bureaucracy evolved from the Administrative and Contracting Unit (ACU), a "joint venture" of the MFA and the UNDP (Slovak Government 2005: 39), but in place to administer the Slovak-UNDP Trust Fund, which was the largest such fund of the UNDP in the region.

The creation of SlovakAid however did not lead to a centralization of the aid budget and a reduction in fragmentation as reforms did in the Czech Republic and partially in Slovenia. The 2007 Act did strengthen the MFA in its lead role of coordinating Slovakia's development cooperation, and it is now seen as the point of contact for policy leadership and strategy. The department with responsibility for foreign aid is the Department for Development Assistance and Humanitarian Aid (ORPO). The department has a director and a staff of 5 people, and forms part of the Directorate General for International Organizations, Development Assistance and Humanitarian Aid (SMOP). The Director General of SMOP reports to the State Secretary, who deputizes for the Minister of Foreign Affairs.

The OECD DAC Special Review (OECD 2011b: 10) highlighted that the Ministry of Finance "plays a key role in ODA allocations and multilateral channel," whilst the Ministry of Education manages scholarships, which form a large proportion of Slovak bilateral aid. These two ministries, along with the MFA, Defense, Agriculture and the Interior are responsible for the lion's share of Slovak foreign aid, although the Special Review identified 15 ministries and other state authorities in total that have a stake in Slovak aid. It is interesting to note that the biggest share of foreign aid goes through the Ministry of Finance (around 77 percent), while only 13 percent of it is managed by the MFA, despite its role as the lead ministry (OECD 2011b). Thus, one can see the MFA's coordination role as one "shared" with the MoF.

Slovakian aid underwent further reform in 2011. The 2011 National Programme reduced the number of priority countries and narrowed the scope of
sectors addressed in order to increase the effectiveness of Slovak aid, reforms
in-line with the recommendations of the Global Consensus on foreign aid.
This also fitted a broader streamlining of foreign policy priorities (Bátora and
Pulišová 2013: 73). The Mid-Term Strategy of Development Cooperation for
2014–2018 set out the program countries as Kenya, Afghanistan and Moldova.
The priority countries are mostly in the Eastern Partnership and Western
Balkan region. South Sudan has been given a special category of a country
with exceptional development and humanitarian needs. The 2011 reform also
included some degree of centralization: while the line ministries retained their
aid budgets, implementation has been streamlined as ministries must use
SlovakAid for implementation.

7.5.1. Explaining the Slovak case

Slovakia's international development policy has clearly matured, and puts the
country in the leading group of ECE states when it comes to international development. We have seen terms such as "unpredictable" replaced by "remarkable
transformation"[30] when discussing Slovakia as a donor. While the coherence
of strategic planning may still show problems as line ministries continue to
dispose over their own aid budgets and the MFA may have difficulties in
altering their priorities, the centralization of implementation activities via
SlovakAid can be seen as a major step. The influence of external actors has
been perhaps stronger in Slovakia than in the other ECE donors, especially
that of the UNDP due to the large Trust Fund. The MFA may have used the
UNDP as an external source of reference in negotiation games with other
government agents, similarly as the Czech MFA used the OECD DAC.
Slovak NGDOs and their advocacy platform MVRO have been growing in
importance *vis-à-vis* the MFA, and like the Czech platform have been able to
exert some influence within the policy field (Végh 2013; CRPE 2013).

Institutions. Like the situation in the Czech Republic, Slovak international
development policy did not stand out among the other ECE countries in
terms of institutional structures and capacities. Broader government foreign
policy strategies before EU accession did not give a strong role to development policy (see Bátora and Pulišová 2013) and once again the fixation was
on EU integration and security issues. The Slovak government publishes
annual foreign policy guidelines, and these have included short sections on
development cooperation since 2004. These documents, prepared by the MFA
and approved by the government, however seem to have treated international
development policy as a standalone policy area and have never tied it to
wider foreign policy priorities (see for example Slovak Government 2007).
They did however lay down plans for the necessary changes in the system and
stressed the need to increase aid quantity and effectiveness. The relative length
of the parts on development in the annual guidelines has also gradually been

increasing, from only 5 lines in 2004 to two pages in 2007, which may be evidence of the policy field's increasing importance. The fact that these annual guidelines were accepted by the government could have allowed the MFA to use them as a point of reference when bargaining with other ministries.

Since 2011, the MFA has increasingly become the main policy player, although the finance issue continues to weaken its position. The OECD DAC Special Review called on the MFA to work more closely with the MoF on foreign aid. In particular, the review highlighted issues associated with coordination between the two Ministries over the European Development Fund, international organizations, as well as issues around developing a multilateral aid strategy. Commitments to increase aid volumes and thus meet EU/UN targets were hampered by the fact that the MFA was not involved in budget development within other ministries nor was there an overarching framework to guide Ministries in the allocation of aid (OECD 2011b). The MoF played a key role in the formulation of all the ministries' "budgets but it does not get involved in the detail of these and thus doesn't look specifically at the ODA components of allocations. The ministries are free to develop the ODA components in their respective budgets in accordance with their own priorities and obligations" (OECD 2011b: 27).[31]

Capacities. There is evidence that the Slovak MFA in the "growth" years did have some capacities which made it stronger than its peers in the other ECE countries, Czech Republic excepted. In particular, the Department for Development Assistance has been able to accumulate expertise, despite rotation. Some staff have been able to build up development experience in secondment posts within the UN or the OECD DAC. The close ties between the MFA and the UNDP's regional center in Bratislava was key in strengthening MFA staff capacities, and also sensitizing staff to the Global Consensus on foreign aid and the importance of poverty focused aid.[32] SlovakAid itself was created based on the administrative unit of the Slovak–UNDP Trust Fund. Like in the Czech case, there does seem to be some level of continuity, as many key development staff members have remained in development throughout the years. However, rotation within the MFA is still identified as an issue (see Beňáková 2010) and NGOs have been especially vocal about the lack of "in-country" experience within the SlovakAid.[33] The OECD DAC Special Review stressed the importance of creating a development cooperation career path within the MFA, as well as the need to "attract and retain a cadre of development professionals in the Ministry and the Agency; professionalize its approach to development cooperation; address the Ministry's frequent staff turnover; provide training for all Ministry staff in development issues; and ensure a proper set of career incentives are available" (OECD 2011b: 8).

While the proximity of the UNDP has helped to some extent professionalize and retain development staff (especially in SlovakAid), their numbers were not large. Staff numbers grew to 20 in 2012, with six officials in the MFA, 11.5 in SlovakAid, and contract staff (see CRPE 2013). As a small state, Slovakia had limited diplomatic presence around the world (Bátora and Pulišová 2013: 71), which created issues in terms of expertise and profile-raising and could have also hindered NGOs working in the field.

Coalitions. The nature of "post-Velvet divorce" politics in Slovakia was markedly different to that in the Czech Republic (Kopecký and Mudde 2000; Henderson 2004). After the end of the Mečiar-regime in 1998, Slovak politicians felt a need to show their European commitment, which resulted in a clear Europeanization of Slovakian politics in general (Harris 2004; Pridham 2008), whilst foreign policy has also become more Euro-centric (Duleba 2012; Mikulova and Simecka 2013). Bátora and Pulišová (2013) show the socialization effect of the EU in relation to foreign and related policies and to some extent we can see this in development policy. We can also argue that outside pressures, coming from the NGDO sector and internationally, mainly from the UNDP through its presence in Bratislava and capacity-building efforts, have not only had a clear impact in formulating the preferences on the government level, but the MFA was able to use these strategically and build coalitions with these actors. The fact that the Czech Republic was seen to be ground breaking in relation to development policy was in a way also a spur to activities in Slovakia. The OECD DAC Special Review also could have helped to promote change, as the reforms in 2011 were in the spirit of the review's recommendations, even though a majority of recommendations were not really acted upon.[34]

However, in order for international pressure to have an impact, there must be a certain willingness domestically to engage in reform. MVRO has been active since before legislation was put in place and has managed to secure a rather strong position for itself, even if problems remain (see Chapter 6). MVRO is the only platform in the five case study countries which has obtained a memorandum of understanding with the MFA and receives direct government funding. This is seen as "very beneficial to secure the position of the platform, especially in times of government change" (see Végh 2013: 15). While this may have impacts on how credible the platform can perform its watchdog role,[35] it can be seen as indicative of close ties existing between the MFA's development department and the platform. The OECD DAC Special Review highlights that NGDOs "enjoy good relations with the Ministry of Foreign Affairs, other ministries and the Slovak Agency for International Development Co-operation" (OECD 2011b: 28), although statements like this must be taken with a pinch of salt. Slovak NGDOs are regarded by themselves and by the Ministry of Foreign Affairs as "partners" in Slovakian aid.[36] The role of specific people in creating this alliance must also be taken into consideration. Marián Čaučík, co-founder and former chairman of MVRO, while not as high profile a person as Šimon Pánek in the Czech Republic, but his efforts clearly helped promote development aid in Slovakia.

A clear example of NGDO influence is the MFA's decision to create a special assistance category for South Sudan in 2011, as there was a risk that the country would have been excluded from the list. More generally, the relatively high volume of Slovak aid going to Sub-Saharan Africa, especially in comparison to the other four case study countries, can also be partially explained by NGO (and also international, mainly UNDP) influence. Bátora and Pulišová (2013: 70–72) highlighted that Slovakia is passive in a number of world regions that are high on the EU foreign policy agenda but of only limited interest to Slovak foreign policy. However, they showed that EU priorities are visible in Slovak aid allocation, arguing that Slovakia launched projects in EU priority countries with limited Slovak ties, such as Kenya, Afghanistan, Sudan, Ethiopia and Vietnam. Their analysis is supported by interviews[37] and Gažovič, who quotes a representative of the MFA who paraphrases the MFA's state secretary by stating "that we have chosen Serbia because of ourselves, Kenya because of the EU and Afghanistan because of the NATO" (Gažovič 2012: 34).

The UNDP's Regional Centre in Bratislava was also a clear ally for the MFA's development department. The Centre was responsible for coordinating UNDP's development work in Eastern Europe and the former Soviet Union, and was thus an important and well staffed office. It also managed the UNDP's Emerging Donors Initiative, and being located in Bratislava, it could easily reach the Slovak MFA, and it has indeed developed close ties. Using a well known and respected international organization, which has worked with several Slovak ministries as a point of reference clearly strengthened the bargaining position of the development department. The department however was less willing to engage in mustering the support of the OECD, and a conference in Bratislava in 2012, discussing the OECD DAC Special Review and the implementation of its recommendations clearly showed that the MFA does not agree with some of the reforms the OECD DAC called for, especially in terms of using budget support, and does not have enough power to implement others, such as increasing the volume of aid.

The Slovak case highlights the interconnection of domestic and international pressures. Support from NGDOs and the UNDP seems to have been enough for two rounds of reform (2007 and 2011) in Slovak development policy, but so far it has not been adequate to combat the influence of the other line ministries and centralize the aid budget to the MFA. We argued that the support from high level politics was crucial in achieving this in the Czech Republic, thus it may be worth examining how politicians related to foreign aid in Slovakia.

The level of debate among Slovakian elites was relatively high compared to some other ECE states, especially Hungary. In the run up to the 2012 elections for example, development cooperation (or human rights/democratic principles in foreign policy) issues received a mention in the manifestos of seven political parties. SMER, the social democratic party winning the elections (and also in power between 2006 and 2010), included a section on development issues in its program for government, including a commitment to revise the 2007 Act on Development Assistance (SMER 2012). Criticism from NGDOs is that SMER has a verbal commitment to raise awareness of development issues amongst MPs, but has no practical plans on how to achieve this.[38] An example was a V4 study trip to Ethiopia, where on returning to Slovakia a briefing on the trip had no MPs from SMER attend.[39] There was a sense that because the trip had been undertaken by opposition MPs this would explain the lack of SMER MPs. SMER also clearly links development and Slovak exports as the following section from their manifesto testifies (SMER 2012):

> The Government will provide versatile and effective support to all Slovak businesses. As part of its pro-export policy, the Government will seek to tap the potential of the fastest-growing economies in terms of identifying new business opportunities and will align the priorities of the development assistance to fit this purpose.

The country has stepped up to the plate when it comes to development aid, which was even made part of the government's "foreign policy decalogue" (Beňáková 2010: 3). Development aid however is sold not as charity but an "investment in the future." The trade advantages are also stressed with some seeing development as leading into business opportunities. Slovak politicians have thus seen the value of international development cooperation, but not necessarily in terms of decreasing poverty or reacting to wishes of the Slovak people, but also as a tool to gain markets and to increase the international prestige of the country. This narrative utilized to defend foreign aid may go against the principles of the global consensus, but it is seen to benefit Slovakia and can serve to empower government agencies like the Ministry of Economy as opposed to the MFA.

Summing up the Slovak case, we see an initial state of a fragmented and inefficient institutional and policy structure, in which all actors were basically free to pursue their own agendas, despite the coordinating role of the MFA, which underwent a revision after 2007 and emerged as a much more effective actor, further strengthened by reforms in 2011. Issues remain, especially around the role of the MFA and its ability to plan development policy strategically with all other line ministries having aid budgets of their own (even though implementation has been centralized), and the visibility of development cooperation within Slovakia (OECD 2011b).[40] The MFA is clearly emerging as the main player in aid in Slovakia but the fact that so little of the bilateral aid budget is in its direct control weakens its position.

None the less, Slovakian aid underwent a highly visible transformation in the last 10 years. The MFA was able to achieve much of this reform due to close links with the UNDP, which helped professionalize it and especially SlovakAid, and has also been a constant point of reference. Close links with the NGDO platform have also played a vital role, and even if some misgivings are apparent between the two sides, the fact that MVRO has a memorandum of understanding with the MFA and receives funding is a sign of a close relationship. Development issues have some visibility in party manifestos, especially that of SMER, the current governing party, but their emphasis on using aid for promoting Slovakian businesses abroad may have hindered the centralization of the aid budget to the MFA.

Most observers and practitioners are aware of the need to build awareness among both the public and MPs (see OECD 2011b). Sonja Licht argues that Slovakia can punch above its weight when it puts its mind to it[41] in relation to aid. However, the regional variations in wealth between different parts of Slovakia mean that the development discourse is situated in a very specific demographic of the Slovak population and the "development at home" discourse still dominates.[42] For this reason, despite the transformation over the years, Slovak aid is still seen as "an unemployed foreign policy tool" (Beňáková 2010: 3).

7.6 Slovenia: partial reform, but still issues

Slovenia's international development policy has also undergone reform since its creation, but this reform was not as ambitious in the Czech case, and has produced a hybrid system which shows signs of both fragmentation and centralization, to some extent similar to Slovakia. Post-independence foreign policy in Slovenia has been characterized as the search for an identity (Bunič and Šabič 2011) and even "searching for a Foreign Policy Identity via the EU" (Kajnč 2011). This included distancing Slovenia from other former Yugoslavian countries, and one potential means for this was to position the country on the donor side of supporting stabilization and post-conflict reconstruction in the region. Indeed, Slovenia's foreign aid efforts began in the late 1990s, when the country became involved in the international efforts to support stabilization and reconstruction in the Western Balkans through supporting the Stability Pact for Southeast Europe. In the run-up to EU accession, a dedicated unit was created within the MFA to coordinate the policy (the Office for International Development Cooperation and Humanitarian Assistance), as well as an inter-ministerial working group. Even though the MFA acted as coordinator, most observers agree that the Ministry of Finance was actually the central actor (Timofejevs Henriksson 2013: 121). All other line ministries also played a role and had some development budget, thus the initial institutional set-up was highly fragmented and not different than that in the other ECE countries. This issue was acknowledged in 2007 by the head of the International Development Cooperation department (Adanja 2007):

> At the moment our activities in the field of international development cooperation are rather dispersed. Each Ministry is planning the corresponding funds and carrying out relevant projects autonomously. At times, it appears difficult even to collect information on development assistance provided in the previous year.

Fragmentation was not only present in terms of line ministries involved, but also in terms of implementing agencies. Throughout the years, a number of specialized implementing agencies or "centres" have been created in Slovenia to manage parts of the country's foreign aid program. While the government played a role in their creation in all cases, private actors were also present, and the centres are non-profit and also seek out alternative sources of funding beyond what they receive from the government. They have been given sole authorization to act for and on behalf of the government in dealing with the private sector. In interviews it was acknowledged that the government did not interfere with the activities of the Centres.[43] Each of these institutions has been created to cover the day-to-day implementation of particular areas where Slovenia has identified its partners' development needs (e.g. mine clearance) or its own strengths as a donor (such as good governance, experiences with the EU, and human rights, see Bunič and Šabič 2011). The creation of dedicated agencies was seen as a way of ensuring sustained government support for the given area and "locking in" the aid program (Timofejevs Henriksson 2013: 181). The centres are the following:

- the International Trust Fund Enhancing Human Security (ITF), previously known as International Trust Fund for Demining and Mine Victim Assistance, created in 1998;
- the Centre of Excellence in Finance (CEF), created at the initiative of the Ministry of Finance in 2001, to support capacity development in public finances and central banking in South East European partners;
- the Together Foundation Regional Centre for the Psychosocial Well-Being of Children, established by the MFA, the Municipality of Ljubljana and Slovene Philanthropy in 2002;
- the Centre for European Perspective (CEP), created in 2004 to share Slovenian EU integration experience with countries wishing to join;
- the Centre for International Cooperation and Development (CMSR), created in 2006, but with roots going back to the 1960s. CMSR also has the role of supporting Slovenian companies in getting business abroad, and was originally jointly controlled by the MFA, MoE and the MoF (Timofejevs Henriksson 2013: 181);
- the Centre for e-Governance Development (CeGD), created in 2008 to carry out ICT education projects in South East Europe in the field of eGovernance.[44]

Criticisms have been raised about this network of quasi-governmental centres, such as issues about transparency and accountability, cost effectiveness and about ensuring that Slovenia is getting the maximum development impact from its aid (OECD 2011c).

The lack of a strategy on Slovenian foreign aid meant the policy was rather *ad hoc* until 2007, although there was a strong focus on the Balkans. Reforms to change this structure began in 2006 with the adoption of the International Development Cooperation of the Republic of Slovenia Act (*Official Gazette of the Republic of Slovenia No. 70/06*). The Act defined the objectives and methods of long-term planning, financing and implementation of international development cooperation. It reaffirmed the central role of the MFA in coordination, but it did not change the fragmented system by creating a single implementing agency or centralizing the development budget. The act mandated the creation of a long term strategy document, which was accepted by Parliament in 2008. Entitled the Resolution on International Development Co-operation, it set out the priorities for Slovenia's bilateral and multilateral aid up to 2015 and promised to "strengthen the relevant organizational structure as an integral part of the Ministry of Foreign Affairs of the Republic of Slovenia and grant it an appropriate level of autonomy."

Centralization efforts began after the adoption of the resolution, but have only achieved partial results (Timofejevs Henriksson 2013: 176). An important element of this process was the consolidation of the country's aid budget in the MFA. The reforms moved Slovenia into a more standard model of development cooperation, with the Department for International Development Cooperation and Humanitarian Assistance within the Directorate for Economic Diplomacy and Development within the MFA, acting as the coordinating body and in control of the consolidated budget. The Director-General reports to the State Secretary at the Ministry of Foreign Affairs, who deputizes for the Minister of Foreign Affairs. This provides Slovenia with clear responsibility at the political level for its foreign aid program. It also places the MFA at the center of Slovenia's aid program, as the Directorate now manages a consolidated budget for ODA which is implemented through a multiannual Government Action Plan (sometimes known as a "framework program" or GAP) negotiated with other ministries. At the Government level, an Inter-ministerial Working Body for International Development Cooperation was set up to aid the planning, coordinating and monitoring the implementation of international development cooperation.

Unlike the Czech case, the Slovenian MFA did not receive total control of the aid budget and line ministries still retain an important role. The MFA has authority to decide on about half of Slovenia's bilateral aid budget (Timofejevs Henriksson 2013: 177), which is a significant increase compared to the pre-centralization era, but also shows the importance that line ministries have managed to retain. The GAP involves the MFA asking other ministries to provide financial planning for their contribution for the following two years. Previously, the MFA was largely only able to count up aid expenditures that other ministries had already disbursed (OECD 2011c). The introduction of a multi-annual GAP in 2010 was an important step in strengthening the coordination role of the MFA, as it gave the Department for International Development Cooperation more authority in preparing the budget. However, dispersing aid activities across different ministries means that the planning process is still very complex (Zrinski and Bučar forthcoming). The fragmented system also means that the MFA finds enforcement of priorities nearly impossible (see Zrinski and Bučar forthcoming), and there is still often little consistency as individual projects seem to prevail. These projects seem to reflect more the interests of the line ministries rather than an overarching coherent strategy (Bunič and Šabič 2011).

The aims of introducing a program budget like the GAP were to move to results-oriented budgeting and to improve coherence across ministries. The MFA's share of the aid budget now results from negotiations among three ministries—foreign affairs, defense and internal affairs—that share one of the 16 main items in the national budget. Ensuring that sufficient funds are allocated thus requires a champion to advocate for international development in these negotiations. In 2011, the budget for aid was insufficient for Slovenia to make its first contribution to the European Development Fund and the MFA had to revert to the Ministry of Finance. This indicates that aid may not have been a high priority during the budget negotiations (OECD 2011c: 16).

7.6.1 Explaining the Slovenian case

The Slovenian case can be seen as one of partial reform: the reforms after 2008 did put the directorate within the MFA in a stronger position both within the MFA and in the government more broadly, the system however remains fragmented. Also, the directorate is still relatively weak, and the MoF and MoE both continue to have strong roles. The number of semi-autonomous implementing agencies has grown throughout the years, increasing the fragmentation and complexity of the system even further. This partial reform can be explained by the relative strengths and traditionally strong roles of the MoF and MoE in foreign aid policy, and the inability of the MFA to muster allies to counter the influence of these two ministries. The increasing fragmentation of the system also meant more and more players and interests, with all of them wanting to keep their role and budget. The Slovenian NGDO community was rather late in organizing itself, and the MFA only began regular consultation with the NGDO platform in 2008 (Timofejevs Henriksson 2013: 200). While relations between them have improved since (Bučar 2012), there still seems to be a lack of trust. The fact that some centralization did happen was due to the drive provided by the coalition government of Borut Pahor after 2008, which stressed the usage of foreign aid to stabilize the Balkans, and the minister of foreign affairs in his government paid a much stronger attention to aid than his predecessors did (Timofejevs Henriksson 2013: 187).

Institutions. Timofejevs Henriksson (2013: 171) provides an overview of the various broader government foreign policy documents and how they relate to foreign aid. Early on, such documents did not have any explicit mention of international development, but the coalition agreement in 2004, which can be seen as the most important policy statement of a government in Slovenia, highly emphasized the need to stabilize the Balkans. It did not however explicitly mention foreign aid as a tool for this. The 2008 coalition agreement however, also in the context of the Balkans, explicitly argued for using foreign aid in stabilization, and most crucially, stated that foreign aid must be made an integral part of the country's foreign policy. This document can thus be seen as an expression of government will to integrate aid policy more strongly into foreign affairs.

This government direction clearly increased the weight of the MFA *vis-à-vis* the other ministries, with a symbolic shift happening, as historically development issues were seen as finance issues not foreign policy one (see OECD 2011c: 6). Since July 2011, the aid program has been managed by one of five directorates within the MFA (it was previously a department and, before then, a unit). This organizational upgrading strengthened the position of the aid program within the MFA and across government. Bučar (2012) argues that "the overall institutional framework for international development cooperation has evolved and become much more firmly embedded within the MFA." Centralization is clearly seen as positive in terms of aligning Slovenia with other donors in terms of granting the MFA the lead role. It was also said to make aid reporting easier to conform to OECD DAC standards and increases NGO influence. However, it is also argued that by making aid more visible, centralization has had an unanticipated negative effect, as larger visibility of funds may lead to budget cuts.[45]

Capacities. The staff issues are relatively similar to other countries in our case study. When the development unit was created in the MFA in 2002, it had a staff of two people, which gradually grew during the years, pushed by Slovenia's presidency of the EU in the first half of 2008 and increasing to 13 in 2011 (OECD 2011c). This is a relatively large number, especially when one takes into account the number of people working in the various centres as well.

Staff capacities in the MFA however have also entered the bargaining game as an issue. Line ministries have regularly argued that centralizing the foreign aid budget to the MFA was not feasible as the MFA had little capacities to run everything, and it had difficulties in retaining experts due to its policy of staff rotation (Timofejevs Henriksson 2013: 183). The fact that rotation was a problem could also be inferred from the recommendations in the OECD DAC Special Review, as it called for "attractive career incentives and recognition may encourage staff not to rotate out of the Directorate too quickly" (OECD 2011c: 24). The lack of development expertise was also confirmed by the review team, "encouraging the MFA to pursue plans to establish a cadre of development professionals, recruited as officials. This will provide the ministry with a core group of staff who are knowledgeable about development co-operation principles, standards, methods and procedures." Development is clearly not seen as an equally valid career choice within the MFA as more traditional diplomacy (Zrinski and Bučar forthcoming).

The OECD DAC Special Review also highlighted that given the number of small allocations made by Slovenia in relation to bilateral aid, "managing these activities absorbs a large amount of time given the limited human resource capacity Slovenia has available for its ODA programme" (OECD 2011c). Thus, the capacities of the MFA, can be seen as rather low throughout the period, despite increasing staff numbers, which have not necessarily led to increased professionalization. In general, the wider MFA has not prioritized foreign aid policy, although observers agree that this changed after 2008 with the socialist coalition government and the new foreign minister, Samuel Žbogar, who was seen as supportive of development aid (Timofejevs Henriksson 2013: 187).

Coalitions. Centralization of the aid budget in the Czech Republic was possible because the MFA was able to strategically mobilize support from the NGDO community (which had good ties to higher level politics) and the OECD DAC. The Slovenian MFA has not been able to do this, and the following quote shows how difficult a time it has in general (Zrinski and Bučar forthcoming):

> [T]he valiant efforts of the small team in the Directorate for international development cooperation to implement the strategy appear to be an uphill struggle. Even the small steps made so far in attempts to centralize bilateral ODA have been met with heavy resistance. Each line ministry has struggled hard not to relinquish its small ODA budget and the ministries are not at all enthusiastic about the centralization efforts of MFA.

It seems the struggles between the ministries are mainly about retaining budgets, but some evidence is also available on different views on how to use foreign aid, making coalition-building for the MFA even more difficult due to the absence of like-minded government partners. The 2006 Act can be seen as a reflection of the status quo. According to an MFA interviewee, the law was "more or less" prepared by the Ministry of Finance.[46] The MoF and the Ministry of Economy prioritized the use of aid to support Slovenian businesses, and this is reflected in clear references in the act about the need to engage companies (but not civil society). One of the implementing agencies, CMSR, also has a mandate to support Slovenian business abroad. While the development department in the MFA can be seen as supporting goals like poverty reduction, it can have a difficult time getting this through. An interviewee argued that there is some degree of "bureaucratic rivalry" between the centres, and also between the MFA and the centres,[47] which indicates that they may not see each other as partners in terms of increasing the aid budget.

As mentioned, the MFA has traditionally not seen the NGDO sector as a partner, but relations have improved. SLOGA has become a well organized, unified lobby group with a clear desire to "make a compact" between itself and the MFA.[48] SLOGA has had difficulties in achieving this, as the MFA was seen as unwilling to cooperate and argues that there is no legal basis for such an arrangement. Most likely, the MFA saw the set of quasi-governmental implementing agencies as a sufficient network for development policy implementation, and did not want to deal with further groups. SLOGA claims that the centralization of funds happened due to pressure from the NGDO community to make the Slovenian aid system more effective,[49] although it is also clear that this suited the MFA in its power play with other government ministries.

The OECD DAC has been calling on Slovenia to clarify roles and responsibilities. To do this they recommend that the 2006 Act be revised and a higher proportion of the aid budget consolidated in the MFA. The MFA however has not been able to leverage this international pressure in its bargaining with the other government actors.

Higher level politics has generally also been unreceptive, with the exception of the socialist-led coalition government between 2008 and 2012. Slovenian Prime Ministers have not paid much attention to foreign aid, and in fact there are hardly any examples of them mentioning it. There is a similar view around MPs and the Parliament. There is a clear appreciation that political will is lacking. For example, in 2008 one interviewee argued that "what lacks is backing from the Parliament and from politicians in our country"[50] whilst another highlighted in relation to achieving aid targets: "it is still possible. It is up to politicians, but there is need for political will."[51]

Summing up the Slovenian case, one can see an initial institutional structure which was fragmented and ministries other than the MFA played a leading role. The 2006 Act on International Development Cooperation mostly reaffirmed this system, but momentum for changed gather with the socialist-led coalition government coming into power in 2008. The government explicitly called on aid being used as a tool of foreign affairs, and together with an activist foreign minister managed to centralize a part of the bilateral aid budget to the MFA. However, this reform remains partial as other line ministries have retained strong roles. There are also issues related to the position and prestige of the development department within the MFA, and the MFA within the government bargaining system. The development department has started to appreciate the benefits of collaboration with the NGDO platform, SLOGA, although interviews suggest that there is still room for improvements here. The major dissonance for Slovenia lies around the implementation of aid. The use of the quasi-governmental centres is seen to have certain advantages but at the same time they raise questions of coordination, tied aid, transparency and value for money. The CSMR "does not fit in" with the ways other new donors do things.[52] Slovenia has seen a decline in support for aid spending since accession to the EU and this links to broader issues on a lack of political will that are common across the region.

7.7 Summary

This chapter aimed to explain reforms in the foreign aid policies (or the lack of them) in the ECE countries using the theoretical framework presented in Chapter 2. All ECE countries started off with highly fragmented international development policies in the early 2000s, which seemed practical at the time: all line ministries had international activities which could be classified as ODA. In time however, this fragmentation proved to be a strong bottleneck in making foreign aid policy more strategic and led to a proliferation of partner countries, sectors and projects. Reducing fragmentation therefore became a key issue in terms of meeting the requirements of the Global Consensus on Foreign Aid. However, centralizing aid strategy and the aid budget to the

MFA proved highly difficult in most cases. The Czech Republic has gone the farthest in these attempts, but a few line ministries retain aid budgets even there. Reforms were half successful in Slovakia and Slovenia, while not much has happened to change the systems in Poland and Hungary.

We attempted to explain reforms with three sets of variables: institutions, capacities, and coalitions. In terms of institutions, wider government foreign policy seems to have been a key explanatory factor, as it could empower the MFA to argue for more strategic aid. As shown for example by the Hungarian government's "global opening" policy after 2011, or the Slovenian government's clear position of using aid for stabilizing the Balkans, wider government support can lead to reform. In terms of MFA capacities, it has been difficult to identify significant differences between the five countries. All of them have been plagued by difficulties in terms of building a professional cadre of development policy experts due to staff rotation and the low prestige of development policy within foreign affairs. Possible exceptions are the Czech Republic which has maintained relatively high staff numbers and has retained some key senior staff, and Slovakia where the UNDP's presence clearly helped professionalize development policy. Out of the three sets of variables however, it seems the third group, the ability of the MFA to build coalitions with other development policy actors has proven to be the most important factor. Likeminded actors in the government were usually non-existent, as MoFs and MoEs had very different visions of foreign aid, thus MFAs had to look outside of the government. The Czech MFA has especially realized the potential of working together with the NGDO sector, and so have their counterparts in Slovakia and, although late in the day, Slovenia. Internal tensions within the NGDO sectors in Poland and Hungary, among other factors, have hindered more meaningful cooperation. Leveraging pressure from international organizations has also been a successful strategy: the Czech MFA relied heavily on the OECD DAC, while the Slovak MFA used the local presence of the UNDP strategically. Interestingly, the EU seems to have played little direct role in any of the countries.

Using the three sets of variables, and more generally the model outlined in Chapter 2, it has been possible to explain why some of the five ECE countries have been able to converge their foreign aid policies towards the recommendations of the Global Consensus on Foreign Aid (and its European interpretation), while others have not, which was the second research question of this book. The complex bargaining game between governmental actors, who are not only influenced by external actors, but also attempt to leverage this external pressure in their bargaining strategies seems like a useful approach to understanding the politics of foreign aid decision-making in the ECE context.

Notes

1 Interview with ECE MFA official S, May 2008.
2 Interview with ECE MFA official H, March 2013.

3 Interview with ECE MFA official S, May 2008.
4 Interview with ECE MFA official M, January 2013.
5 Interview with two ECE MFA officials, March 2013.
6 Interview with ECE NGO representative G, March 2013.
7 Interview with ECE NGO representative G, March 2013.
8 Interviews with ECE NGO representative G, March 2013, and a Czech NGO expert, October 2013.
9 Interview with a Czech NGO expert, October 2013.
10 In a 2007 interview, Deputy Minister of Finance Tomáš Zídek argued that the 0.17 percent aid target is not compulsory, and the Czech Republic places priority on meeting the Maastricht debt and budget deficit criteria. He also argued that the Ministry of Finance and the Ministry of Industry agree that foreign assistance should serve as a "pioneer" of trade cooperation and investment (Hořejš 2008).
11 Interview with EU official D, February 2012.
12 Interview with ECE MFA official O, June 2013.
13 Interview with ECE MFA official T, March 2008.
14 Interview with ECE NGO representative M, April 2014.
15 Interview with ECE MFA official O, June 2013.
16 Interview with ECE NGO representative N, March 2011. This was substantiated by ECE MFA official A, who argued that they "struggle to get [their] voice heard."
17 Interview with a non-MFA ECE official, October 2012.
18 Interviews with ECE MFA officials U, March 2011 and O, June 2013.
19 Interview with ECE NGO representative G, March 2013.
20 For an excellent overview of Polish Aid policy (in Polish), see Kopiński (2011).
21 Interview with ECE development policy expert, April 2014.
22 Interview with ECE MFA official B, October 2008.
23 Interview with an ECE diplomat, October 2008.
24 Interview with ECE NGO representative C, July 2010.
25 Interview with an ECE NGO expert, April 2014.
26 Interview with ECE NGO representative C, July 2010.
27 Interview with ECE NGO representative O, June 2014.
28 Interview with ECE NGO representative O, June 2014.
29 This framework was first utilized in Vittek and Lightfoot 2009. This section builds upon and updates that analysis.
30 Comment made by former EU Commissioner for Development Andris Piebalgs at the *Ten years of Slovak Aid Conference*, Bratislava, 16 October 2013.
31 The tension in the relationship between the MFA and the MoF was nicely outlined in an exchange between Vazil Hudák, State Secretary in the MoF and Peter Burian, State Secretary in the MFA, at the conference to celebrate ten years of Slovak aid in 2014. Mr Hudák opened his presentation with a light hearted remark about increasing Slovak ODA, which prompted a knowing laugh from the audience. The retort from Mr Burian suggested that the MFA asking the MoF for money was a common occurrence.
32 Interview with UNDP expert, April 2012.
33 Interview with ECE NGO representative M, April 2014.
34 Interview with ECE NGO representative H, April 2013. See also Chapter 5.
35 As noted by the OECD DAC: "the closeness of the relationship with the Ministry and the dependence of most of the NGOs on Slovakia's bilateral programme for funds is a constraint to the policy watchdog role that these key stakeholders could and should be playing" (OECD 2011b: 28).
36 Interview with ECE NGO representative H and group interview with ECE MFA officials, April 2013.
37 Group interview with ECE MFA officials, April 2013.

38 Interview with ECE NGO representative M, April 2014.
39 Interview with ECE NGO representative M, April 2014.
40 Interview with an ECE development policy expert, May 2014.
41 Contribution at the *Ten years of Slovak Aid Conference*, Bratislava, 16 October 2013.
42 Interview with an ECE development policy expert May 2014; Interview with a CIDA official, November 2013.
43 Interview with non MFA ECE official, January 2013
44 At the time of writing the future of some of these centres was unclear.
45 Interview with an ECE development policy expert, January 2013.
46 Interview with a non-MFA ECE official, January 2013.
47 Interview with a non-MFA ECE official, January 2013.
48 Interview with ECE NGO representative F, January 2013.
49 Interview with ECE NGO representative F, January 2013.
50 Interview with ECE diplomat, October 2008.
51 Interview with ECE diplomat, October 2008.
52 Interview with ECE NGO representative F, January 2013.

8 Conclusions

This book aimed to provide an understanding of how international development policies have changed, or have failed to change in five ECE countries (the Czech Republic, Hungary, Poland, Slovakia and Slovenia) in the ten years following their EU accession. Specifically, the book asked two research questions: (1) To what extent have the international development policies of the five countries conformed to the Global Consensus on Foreign Aid?; and (2) What factors and dynamics account for the paths and trajectories taken in this policy area? This concluding chapter reviews the main insights that the book has generated regarding these two research questions, and presents areas for future research.

Concerning adherence to the Global Consensus, we have found that rhetorically, the ECE countries are strong supporters: they have signed up to all documents which embody the Consensus, and formally take part in the creation of the EU's development *acquis* which embodies a European interpretation of the Global Consensus. In the past ten years, they have clearly learnt to "talk the talk" of the global development system, as evidenced by frequent references to the principles and norms of the Global Consensus in development strategies and government communication. Compliance in practice however is highly problematic, and the principles and norms referred to are often not reflected in international development practice: the ECE countries have done little to increase their relative aid efforts since 2006; they have done little to implement principles like ownership and partnership, donor coordination, alignment, transparency, results orientation or accountability. While we have noted that many of the more established donors do not comply with the elements of the Global Consensus either, the shortfall of the ECE countries is even more spectacular.

More broadly, compliance in rhetoric and non-compliance in practice relates to a strange ambivalence: on the one hand, the ECE countries emphasize that they do not want to be treated as a distinct group of donors, and have made their intentions clear of wishing to join the "club" of Western donors, as represented by the OECD DAC. Four out of the five countries have joined the OECD DAC in 2013, not least because the DAC itself has been keen on admitting new members. However, there are several instances when the ECE countries actually emphasize that they are special and different to most "traditional" donors: they had different historical trajectories (most importantly, they never had colonies), they have a comparative advantage in Eastern countries as opposed to those of the global South, they possess a unique experience in managing transition and EU integration reforms, and many elements of the Global Consensus "do not fit their realities." Within the EU framework, there are examples of them requesting preferential treatment in certain areas of development policy, which does not seem to fit well with their rhetoric which implies the opposite.

What is the explanation for this general reluctance to implement the globally agreed standards which they themselves have signed up to? An easy, but highly misleading answer, often repeated in the literature, would be the lack of money, or to be more precise, the high alternative cost of allocating resources to foreign aid. The ECE countries are less developed than most of the OECD DAC members are, and thus have less money to spare for international development. "Money is needed at home," as the standard argument goes. Signing up to non-binding global commitments or endorsing the EU's development *acquis* soft law in the Council costs next to nothing, and can even be used to project an image of being a responsible high income country. Actually implementing some of these commitments however may cost money, thus the ECE countries are only willing to engage in rhetorical compliance.

While clearly a factor, the lack of money cannot explain everything, and when going into details on the ECE countries' failure to comply with the Global Consensus, it actually explains strikingly little. Clearly, the lack of resources can explain why the ECE countries have not met quantitative aid targets or why they have been reluctant in drawing up roadmaps to meet these targets. But then one may ask why do they do development policy in the first place if their scarce resources could be spent elsewhere? Also, it does not explain why they do not engage in implementing aid effectiveness measures such as untying aid, working together with other donors, engaging in better strategic planning, creating effective and efficient aid delivery structures, or increasing the transparency of their international development policies. Many of these could be implemented with little costs, and, to be fair, some ECE countries have taken certain measures, but, in general, little is being done. This reluctance is puzzling because implementing aid effectiveness measures would contribute to the responsible image the ECE states would like to project internationally. A standard explanation in the literature for this reluctance is the "lack of political will." This may sound reasonable, but without further definition and expansion of the concept, it is little more than a tautology.

In explaining the reluctance of the ECE countries to implement the Global Consensus on Foreign Aid (or its European interpretation), the book reconceptualized the "lack of political will" argument. It's not a lack of will which is the main issue, but rather a lack of political attention to development policy. As argued in Chapter 2, higher level decision makers, including Members of

Parliament, Ministers and even Prime Ministers in ECE countries have very little knowledge about international development. Whilst we accept this may also be the case in other donors (see Breuning 2013), the relative infancy of the ECE countries' development policies make the situation more pronounced. Without strong guidance from politicians, international development policy-making becomes a bureaucratic bargaining game between governmental agencies involved in the policy. The outcomes of this bargaining game tend to reflect a policy which is acceptable for all, but is not necessarily optimal, nor does it necessarily comply with international requirements. Government bureaucracies are interested in protecting their turf, and expansion in both in budgets and responsibilities. Implementing the Global Consensus would mainly strengthen the International Development Cooperation Department in MFA, but many government bureaucracies would have other goals with foreign aid which they would want to promote. Examining these government dynamics, often at the technical level, can provide us with a much more fruitful way of interpreting development policy outcomes in the ECE countries as opposed to using more simplified explanations like pointing at political will or the lack of money.

The core of our explanatory model in this book is therefore based on the government politics model of foreign policy analysis, but we have expanded this with the influence of actors outside of the state: international actors like the European Union and the OECD DAC, as well as domestic stakeholders like non-governmental development organizations. The major driver in the (re-)creation of ECE development policies was accession to the EU, and these other external forces were more or less consistent among all five countries. Thus, any variation among the five countries needs to be explained with domestic reasons: differences in the influence of national NGOs, and different dynamics within governments.

Applying our framework to the five countries shows that it is indeed possible to explain ECE development policies using government bargaining and exter-nal influence as sets of explanatory variables. Reform of the Czech Republic's aid system between 2007 and 2011 was clearly a bottom-up process, with the need for reform initiating from the technical level and eventually spilling over to politics. Reform mainly served the interests of the MFA (and especially the International Development Department within it), which was able to mobilize both the OECD DAC and the NGO community. But the outcome was never certain due to large number of other government actors interested in protect-ing their responsibilities and maintaining the pre-reform *status quo*. Conces-sions clearly needed to be made. In case of Hungary, conflicting interests between ministries and the MFA's inability to build coalitions with outside actors hindered any reform for a decade. The country's first aid strategy was only accepted in 2014, and was seen as major breakthrough: it is a result of strategic advocacy by NGOs and recognition by the MFA that reform would fit well with the broader foreign policy goals of "Global Opening" of the right-wing government in power after 2010. However, the new strategy clearly reflects the interests of the line ministries as well as it does not reform the fragmented system or centralize funds.

Poland presents an interesting case as it is the only one of the five case studies with the potential to be a major foreign policy player (see Kaminska 2013), yet its aid policy lags behind in many respects. It is only relatively recently that a law on development policy articulating a clear and to some extent unique vision has been created, but the situation is still that the MFA is only the central player on paper, with line ministries and the MoF in particular playing a key veto role. The Polish government sees regional stability through democratization the key to Poland's security, and democracy promotion concerns have dominated international development policy (see Pospieszna 2014). Democracy aid resonates well not only with broader government foreign policy goals, but also the self image of Poles, and the activities of a number of democracy promotion NGDOs. Against this backdrop, the MFA was unable to mobilize allies for stronger poverty reduction focused aid.

Slovakia's aid policy was a slow starter but underwent a major reform in 2007. We see a crucial role in the development of Slovak aid policy being played by external actors, most importantly the UNDP. The reform has increased the coordination role of the MFA and centralized implementation tasks through the creation of an agency, but issues remain with other ministries. NGOs and the MFA have developed a mature working relationship, evidenced by the fact that the NGDO advocacy platform receives direct government funding. Unusually in the region, we see international development issues appearing in the election manifestos of political parties, although with a strong emphasis on links with foreign trade. None the less, this is a sign that public debate can be shaped in the future.

Slovenia's aid policy, like the Slovak case, has undergone partial reform since the development began taking shape in the late 1990s. A fragmented system has become more centralized, with the MFA playing a key role. The existence of many implementing agencies or "centres" is unique to Slovenia and subject of some criticism from the OECD DAC and NGOs. Partial centralization was made possible by momentum from the government in power between 2008 and 2012. The relationship between the MFA and NGOs, although initially strained and uncooperative, has become a supportive one, although this has not been sufficient to break down bureaucratic barriers to increased centralization. The impact of the financial crisis also appears to be a significant factor in Slovenia, both in terms of financial contributions for development and public support.

Our analysis reveals clear differences between the five countries: some have undertaken strong reforms, while others have hardly touched their initial development policy setups. While even the Czech Republic falls short of many elements of the Global Consensus, it has done the most in making its international development more effective. Hungary on the other hand has scarcely done anything up to 2014. These differences also reflect differences in trajectories and thus a process of divergence and differentiation is present. In the mid-2000s, all the five ECE countries had rather similar institutional setups and all lacked clear policy frameworks. Today however they seem to be increasingly distinct from each other, questioning voices which talked about the "ECE face of donorship." With these divergent trajectories, the legacy of the Communist past and the impact of international cooperation policies of the time also seem to be waning. These legacies are still present in some countries in terms of partner country selection, but it is less apparent there as well: Poland is increasingly conscious of supporting democratization in the former Soviet space, Slovenia focuses most of its efforts on the Western Balkans and Slovakia has focused heavily on Sub-Saharan African countries which had little connections with Communist Eastern Europe.

International organizations, and especially the EU, have played a key role in re-starting ECE development policies. However, their impact in subsequently shaping these policies has been highly limited. The EU seems to have offered only limited possibilities for social learning in the post-accession phase, and the OECD DAC has failed to impose credible conditionality during the accession process of the ECE countries. While both the European Commission and the OECD DAC can be thought norm entrepreneurs which promote adherence to the Global Consensus for their members, they have limited scope to influence members in the adoption of soft law. Pressures for social learning may be stronger in the future now that four of the ECE countries are members of the OECD DAC. They will be subject to the OECD DAC's peer review process, which is likely to be much more thorough than the initial Special Reviews, and the countries will face stronger pressures to act on recommendations in the reviews. As the Czech case has shown, peer reviews can be vital in empowering certain domestic actors (the MFA) in the government bargaining game. However, too harsh criticism can also alienate certain actors, as shown by the Polish case. Clearly, future research will be needed on the transformative power of the OECD DAC, especially in the ECE context.

Our research has also revealed the key role of the development NGO sectors in shaping the international development policies of their countries. NGDOs have clearly become more mature and professional, and EU accession has played a key role in this by exposing them to European-wide networks and the need to work together in order to obtain EU grants. NGDOs in some of the five countries have realized that "they are in this together" with the MFA and need to cooperate. This necessitates tempering criticism, which has proven to be counterproductive. Criticism of the government's practice can only work if a constituency for foreign aid exists, such as an informed and interested public opinion which would increase pressure on the government to react. Development policy reform has been successful in countries where the NGDO sector has been strategic in its criticism and advocacy, and has rather opted to work together with the MFA in overcoming resistance to reform among other government actors. NGDOs can be engines of change in the future, but their possibilities are limited by wider public support. Indeed, development NGOs in the ECE countries are detached from their societies in a sense that they do not rely on grassroots support. Building a public base which is better informed and active on global issues is crucial for the long term success of NGDOs. This is another area in which future, policy-oriented research is necessary on how public awareness can be strengthened. A more informed public may also empower certain government actors, and may also force higher level politics to pay more attention to international development. NGO projects aimed at fostering awareness, often involving the media and academia and at times funded by the EU are underway, but reaching new people is a challenge.

Future research is needed on how the ECE countries relate to the issue of policy coherence for development. So far, this has only entered development policies in the region on a marginal level, and these policies remain almost solely focused on aid. However, policy coherence, and "beyond aid" are gaining importance both globally and within the EU, with the post-2015 development agenda likely to feature non-aid tools to promote development strongly. The ECE countries must also focus more on these issues, and they cannot continue saying that "policy coherence is an issue for rich Western countries, not us." However, only the Czech Republic has created institutions for explicitly dealing with policy coherence issues, but this inter-ministerial committee has never met on high level. All countries, but especially Poland and Hungary are supporters of the EU's Common Agricultural Policy which provides their farmer with high agricultural subsidies. The ECE countries do seemingly well on climate-related issues as emissions of CO_2 have drastically decreased in the region since 1990. This is due to the collapse of polluting Communist industry and a rapid shift to services and less polluting manufacturing. However, four of the ECE countries (with the exception of Slovenia) have been rather strong in opposing climate goals on the EU level (van Renssen 2014; *The Guardian* 2014) and seem to put national economic considerations before reducing emissions. These opposing interests do not bode well for the creation of coherent policies, but need to be better understood before policies can be formulated to deal with it. So far, Horký (2010c) is the only academic research on the topic.

Comparative donor studies like this book have a long tradition in the development studies literature, and have generated important insights on what works in policy terms, how reforms can be done, and whether best practices are transferable from one donor to another. In future research, it may be insightful to compare ECE donor countries with more established donors or other emerging donors. So far, such comparisons have been seen as irrelevant as there were so large differences between these countries. However, due to the different trajectories and heterogeneity observed among the ECE donors, it may make sense to compare them with donors like Austria, Spain or non-ECE new OECD DAC members like South Korea and Iceland. Indeed, studies on South Korea's donorship (Kim 2010, 2011) reveal that the country is coping with many similar problems and issues as the ECE countries. The Czech Republic on the other hand ranks among the middle of OECD DAC donors in many respects, which can also make comparisons interesting. These comparisons can also help break down the new donor/old donor distinction which, rhetorically at least, many of the ECE countries would wish to achieve. New vs. old donor comparisons can be used in a broader sense to help increase our understanding of how foreign aid policy is made as a part of foreign policy. The model developed in this book can be used and adapted for such comparisons, although it would need to be expanded with further groups of actors and explanatory variables, such as public opinion, the role of parties, a stronger role for Parliament and the chief executive level, private businesses working in the "aid business," etc. These would increase the complexity of the model, potentially to a point where it would no longer be manageable. None the less, we argue that future comparative donor studies will need to make better use of theoretical frameworks, and this book can be seen as a pioneer in this regard.

As a final issue, when comparing the international development policies of the ECE countries to the Global Consensus on Foreign Aid, one must not forget that these countries only have ten years of experience of donorship, and their re-emergence as donors was a rather hurried process. We may take the fact into account that they had development policies during Communism, but these policies were very different and most ECE countries experienced a more than ten year break. The question arises whether we simply expect too much from these countries after such a short period of time? Has the era of globalization inflated our expectations compared to what is realistic? Other donors often had much longer journeys than the ECE countries: South Korea started its aid program after transitioning to democracy in 1987 and joined the OECD DAC only in 2010, even though its ODA/GNI at the time of accession was comparable to that of the ECE countries. Ireland on the other hand, today seen as a good model of aid, took much less time to mature: its aid program began in 1974 (also around the time of the country's accession to the EU) and it joined the OECD DAC about a decade later in 1985, with ODA/GNI levels around 0.2 percent, roughly double of what the ECE countries contribute. This quick growth in aid happened before the "economic miracle years" of the Irish economy during the 1990s, when income levels in the country were not much different than those of the ECE countries in the past decade. Ireland may be an exception, but it shows that relatively quick donor trajectories are possible and points to the fact that it may not be unreasonable to expect more from the ECE countries.

In the end, aid is a tool of foreign policy. How countries use aid and what relative importance they place on it tells much about their foreign policy priorities. The ECE countries have found aid to be useful tool to some degree in their neighborhood, but are still struggling to justify using aid in poor regions like Sub-Saharan Africa, regions which are not really in the focus of their foreign policies either. This may also change gradually: with increasing living standards and becoming destination countries for migrants, the contacts between the ECE region and the developing world, once thought of as a far away exotic place which does not really concern them, will intensify, forcing these countries to rethink their foreign policies, which may also lead to a re-evaluation of how, how much, and to whom they give foreign aid.

Bibliography

Acemoglu, D. and Robinson, J. (2012) *Why Nations Fail*, London: Crown Publishers.

Acemoglu, D., Johnson, S. and Robinson, J. (2005) 'Institutions as the fundamental cause of long-run growth', in P. Aghion and S. Durlauf (eds) *Handbook of Economic Growth*, Oxford: North Holland, pp. 384–473.

Adamcová, N. *et al.* (2006) *International Development Cooperation of the Czech Republic*, Prague: Institute of International Relations.

Adanja, M. (2007) 'New EU Donors', presentation at the Public Hearing of the European Parliament Committee on Development, Brussels, 30 January.

Agnew, J.J. and Entrikin, N. (2004) *The Marshall Plan Today: Model and Metaphor*, Oxford: Routledge.

Ahmed, S. and Potter, D. (2006) *NGOs in International Politics*, West Hartford: Kumarian Press.

Aldasoro, I., Nunnenkamp, P. and Thiele, R. (2010) 'Less aid proliferation and more donor coordination? The wide gap between words and deeds', *Journal of International Development*, 22(7): 920–940.

Alesina, A. and Dollar, D. (2000) 'Who gives foreign aid to whom and why?', *Journal of Economic Growth*, 5(1): 33–63.

Alesina, A. and Weder, B. (2002) 'Do corrupt governments receive less foreign aid?', *American Economic Review*, 92(4): 1126–1137.

Allison, G.T. (1969) 'Conceptual models and the Cuban missile crisis', *The American Political Science Review*, 63(3): 689–718.

Allison, G.T. (1971) *The Essence of Decision: Explaining the Cuban Missile Crisis*, Glenview, IL: Scott and Foresman.

Allison, G.T. and Halperin, M.H. (1972) 'Bureaucratic politics: a paradigm and some policy implications', *World Politics*, 24: 40–79.

Alonso, J.A. (2012) 'From aid to global development policy', *United Nations Department of Economic and Social Affairs Working Paper*, 121.

Asiaport (2014) 'A fejlesztéspolitika csak nyerhet a globális nyitással' ['Development policy can only win with global opening'], available online: www.asiaport.hu/index.php/2013-05-22-07-23-2/8215-a-fejlesztespolitika-csak-nyerhet-a-globalis-nyitassal (accessed 25 June 2014).

Baginski, P. (2002) 'Poland', in M. Dauderstädt (ed.) *EU Eastern Enlargement and Development Cooperation*, Bonn: Friedrich Ebert Stiftung.

Baginski, P. (2007) 'Polish foreign assistance in the EU Context', presentation at the Public Hearing of the European Parliament Committee on Development, Brussels, 30 January.

Batory, A. and Cartwright, A. (2011) 'Re-visiting the partnership principle in cohesion policy: the role of civil society organizations in structural funds monitoring', *JCMS: Journal of Common Market Studies*, 49(4): 697–717.

Baun, M. and Marek, D. (eds) (2013) *The New Member States and the European Union: Foreign Policy and Europeanization*, Abingdon: Routledge.

Bátora, J. (2012) 'Europeanization of foreign policy: whither Central Europe?', in Z. Šabič, and P. Drulák (eds) *Regional and International Relations of Central Europe*, London: Palgrave Macmillan, pp. 220–238.

Bátora, J. (2013) 'Compliance and non-compliance as sources of recognition: Slovakia and NATO', *Communist and Post-Communist Studies*, 46(3): 387–396.

Bátora, J. and Pulišová, V. (2013) 'Slovakia: learning to add value to EU foreign policy', in M. Baun and D. Marek (eds) *The New Member States and the European Union: Foreign Policy and Europeanization*, London: Routledge, pp. 68–83.

Beasly, R. (1998) 'Collective interpretations: how problem representations aggregate in foreign policy groups', in D.A. Sylvan and J.F. Voss (eds) *Problem Representation in Foreign Policy Decision Making*, Cambridge: Cambridge University Press, pp. 80–115.

Benczes, I. (2013) 'The impossible trinity of denial: European economic governance in a conceptual framework', *Transylvanian Review of Administrative Sciences*, 9(39): 5–21.

Bendor, J. and Hammond, T.H. (1992) 'Rethinking Allison's models', *American Political Science Review*, 86: 301–322.

Beňáková, N. (2010) 'SlovakAid – an unemployed foreign policy tool', *International Issues and Slovak Foreign Policy Affairs*, 19(3): 3–22.

Berthélemy, J.-C. (2006) 'Bilateral donors' interest vs. recipients' development motives in aid allocation: do all donors behave the same?', *Review of Development Economics*, 10(2): 179–194.

Beyers, J. (2005) 'Multiple embeddedness and socialization in Europe: the case of council officials', *International Organization*, 59(4): 899–936.

Biesemans, S. (2007) 'New EU Donors', Presentation at Public Hearing of European Parliament, Committee on Development, 30 January, available online: www.europa rl.europa.eu/comparl/deve/hearings/default_en.htm (accessed 11 November 2009).

Birdsall, N. and Kharas, H. (2010) *Quality of Official Development Assistance Assessment*, Washington, DC: Brookings Institution and Center for Global Development.

Bister, A. (2005) *Development NGOs in Slovenia*, Trialog: Vienna.

Boschini, A. and Olofsgård, A. (2007) 'Foreign aid: an instrument for fighting communism?', *The Journal of Development Studies*, 43(4): 622–648.

Bördős, É. and Gregor, A. (2014) *How Much Solidarity Do Hungarians Have? To Whom and in What Ways Would the Population of Hungary Give Aid at Home and Abroad?*, Budapest: Demnet Foundation.

Börzel, T. (2010) 'Why you don't always get what you want: EU enlargement and civil society in Central and Eastern Europe', *Acta Politica*, 45(1–2): 1–10.

Börzel, T. and Buzogány, Á. (2010) 'Governing EU accession in transition countries: the role of non-state actors', *Acta Politica*, 45(1–2): 158–182.

Brainad, L. (ed.) (2003) *The Other War: Global Poverty and the Millennium Challenge Account*, Washington, DC: Brookings Institution Press.

Breuning, M. (2013) 'Roles and realities: when and why gatekeepers fail to change foreign policy', *Foreign Policy Analysis*, 9(3): 307–325.

Browne, S. (1990) *Foreign Aid in Practice*, London: Pinter.

Brubacher, B. (2003) 'European Union Enlargement: Opportunities and Challenges for Western and Eastern European NGOs', Oxford: INTRAC, available online: www.intrac.org/data/files/resources/200/European-Union-Enlargement-Opportunities-and-Challenges-for-NGOs.pdf (accessed 5 June 2013).

Bruszt, L. (2008) 'Multi-level governance – the Eastern versions: emerging patterns of regional development governance in the new member states', *Regional and Federal Studies*, 18(5): 607–627.

Bučar, M. (2012) 'Involving civil society in the international development cooperation of 'new' EU member states: the case of Slovenia', *Perspectives on European Politics and Society*, 13(1): 83–99.

Bučar, M. and Mrak, M. (2007) 'Challenges of Development Cooperation for EU New Member States', paper presented at the ABCDE World Bank Conference, Bled, Slovenia, 17–18 May, available online: http://siteresources.worldbank.org/INTABCDESLO2007/Resources/PAPERABCDEBucarMrak.pdf (accessed 11 November 2009).

Bučar, M., Marques, M.-J., Mesic, A. and Plibersek, E. (2007) 'Towards a division of labour in European development co-operation: case studies', *Deutsches Institut für Entwicklungspolitik Discussion Paper*, 11/2007.

Bunič, P. and Šabič, Z. (2011) 'Slovenia and the Eastern neighbourhood', *Perspectives: Review of International Affairs*, 2: 165–181.

Burnell, P. (1997) *Foreign Aid in a Changing World*, Milton Keynes: Open University Press.

Burnell, P. (2005) 'Foreign aid resurgent: new spirit or old hangover?', in T. Addison and G. Mavrotas (eds) *Building the New International Financial Architecture: Issues, Challenges and Agendas*, London and Helsinki: Palgrave Macmillan and UNU-WIDER.

Burnside, C. and Dollar, D. (2000) 'Aid, policies and growth', *American Economic Review*, 90(4): 847–868.

Burnside, C. and Dollar, D. (2004) 'Aid, policies and growth: revisiting the evidence', *World Bank Policy Research Working Paper*, 3251.

Cabral, L., Russo, G. and Weinstock, J. (2014) 'Brazil and the shifting consensus on development co-operation: salutary diversions from the "aid-effectiveness" trail?', *Development Policy Review*, 32: 179–202.

Calleja-Ragonesi, I., Khakee, A. and Pisani, M. (2014) 'Blessed is he who considers the human rights paradigm: Maltese aid between charity and human rights and between Catholicism and Secularism', *Mediterranean Quarterly*, 25(3): 99–122.

Carbone, M. (2004) 'Development policy', in N. Nugent (ed.) *EU Enlargement*, Basingstoke: Palgrave Macmillan, pp. 242–252.

Carbone, M. (2007) *The European Union and International Development*, London: Routledge and UACES.

Carbone, M. (2011) 'Development policy in a changing Europe – more donors, new challenges?', in F. Bindi and I. Angelescu (eds) *The Frontiers of Europe: A Transatlantic Problem?*, Washington, DC: Brookings Institute, pp. 151–165.

Carmin, J. and Fagan, A. (2010) 'Environmental mobilisation and organisations in postsocialist Europe and the former Soviet Union', *Environmental Politics*, 19(5): 689–707.

Cassen, R. *et al.* (1986) *Does Aid Work? Report to an Intergovernmental Task Force*, Oxford: Clarendon Press.

Chandy, L. (2011) 'It's complicated: the challenge of implementing the Paris Declaration on aid Effectiveness', available online: www.brookings.edu/research/opinions/2011/09/22-paris-declaration-chandy/ (accessed 15 January 2014).

Chaney, P. (2013) 'Unfulfilled mandate? exploring the electoral discourse of international development aid in UK Westminster elections 1945–2010', *European Journal of Development Research*, 25: 252–270.

Checkel, J.T. (2001) 'Why comply? Social learning and European identity change', *International Organization*, 55(3): 553–588.

Checkel, J.T. (2005) 'International institutions and socialization in Europe: introduction and framework', *International Organization*, 59(4): 801–826.

Chelotti, N. (2013) 'Analysing the links between national capitals and Brussels in EU foreign policy', *West European Politics*, 36(5): 1052–1072.

Chimiak, G. (2014) 'The rise and stall of non-governmental organizations in development', *Polish Sociological Review*, 1(185): 25–44.

Císař, O. (2010) 'Externally sponsored contention: the channelling of environmental movement organisations in the Czech Republic after the fall of Communism', *Environmental Politics*, 19(5): 736–755.

Claessens, S., Cassimon, D. and Van Campenhout, B. (2007) 'Empirical evidence on the new international aid architecture', *IMF Working Paper WP/07/277*.

Clark, I. (2007) 'Legitimacy in international or world society', in A. Hurrelmann, S. Schneider and J. Steffek (eds) *Legitimacy in an Age of Global Politics*, New York: Palgrave Macmillan, pp. 193–210.

Clemens, M.A. and Moss, T.J. (2007) 'The ghost of 0.7 per cent: origins and relevance of the international aid target', *International Journal of Development Issues*, 6(1): 3–25.

Collier, P. and Dollar, D. (2002) 'Aid allocation and poverty reduction', *European Economic Review*, 46(3): 1475–1500.

Collier, P. and Gunning, J.W. (1999) 'The IMF's role in structural adjustment', *The Economic Journal*, 109(459): 634–651.

CONCORD (2007) *AidWatch 2007: Hold the Applause! EU Governments Risk Breaking Aid Promises*, Brussels: CONCORD.

CONCORD (2011) *AidWatch 2011: Challenging Self-Interest. Getting EU Aid Fit for the Fight Against Poverty*, Brussels: CONCORD.

CONCORD (2012) *AidWatch 2012: Aid We Can: Invest More in Global Development*, Brussels: CONCORD.

CONCORD (2013) *AidWatch 2013: The Unique Role of European Aid. The Fight Against Global Poverty*, Brussels: CONCORD.

Council of the European Union (2005) 'Council conclusions on an EU strategy for Africa', 14831/05, 22 November.

Council of the European Union (2007) 'Council Regulation (EC) No 617/2007 of 14 May 2007 on the implementation of the 10th European Development Fund under the ACP-EC Partnership Agreement', *Official Journal of the European Union L152/1*.

Council of the European Union (2011a) 'Operational framework on aid effectiveness – consolidated text', 18239/10, 11 January.

Council of the European Union (2011b) 'EU common position for the Fourth High Level Forum on Aid Effectiveness', 14 November.

Council of the European Union (2012a): 'Increasing the impact of EU development policy: an agenda for change', 14 May.

Council of the European Union (2012b) 'Council Conclusions "The future approach to EU budget support to third countries"', 14 May.

Council of the European Union (2012c) 'Council conclusions on policy coherence for development', 14 May.

Cox, T. and Gallai, S. (2013) 'Civil society and policy actors in post-communist Hungary: linkages and contexts', *Perspectives on European Politics and Society*, 15(1): 51–67.

Crawford, B. and Lijphart, A. (1995) 'Explaining political and economic change in post-communist Eastern Europe. Old legacies, new institutions, hegemonic norms, and international pressures', *Comparative Political Studies*, 28(2): 171–199.

CRPE (2013) 'New donors on the CEE block', *CRPE Policy Memo*, 48.

Czech Development Agency (2013) 'Czech Republic Development Cooperation Factsheet', available online: www.dev-practitioners.eu/fileadmin/Redaktion/Docum ents/members_info/factsheet_CzDA.pdf?PHPSESSID=1a01fd11ca0e561492ed239ae d64b1dd (accessed 4 March 2014).

Czech Development Agency (2014) 'Cooperation with other donors', available online: www.czda.cz/czda/cooperation-with-other-donors.htm?lang=en (accessed 4 March 2014).

Czech Government (2002) 'Resolution of the Czech Republic Government no. 91, dated January 23, 2002, "The concept of the international development cooperation of the Czech Republic for the 2002–2007 period"'.

Czech Government (2003) 'Conceptual basis of the foreign policy of the Czech Republic for the 2003–2006 period', unofficial English translation available online: www.opera tionspaix.net/DATA/DOCUMENT/51~v~Conceptual_Basis_of_the_Foreign_Policy_ of_the_Czech_Republic_for_the_2003-2006_Period_.pdf (accessed 20 March 2014).

Czech Ministry of Foreign Affairs (2007) 'Transformace systému zahraniční rozvojové spolupráce ČR' ['Transformation of international development cooperation in the Czech Republic'], available online: www.mzv.cz/jnp/cz/zahranicni_vztahy/rozvojova_ spoluprace/dvoustranna_zrs_cr/transformace_systemu_zahranicni.html (accessed 20 March 2014).

Czech Ministry of Foreign Affairs (2010) 'The development cooperation strategy of the Czech Republic 2010–2017', unofficial English translation available online: www.mzv. cz/file/762314/FINAL__Development_Cooperation_Strategy_2010_2017.pdf (accessed 20 March 2014).

Czech Ministry of Foreign Affairs (2011) 'Harnessing the transition experience in EU's external relations: From policy to implementation', 'Non-paper by the Czech Republic, Estonia, Hungary, Latvia, Lithuania, Romania, Slovak Republic, and Slovenia', available online: www.mzv.cz/file/591175/non_paper_on_the_transition_ experience.pdf (accessed 2 February 2011).

Czech Ministry of Foreign Affairs (2013) 'The Czech Republic has become a member of the OECD Development Assistance Committee', available online: www.mzv.cz/oecd. paris/en/about_the_czech_republic/the_czech_republic_has_become_a_member. html (accessed 17 April 2014).

Dalgaard, C.-J., Hansen, H. and Tarp, F. (2004) 'On the empirics of foreign aid and growth', *Economic Journal*, 114(496): 191–216.

Danielson, A. and Wohlgemuth, L. (2005) 'Swedish development cooperation in perspective', in P. Hoebink and O. Stokke (eds) *Perspective on European Development Co-operation*, Abingdon: Routledge, pp. 518–546.

Dauderstädt, M. (2002) 'Eastern enlargement and development policy', in M. Dauderstädt (ed.) *EU Eastern Enlargement and Development Cooperation*, Bonn: Friedrich Ebert Stiftung.

Degnbol-Martinussen, J. and Engberg-Pedersen, P. (2005) *Aid: Understanding International Development Cooperation*, London: Zed Books.

DemNet (2010) 'Tanulmányutak külföldre – Kenya 2010' ['Study visits abroad – Kenya 2010'], available online: www.demnet.hu/hu/nemzetkozi-fejlesztes/tanulma nyutak-kulfoldre/371-kenya-2010 (accessed 29 July 2014).

Denca, S.S. (2009) 'The Europeanization of foreign policy: empirical findings from Hungary, Romania and Slovakia', *Journal of Contemporary European Research*, 5(3): 389–404.

Després, L. (1987) 'Eastern Europe and the Third World: economic interactions and policies', in R.E. Kanet (ed.) *The Soviet Union, Eastern Europe, and the Third World*, Cambridge: Cambridge University Press, pp. 141–162.

Development Strategies and IDC (2003) 'The consequences of enlargement for development policy. Volume 1', available online: www.edis.sk/ekes/study_conseq_enlarg_vol1.pdf (accessed 3 March 2014).

Doherty, B. and Doyle, T. (2006) 'Beyond borders: transnational politics, social movements and modern environmentalisms', *Environmental Politics*, 15(5): 697–712.

Dollar, D. and Levin, V. (2006) 'The increasing selectivity of foreign aid, 1984–2002', *World Development*, 34(12): 2034–2046.

Doward, J. (2013) 'World poverty: can the G8 deliver on the promise it made at Gleneagles?', *The Observer*, 2 March.

Drążkiewicz, E. (2008) *Official Development Assistance in Visegrad Countries*, Warsaw: Polish Green Network.

Drążkiewicz-Grodzicka, E. (2010) 'An emergent donor? The case of Polish developmental involvement in Africa', unpublished PhD thesis, University of Cambridge.

Drążkiewicz-Grodzicka, E. (2013) 'From recipient to donor: the case of Polish developmental cooperation', *Human Organization*, 72(1): 65–75.

Dreher, A., Fuchs, A. and Nunnenkamp, P. (2013) 'New donors', *International Interactions*, 39: 402–415.

Drezner, D.W. (2000) 'Ideas, bureaucratic politics, and the crafting of foreign policy', *American Journal of Political Science*, 44: 733–749.

Drozd, M. (2007) 'The new face of solidarity: A brief survey of Polish aid', manuscript, available online: http://papers.ssrn.com/sol3/Delivery.cfm/SSRN_ID1132246_code948600.pdf?abstractid=1132246&mirid=2 (accessed 3 February 2014).

Duleba, A. (2012) 'Twenty years of Slovak foreign policy: teething problems, successful integration and post-accession challenges', *International Issues & Slovak Foreign Policy Affairs*, 3(4): 25–63.

Easterly, W. (2003) *The Elusive Quest for Growth: Economists' Adventures and Misadventures in the Tropics*, Cambridge, MA: MIT Press.

Easterly, W. (2006a) 'Reliving the 1950s: the big push, poverty traps, and takeoffs in economic development', *Journal of Economic Growth*, 11(4): 289–318.

Easterly, W. (2006b) *The White Man's Burden: Why the West's Efforts to Aid the Rest Have Done So Much Ill and So Little Good*, New York: Penguin Press.

Easterly, W. (2007) 'Are aid agencies improving?', *Economic Policy*, 22(52): 633–678.

Easterly, W. (2009) 'How the Millennium Development Goals are unfair to Africa', *World Development*, 37(1): 26–35.

Easterly, W. and Pfutze, T. (2008) 'Where does all the money go? Best and worst practices in foreign aid', *Journal of Economic Perspectives*, 22(2): 29–52.

Easterly, W., Levine, R. and Roodman, D. (2004) 'New data, new doubts: a comment on Burnside and Dollar's Aid, Policies and Growth 2000', *American Economic Review*, 94(3): 774–780.

Elster, J., Offe, C. and Preuss, U. (1998) *Institutional Design in Post-Communist Societies: Rebuilding the Ship at Sea*, Cambridge: Cambridge University Press.

Engberg-Pedersen, L. (2014) 'Bringing aid management closer to reality: the experience of Danish bilateral development cooperation', *Development Policy Review*, 32(1): 113–131.

Epstein, R.A. and Sedelmeier, U. (2008) 'Beyond conditionality: international institutions in postcommunist Europe after enlargement', *Journal of European Public Policy*, 15(6): 795–805.

Eurobarometer (2005) *Attitudes towards Development Aid, Eurobarometer 222*, Brussels: European Commission, available online: http://ec.europa.eu/public_op inion/archives/ebs/ebs_222_en.pdf (accessed February 2014).

Eurobarometer (2007) '*Europeans and Development Aid, Eurobarometer 280*, Brussels: European Commission, available online: http://ec.europa.eu/public_opinion/a rchives/ebs/ebs_280_en.pdf (accessed 11 November 2009).

Eurobarometer (2009) *Development Aid in Times of Economic Turmoil, Eurobarometer 318*, Brussels: European Commission, available online: http://ec.europa.eu/public_ opinion/archives/ebs/ebs_318_en.pdf (accessed 16 January 2013).

Eurobarometer (2010) *Europeans, Development Aid and the Millennium Development Goals, Eurobarometer 352*, Brussels: European Commission, available online: http:// ec.europa.eu/public_opinion/archives/ebs/ebs_352_en.pdf (accessed 27 January 2012).

Eurobarometer (2012) *Solidarity that Spans the Globe: Europeans and Development Aid, Eurobarometer 392*, Brussels: European Commission, available online: http://ec. europa.eu/public_opinion/archives/ebs/ebs_392_en.pdf (accessed 21 January 2013).

Eurobarometer (2013) *EU Development Aid and the Millennium Development Goals, Eurobarometer 405*, Brussels: European Commission, available online: http://ec. europa.eu/public_opinion/archives/ebs/ebs_405_en.pdf (accessed 13 August 2014).

European Commission (1998) 'Regular Report from the Commission on Czech Republic's Progress Towards Accession', available online: http://ec.europa.eu/enla rgement/archives/pdf/key_documents/1998/czech_en.pdf (accessed 3 March 2014).

European Commission (1999) 'Regular Report from the Commission on Hungary's Progress Towards Accession', available online: http://ec.europa.eu/enlargement/a rchives/pdf/key_documents/1999/hungary_en.pdf (accessed 3 March 2014).

European Commission (2002) 'Untying: enhancing the effectiveness of aid', COM639, 18 November.

European Commission (2003) 'Comprehensive monitoring report on Poland's pre- parations for membership', available online: http://ec.europa.eu/enlargement/archi ves/pdf/key_documents/2003/cmr_pl_final_en.pdf (accessed 3 March 2014).

European Commission (2006) *EU Donor Atlas 2006*, Brussels: DG Development.

European Commission (2007a) 'Annual report from the Commission to the European Parliament, the Council, the Economic and Social Committee and the Committee of the Regions of 4 April 2007, Keeping Europe's promises on Financing for Development', COM 164 final.

European Commission (2007b) 'EU Code of Conduct on Division of labour in Development Policy', COM 72 final, Brussels: European Commission.

European Commission (2011) 'EU Accountability Report 2011 on Financing for Development Review of progress of the EU and its Member States', COM 218 final.

European Commission (2013a) 'EU 2013 Report on Policy Coherence for Development', SWD 456 final, Brussels: European Commission.

European Commission (2013b): 'EU Accountability Report 2013 on Financing for Development Review of progress by the EU and its Member States', COM 531 final, Brussels: European Commission.

European Consensus (2006) 'Joint declaration by the Council and the representatives of the governments of the Member States meeting within the Council, the European Parliament and the Commission on the development policy of the European Union entitled The European Consensus.', *Official Journal*, C 46 of 24 February.

European Court of Auditors (2010) 'The Commission's Management of General Budget Support in ACP, Latin American and Asian Countries', *Special Report 11*, Luxembourg: European Court of Auditors.

Eyben, R. (2013) 'Struggles in Paris: The DAC and the purposes of development aid', *European Journal of Development Research*, 25(1): 78–91.

Fagan, A. (2005) 'Taking stock of civil-society development in Post-Communist Europe: evidence from the Czech Republic', *Democratization*, 12(4): 528–547.

Faust, J. and Messner, D. (2005) 'Europe's New Security Strategy: Challenges for Development Policy', *The European Journal of Development Research*, 17(3): 423–436.

Faust, J. and Messner, D. (2012) 'Probleme globaler Entwicklung und die ministerielle Organisation der Entwicklungspolitik', *Zeitschrift für Außen- und Sicherheitspolitik*, 5(2): 165–175.

Fink-Hafner, D., Hafner-Fink, M. and Novak, M. (2014) 'Europeanisation as a factor of National Interest Group Political-Cultural Change: The case of interest groups in Slovenia', *East European Politics & Societies*, early view.

Fodor, E. (2003) 'Partnerek a fejlődésben – az Európai Unió fejlesztési politikája' ['Partners in Development – the Development Policy of the European Union'], *Külügyi Szemle*, 2(2): 142–170.

FOND (2009) http://trialog-information-service.blogspot.hu/2009/12/fond-launches-re search-paper-its-our.html.

FoRS (2011) 'Zahraniční rozvojová spolupráce v roce 2010', Prague: FoRS.

FoRS (2012a) 'Zpráva FoRS o zahraniční rozvojovéspolupráci ČR za rok 2011', Prague: FoRS.

FoRS (2012b) 'Briefing paper: Official Development Assistance of the Czech Republic in 2011', Prague: FoRS.

Frot, E. and Santiso, J. (2010) 'Crushed aid: Fragmentation in sectoral aid', *OECD Development Centre Working Papers*, No. 248.

Gąsior-Niemiec, A. (2010) 'Lost in the system? Civil society and regional development policy in Poland', *Acta Politica*, 45(1–2): 90–111.

Gavas, M., Herbert, S. and Maxwell, S. (2012) 'An agenda for change for EU Development Policy', *Overseas Development Institute*, available online: www.odi. org/comment/6040-eu-development-policy-agenda-change (accessed 11 July 2014).

Gažovič, O. (2012) 'Slovak Aid – oficiálna rozvojová pomoc ako nástroj konštituovania identity SR?', *Mezinárodní vztahy*, 47(1): 22–46.

Gažovič, O. and Profant, T. (forthcoming) 'Slovakia: A donor against its will', in O. Horký-Hlucháň and S. Lightfoot (eds) *Development Cooperation of the 'New' EU Member States*, Basingstoke: Palgrave Macmillan.

Gerber, E.R. (1999) *The Populist Paradox. Interest Group Influence and the Promise of Direct Legislation*, Princeton, NJ: Princeton University Press.

Gibler, D.M. and Miller, S.V. (2012) 'Comparing the foreign aid policies of presidents Bush and Obama', *Social Science Quarterly*, 93: 1202–1217.

Gibson, C., Andersson, K., Ostrom, E. and Shivakumar S. (2005) *The Samaritan's dilemma: the political economy of development aid*, Oxford: Oxford University Press.

Glopolis (2010) 'What the elections are not about', available online: http://glopolis.org/en/articles/what-elections-are-not-about/ (accessed 9 September 2014).

Gore, C. (2000) 'The rise and fall of the Washington Consensus as a paradigm for developing countries', *World Development*, 28(5): 789–804.

Gore, C. (2013) 'Introduction. The new development cooperation landscape: actors, approaches, architecture'. *Journal of International Development*, 25(6): 769–786.

Grabbe, H. (2006) *The EU's Transformative Power*, Basingstoke: Palgrave Macmillan.

Granell, F. (2005) 'Can the 5th enlargement weaken the EU's Development Cooperation?', *Jean Monnet/Robert Schuman Paper Series*, University of Miami, 5(24) (Miami: University of Miami), available online: http://www6.miami.edu/EUCenter/granell2final.pdf (accessed 11 November 2009).

Gray, P. (2014) 'Russia as a recruited development donor', *European Journal of Development Research*, advance online publication, 14 August, doi:10.1057/ejdr.2014.34.

Grimm, S. and Harmer A. (2005) 'Diversity in donorship: the changing landscape of official humanitarian aid. Aid donorship in Central Europe', *HPG Background Paper*, London: ODI.

Grimm, S., Humphrey, J., Lundsgaarde, E. and De Souza, S.-L. (2008) 'European Development Cooperation to 2020: Challenges by new actors in international development', *Working Paper 4*, Bonn: European Association of Development Research and Training Institutes (EADI), available online: www.edc2020.eu/index.php?id=69 (accessed November 2011).

Grosse, T. (2010) 'Social dialogue during enlargement: The case of Poland and Estonia'. *Acta Politica*, 45(1–2): 112–135.

Grupa Zagranica (2011a) 'Aid Watch Report "Polish development cooperation 2010"', Warsaw: Grupa Zagranica.

Grupa Zagranica (2011b) 'Act on development cooperation. A missed opportunity or the opening for a new quality', *Opinions, Discussions and Analysis No. 3*, Warsaw: Grupa Zagranica.

Gulrajani, N. (2014) 'Organising for donor effectiveness: an analytical framework for improving aid effectiveness', *Development Policy Review*, 32(1): 89–112.

Hallet, M. (2009) 'Economic cycles and development aid: what is the evidence from the past?', *ECFIN Economic Brief 5*, European Commission's Directorate-General for Economic and Financial Affairs, November.

Halperin, M. (1974) *Bureaucratic Politics and Foreign Policy*, Washington, DC: Brookings Institution.

Hancilova, B. (2000) 'Czech Humanitarian Assistance, 1993–1998', *Journal of Humanitarian Assistance*, available online: http://sites.tufts.edu/jha/archives/146 (accessed 3 March 2014).

Hansen, H. and Tarp, F. (2000) 'Aid effectiveness disputed', *Journal of International Development*, 12(3): 375–398.

Hanšpach, D. (2004) 'V4 countries and development cooperation: (re)emerging donors in (re)United Europe and the role of UNDP', *Medzinárodne otázky* (*International Issues*), 13(4): 23–41.

Hanusová, M. (2012) 'How Slovakia has responded to its special peer review?', Presentation at the conference 'Moving towards accession to the DAC', Bratislava, 3–4 October.

Harmer, A. and Cotterell, L. (2005) 'Diversity in donorship. The changing landscape of official humanitarian aid', *HPG Research Report* 20, London: ODI.

Harris, E. (2004) 'Europeanisation of Slovakia', *Comparative European Politics*, 2(2): 185–211.

Hartmann, S. (2009) 'Between Ambitions and Realities: The Pathway of European Development Cooperation since Maastricht', *OEFSE Discussion Paper* 24, Vienna.

Hattori, T. (2003) 'The moral politics of foreign aid', *Review of International Studies*, 29(2): 229–247.

Haughton, T. (2007) 'When does the EU make a difference? Conditionality and the accession process in Central and Eastern Europe', *Political Studies Review*, 5: 233–246.

Haughton, T. and Malova, D. (2007) 'Emerging patterns of EU membership: drawing lessons from Slovakia's first two years as a member state', *Politics*, 27(2): 69–75.

Helmke, G. and Levitsky, S. (2004) 'Informal institutions and comparative politics: a research agenda', *Perspectives on Politics*, 2(4): 725–740.

Henderson, K. (2004) *Slovakia: The Escape from Invisibility*, London: Routledge.

Hlavičková, Z. (2012) 'Application of OECD DAC special review recommendations in development cooperation of the Czech Republic', Presentation at the conference 'Moving towards accession to the DAC', Bratislava, 3–4 October.

Hoebink, P. (ed.) (2010) *European Development Cooperation – In Between the Local and the Global*, Amsterdam: Amsterdam University Press.

Hoebink, P. and Stokke, O. (eds) (2005) *Perspectives on European Development Cooperation: Policy and Performance of Individual Donor Countries and the EU*, London: Routledge.

Hoeffler, A. and Outram, V. (2011) 'Need, merit, or self-interest – what determines the allocation of aid?', *Review of Development Economics*, 15(2): 237–250.

Holden, P. (2009) *In Search of Structural Power: EU Aid Policy as a Global Political Instrument*, Farnham: Ashgate.

Holland, M. (2008) 'The EU and the global development agenda', *Journal of European Integration*, 30(3): 343–362.

Hook, S.W. (1995) *National interest and foreign aid*, Boulder, CO: Lynne Rienner Publishers.

Hook, S.W. (2008) 'Ideas and change in U.S. foreign aid: inventing the Millennium Challenge Corporation', *Foreign Policy Analysis*, 4: 147–167.

Hořejš, N. (2008) 'Více pomoci až po stabilizaci', available online: www.rozvojovka.cz/clanky/525-vice-pomoci-az-po-stabilizaci.htm.

Horký, O. (2010a) 'Development Cooperation in the Czech Foreign Policy', in M. Kořan (ed.) *Czech Foreign Policy: Analysis*, Prague: Institute of International Relations, pp. 347–361.

Horký, O. (2010b) 'The Europeanization of development policy: accommodation and resistance of the Czech Republic', *DIE Discussion Paper*, 18/2010.

Horký, O. (2010c) 'Policy coherence for development of the Czech Republic. Case studies on migration and trade', in P. Hoebink (ed.) *European Development Cooperation – In Between the Local and the Global*, Amsterdam: Amsterdam University Press, pp. 223–258.

Horký, O. (2011) 'The impact of the shallow Europeanisation of the "new" member states on the EU's actorness: What coherence between foreign and development policy?', in S. Gänzle, S. Grimm and D. Makhan (eds) *EU Policy for Global Development: Superpower in the Making?*, Basingstoke: Palgrave Macmillan, pp. 57–73.

Horký, O. (2012) 'The transfer of the central and Eastern European 'transition experience' to the South: myth or reality?', *Perspectives on European Politics and Society*, 13(1): 17–32.

Horký, O. and Lightfoot, S. (2012) 'From aid recipients to aid donors? Development policies of Central and Eastern European states', *Perspectives on European Politics and Society*, 13(1): 1–16.

Horký, O. and Rusin, P. (2006) 'The Enlarged Europe and Africa's Development: How to Keep Commitments of the Millennium Declaration', Policy Brief, Prague: CEFRES/Institute of International Relations.

Horký-Hlucháň, O. and Lightfoot, S. (eds) (2012) *Development Policies of Central and Eastern European States. From Aid Recipients to Aid Donors*, Abingdon: Routledge.

Hout, W. (2010) 'Governance and development: changing EU policies', *Third World Quarterly*, 31(1): 1–12.

Howard, M. (2002) *The Weakness of Civil Society in Post-Communist Europe*, Cambridge: Cambridge University Press.

Hódosi, R. (2012) 'Mit tesz Magyarország a fejlődő országokért? Stratégiai fordulópont előtt a magyar nemzetközi fejlesztési együttműködés' ['What does Hungary do for the developing countries? The strategic turning point of Hungarian official development policy'], Budapest: HAND.

HTSPE (2011) 'Joint multi-annual programming, final report', available online: http://ec.europa.eu/europeaid/how/ensure-aid-effectiveness/documents/report-joint-multi-a nnual-programming_en.pdf.

Hungarian Government (2008) 'Hungary's external relations strategy', unofficial English translation available online: www.mfa.gov.hu/kum/en/bal/foreign_policy/external_ relations_strategy/ (accessed 20 July 2011).

Hungarian Ministry of Foreign Affairs (2006) 'Hungarian international development policy', Budapest: Ministry of Foreign Affairs, available online: www.mfa.gov.hu/NR/ rdonlyres/933C1461-8F65-403A-B841-B0A37C755BF4/0/061206_newdonor.pdf.

Hungarian Ministry of Foreign Affairs (2011) 'Magyar külpolitika az Uniós elnökség után', ['Hungarian foreign policy after the EU presidency'], Budapest: Ministry of Foreign Affairs, available online: http://eu.kormany.hu/download/4/c6/20000/kulpoli tikai_strategia_20111219.pdf (accessed 25 October 2012).

Hungarian Ministry of Foreign Affairs (2014) 'Magyarország nemzetközi fejlesztési együttműködésére vonatkozó szakpolitikai stratégiája és nemzetközi humanitárius segítségnyújtására vonatkozó szakpolitikai koncepciója (2014–2020)', available online: http://nefe.kormany.hu/download/5/f0/a0000/El%C5%91terjeszt%C3%A9s_ NEFEstrat%20v%C3%A9gleges%20strat%C3%A9gia_561NEFEFO.pdf.

HUN-IDA (2004) 'A magyar műszaki-tudományos együttműködés és segítségnyújtás négy évtizedének rövid áttekintése napjainkig' ['A brief overview of the four decades of Hungarian technical and scientific cooperation and assistance'], manuscript, Budapest: HUN-IDA Kht.

Hulényi, P. (2012) 'OECD/DAC Special Peer Review. Slovak Aid – One Year After', Presentation at the conference, 'Moving towards accession to the DAC', Bratislava, 3–4 October.

Hynek, H. and Marton, P. (eds) (2012) *Statebuilding in Afghanistan: Multinational Contributions to Reconstruction*, Abingdon: Routledge.

ICDT (2014) 'Introduction', available online: www.icdt.hu/about-us/introduction/ (accessed 25 June 2014).

Iłowiecka-Tanska, I. and Pejda, M. (2008) 'Polish Official Development Assistance and Peacebuilding, IFP Capacity-Building Cluster, Country case study: Poland', Initiative for Peacebuilding.

Jacobsson, B. (2006) 'Regulated regulators: global trends of state transformation', in M.-L. Djelic and K. Sahlin-Andersson (eds) *Transnational Governance: Institutional Dynamics of Regulation*, Cambridge: Cambridge University Press, pp. 205–224.

Jacobsson, K. and Saxonberg, S. (2013) *Beyond NGO-ization: The Development of Social Movements in Central and Eastern Europe*, Farnham: Ashgate.

Janulewicz, L. (2014) 'Legislating Foreign Aid: The making of Poland's Act on Development Cooperation between international norms and domestic preferences', Paper for the UACES 44th Annual Conference, Cork, Ireland, 1–3 September.

Johnson, J. (2006) 'Two-Track diffusion and central bank embeddedness: the politics of Euro adoption in Hungary and the Czech Republic', *Review of International Political Economy*, 13(3): 361–386.

Juncos, A.E. (2011) 'Europeanization by decree? The case of police reform in Bosnia', *Journal of Common Market Studies*, 49(2): 367–387.

Juncos, A.E. and Pomorska, K. (2011) 'Invisible and unaccountable? National representatives and council officials in EU foreign policy', *Journal of European Public Policy*, 18(8): 1096–1114.

Kahneman, D. and Tversky, A. (1979) 'Prospect theory: an analysis of decision under risk', *Econometrica*, 47(2): 263–292.

Kajnč, S. (2011) 'Slovenia: searching for a foreign policy identity', in R. Wong and C. Hill (eds) *National and European Foreign Policies: Toward Europeanisation*, London: Routledge, pp. 189–209.

Kaminska, J. (2013) 'Poland: the new agenda setter', in M. Baun and D. Marek (eds) *The New Member States and the European Union: Foreign policy and Europeanization*, Abingdon: Routledge, pp. 22–36.

Kanet, R. (1981) 'Patterns of Eastern European Economic Involvement in the Third World', in M. Radu (ed.) *Eastern Europe and the Third World*, New York: Praeger, pp. 303–332.

Kerényi, S. and Szabó, M. (2006) 'Transnational influences on patterns of mobilisation within environmental movements in Hungary', *Environmental Politics*, 15(5): 803–820.

Kharas, H. (2009) 'Development Assistance in the 21st Century', contribution to the VIII Salamanca Forum 'The Fight Against Hunger and Poverty', 2–4 July.

Kim, S. (2010) 'Korea: 'something old' and 'something borrowed', *NORRAG Newsletter: A Brave New World of 'Emerging', 'Non-DAC' Donors and their Differences from Traditional Donors*, NN44: 76–78.

Kim, S. (2011) 'Bridging two worlds? An analysis of the ethical case for South Korean aid', *Journal of International Development*, 23(6): 802–822.

Kim, Y. (2014) 'How NGOs influence US foreign aid allocations', *Foreign Policy Analysis*, doi: 10.1111/fpa.12064.

Kiss, J. (2007) 'A magyar nemzetközi fejlesztéspolitika a számok tükrében' ['Hungarian official development policy in numbers'], Budapest: HAND.

Kiss, J. (2011) 'A magyar NEFE a válság éveiben' ['Hungarian official development policy in the years of crisis'], Budapest: HAND.

Kleibl, J. (2013) 'Tertiarization, industrial adjustment, and the domestic politics of foreign aid', *International Studies Quarterly*, 57: 356–369.

Knack, S. and Rahman, A. (2007) 'Donor fragmentation and bureaucratic quality in aid recipients', *Journal of Development Economics*, 83: 176–197.

Koch, S., Gavas, M. and Furness, M. (2011) 'EU development policy: ambitious agenda for change or the same old story?', *DIE The Current Column Paper*, available online: www.die-gdi.de/uploads/media/Column_Koch.Gavas.Furness.pdf (accessed 11 July 2014).

Kochanowicz, K. (2012a) 'Country strategy papers: a policy tool to increase effectiveness of Polish development cooperation', *Minority Rights Group Briefing Paper*, available online: www.minorityrights.org/11315/briefing-papers/country-strategy-pap ers-a-policy-tool-to-increase-effectiveness-of-polish-development-cooperation.html (accessed 4 March 2014).

Kochanowicz, K. (2012b) 'The evolution of development cooperation in the EU new member states and the post-2015 debate on development: the case of Poland', in P. Pavlík (ed.) *New Challenges for Cooperation of European and Developing Countries. Proceedings from International EADI Conference*, Prague: University of Economics.

Kopecký, P. and Mudde, C. (2000) 'What has Eastern Europe taught us about the democratization literature (and vice versa)?', *European Journal of Political Research*, 37: 517–539.

Kopiński, D. (2011) *Pomoc Rozwojowa*, Warsaw: Difin.

Kragelund, P. (2008) 'The return of the non-DAC donors to Africa: new prospects for African development', *Development Policy Review*, 26(5): 555–584.

Krasner, S.D. (1971) 'Are bureaucracies important? (Or Allison Wonderland)', *Foreign Policy*, 7: 159–179.

Krichewsky, L. (2003) 'Development Policy in the Accession Countries', Report, 2nd edn, Vienna: Trialog.

Kucharczyk, J. and Lovitt, J. (eds) (2008) *Democracy's New Champions. European Democracy Assistance After EU Enlargement*, Prague: Pasos.

Kugiel, P. (2012a) 'Country strategy papers in Polish development cooperation', *PISM Bulletin*, 81(414).

Kugiel, P. (2012b) 'Slovak development cooperation: lessons for Poland', *PISM Bulletin*, 69(402).

Kugiel, P. (2014) 'The financing and adjustment of EU development cooperation: implications for Poland', *PISM Bulletin*, 51(646).

Kugiel, P., Pędziwiatr, K. and Dańda, A. (2011) *Current Challenges to Peacebuilding Efforts and Development Assistance*, Kraków: Tischner European University.

Kutter, A. and Trappmann, V. (2010) 'Civil society in Central and Eastern Europe: the ambivalent legacy of accession', *Acta Politica*, 45(1–2): 41–69.

Kuuish, R. (2006) 'Estonia's development cooperation: power, prestige and practice of a new donor', in *Estonian Foreign Policy Yearbook*, Tallinn: Eesti Välispoliitika Instituut, pp. 51–67.

Lal, D. (1996) 'Foreign aid: an idea whose time has gone', *Economic Affairs*, 16(4): 9–13.

Lancaster, C. (2006) *Foreign Aid: Diplomacy, Development, Domestic Politics*, Chicago, IL: University Of Chicago Press.

Lewis, D. and Kanji, N. (2009) *Non Governmental Organisations and Development*, Oxford: Routledge.

Lewis, J. (2005) 'The janus face of Brussels: socialization and everyday decision making in the European Union', *International Organization*, 59(4): 937–971.

Lightfoot, S. (2008) 'Enlargement and the challenge of EU development', *Perspectives on European Politics and Society*, 9(2): 128–142.

Lightfoot, S. (2010) 'The Europeanisation of international development policies: the case of Central and Eastern European states', *Europe-Asia Studies*, 62(2): 329–350.

Lightfoot, S. and Lindenhovius Zubizarreta, I. (2011) 'The emergence of international development policies in Central and Eastern Europe', in P. Hoebink (ed.) *European Development Cooperation – in Between the Local and the Global*, Amsterdam: Amsterdam University Press, pp. 175–194.

Lightfoot, S. and Szent-Iványi, B. (2014) 'Reluctant donors? The Europeanization of international development policies in the new member states', *JCMS: Journal of Common Market Studies*, 52(6): 1257–1272.

Lim, S. (2014) 'Determinants for compliance: Implementing the OECD DAC principles in South Korea and the implications for future DAC member states', *globalizations*, early view.

Lister, M. and Carbone, M. (2006) *New Pathways in International Development. Gender and Civil Society in EU Policy*, Aldershot: Ashgate.

Liverani, A. and Lundgren, H.E. (2007) 'Evaluation systems in development aid agencies: an analysis of DAC peer reviews 1996–2004', *Evaluation*, 13: 241–256.

Lomoy, J. (2013) '2013 – An exceptional year for the DAC', available online: www.oecd. org/dac/dac-global-relations/2013%20Exceptional%20year%20for%20DAC.pdf.

Longhurst, K. (2013) 'Where from, where to? New and old configurations in Poland's foreign and security policy priorities', *Communist and Post-Communist Studies*, 46: 363–372.

Lumsdaine, D.H. (1993) *Moral Vision in International Politics*, Princeton, NJ: Princeton University Press.

Lundsgaarde, E. (2013a) *The Domestic Politics of Foreign Aid*, London: Routledge.

Lundsgaarde, E. (2013b) 'Bureaucratic Pluralism and the Transformation of Development Cooperation', DIE Working Paper, German Development Institute.

Mahon, R. and McBride, S. (2008) 'Introduction', in R. Mahon and S. McBride (eds) *The OECD and Transnational Governance*, Vancouver: UBC Press, 3–24.

Mahon, R. and McBride, S. (2009) 'Standardizing and disseminating knowledge: the role of the OECD in global governance', *European Political Science Review*, 1(1): 83–101.

Majerová, I. (2013) 'Czech international development policy in the context of EU enlargement', *Journal of Eastern Europe Research in Business & Economics*, 1–10.

Manning, R. (2006) 'Will 'emerging' donors challenge the face of international co-operation?', *Development Policy Review*, 24(4): 371–383.

Manning, R. (2010) 'The impact and design of the MDGs: some reflections', *IDS Bulletin*, 41(1): 7–14.

Marcussen, M. (2004) 'Multilateral surveillance and the OECD: playing the ideal game', in M. Beyeler and K. Armingeon (eds) *The OECD and the European welfare States*, Cheltenham: Edward Elgar Publishing, pp. 13–31.

Martens, B. (2008) 'Why do aid agencies exist?', in W. Easterly (ed.) *Reinventing Foreign Aid*, Cambridge, MA: MIT Press, pp. 285–310.

Martini, J., Mongo, R., Kalambay, H., Fromont, A., Ribesse, N. and Dujardin, B. (2012) 'Aid effectiveness from Rome to Busan: some progress but lacking bottom-up approaches or behaviour changes', *Tropical Medicine & International Health*, 17: 931–933.

Marton, P. (2013) *A külpolitika elemzése. Fogalmak és módszerek a külpolitika forrásainak feltárására*, Budapest: Antal József Tudásközpont.

Marton, P. and Eichler, J. (2013) 'Between willing and reluctant entrapment: CEE countries in NATO's non-European missions', *Communist and Post-Communist Studies*, 46: 351–362.

Mawdsley, E. (2012) *From Recipients to Donors: Emerging Powers and the Changing Development Landscape*, London: Zed Books.

Maxwell, S. *et al.* (2010) 'New Challenges, New Beginnings: Next steps in European development cooperation', ODI/European Think tanks Group.

Meernik, J., Krueger, E. and Poe, S. (1998) 'Testing models of U.S. foreign policy: foreign aid during and after the Cold War', *The Journal of Politics*, 60: 63–85.

Meislová, M. (2010) 'Czech Republic's 2010 elections and foreign development cooperation', *Contemporary European Studies*, 2: 29–41.

Michaux, V. (2002) 'EU enlargement: A brake on development cooperation?', *The Courier ACP-EU*, July–August.

Mikulova, K. and Berti, B. (2013) 'Converts to missionaries: Central and eastern European democracy assistance in the Arab world', Washington, DC: Carnegie Endowment for International Peace.

Mikulova, K. and Simecka, M. (2013) 'Norm entrepreneurs and Atlanticist foreign policy in central and Eastern Europe: the missionary zeal of recent converts', *Europe-Asia Studies*, 65(6): 1192–1216.

Miles, R.E. (1978) 'The origin and meaning of Miles' law', *Public Administration Review*, 38(5): 399–403.

Milner, H. and Tingley, D. (2013) 'Public opinion and foreign aid: a review essay', *International Interactions*, 39(3): 389–401.

Mintz, A. (2004) 'How do leaders make decisions? A poliheuristic perspective', *Journal of Conflict Resolution*, 48: 3–13.

Mintz, A. and DeRouen, K. (2010) *Understanding Foreign Policy Decision Making*, Cambridge: Cambridge University Press.

Miszlivetz, F. and Ertsey, K. (1998) 'Hungary: civil society in the post-socialist world', in A. Van Rooy (ed.) *Civil Society and the Aid Industry*, London: Earthscan Publications, pp. 71–103.

Morrissey, O. (2005) 'British aid policy in the 'short-Blair' years', in P. Hoebink and O. Stokke (eds) *Perspective on European Development Co-operation*, Abingdon: Routledge, pp. 161–183.

Mosley, P. (1985) 'The political economy of foreign aid: a model of the market for a public good', *Economic Development and Cultural Change*, 33(2): 373–393.

Moss, T., Pettersson, G. and Van de Walle, N. (2006) 'An aid-institutions paradox? A review essay on aid dependency and state building in sub-Saharan Africa', *Center for Global Development working paper*, 74: 11–15.

Moyo, D. (2009): *Dead Aid: Why Aid is Not Working and How There is a Better Way For Africa*, London: Penguin.

Mrak, M. (2002) 'Slovenia as a Donor Country: Where It Is and Where It Should Go?', Paper presented at the EADI Conference in Ljubljana, August.

MTI (2014) 'Németh Zsolt: a magyar gazdaság diverzifikálását szolgálja a globális nyitás', available online: www.galamuscsoport.hu/tartalom/cikk/355633_nemeth_zsolt_a_magyar_gazdasag_diverzifikalasat_a.

Murphy, J. and Gray, P.A. (2013) 'Developing Development (Education) in Russia', in Proceedings of the 12th UKFIET International Conference on Education and Development, 10–12 September, Oxford University.

194   *Bibliography*

MVRO (2011) 'Slovenská rozvojová pomoc v roku 2011', Bratislava: MVRO.
MVRO (2012) 'Slovenská rozvojová pomoc v roku 2012', Bratislava: MVRO.
Najslová, L. (2013) 'Foreign Democracy Assistance in the Czech and Slovak Transitions: what lessons for the Arab world?', FRIDE Working Paper.
Naurin, D. and Wallace, H. (2010) *Unveiling the Council of the European Union: Games Governments Play in Brussels*, Basingstoke: Palgrave Macmillan.
Nayyar, D. (1977) *Economic Relations Between Socialist Countries and the Third World*, London: Macmillan.
Népszava (2013) http://nepszava.hu/cikk/1006179-bun-es-bunhodes?print=1.
Nielsen, K., Berg, E. and Roll, G. (2009) 'Undiscovered avenues? Estonian civil society organisations as agents of Europeanisation', *TRAMES*, 13(3): 248–264.
Niskanen, W.A. (1968) 'The peculiar economics of bureaucracy', *American Economic Review*, 58(2): 293–305.
Nissen, S. (2014) 'The Eurobarometer and the process of European integration', *Quality & Quantity*, 48(2): 713–727.
Nunnenkamp, P. and Thiele, R. (2013) 'Financing for development: the gap between words and deeds since Monterrey', *Development Policy Review*, 31(1): 75–98.
Nunnenkamp, P., Öhler, H. and Thiele, R. (2013) 'Donor coordination and specialization: did the Paris Declaration make a difference?', *Review of World Economics*, 149(3): 537–563.
O'Dwyer, C. (2012) 'Does the EU help or hinder gay-rights movements in post-communist Europe? The case of Poland', *East European Politics*, 28(4): 332–352.
OECD (1996) 'Shaping the 21st Century: The Contribution of Development Co-operation', Paris: OECD.
OECD (2005) 'Ireland. Development Assistance Committee (DAC) Peer Review', Paris: OECD.
OECD (2006) 'DAC in Dates. The History of OECD's Development Assistance Committee', Paris: OECD.
OECD (2007) 'DAC Special Review of the Czech Republic', Paris: OECD.
OECD (2008) 'The Paris Declaration on Aid Effectiveness and the Accra Agenda for Action', available online: www.oecd.org/dac/effectiveness/34428351.pdf (accessed 10 July 2014).
OECD (2009a) 'Managing Aid: Practices of DAC Member Countries', Paris: OECD.
OECD (2009b) 'Untying Aid: Is It Working?', Paris: OECD.
OECD (2010) 'DAC Special Review of Poland', Paris: OECD.
OECD (2011a) 'Aid Effectiveness 2005–10: Progress in Implementing the Paris Declaration', Paris: OECD.
OECD (2011b) 'DAC Special Review of the Slovak Republic', Paris: OECD.
OECD (2011c) 'DAC Special Review of Slovenia', Paris: OECD.
OECD (2011d) 'Concept and Experiences of the EU Fast Track Initiative on Division of Labour', available online: www.oecd.org/dac/effectiveness/47823319.pdf.
OECD (2012) 'European Union. Development Assistance Committee (DAC) Peer Review 2012', Paris: OECD.
OECD (2013) 'Information Note on the DAC Peer Review Process', available online: www.oecd.org/dac/peer-reviews/DCD%282013%296.pdf.
OECD (2014) 'DAC Datasets on OECD.stat', available online: www.oecd.org/dac/aidstatistics/internationaldevelopmentstatisticsidsonlinedatabasesonaidandotherresourceflows.htm (14 July 2014).
OECD (n.d.a) 'DAC Members', available online: www.oecd.org/dac/dacmembers.htm.

OECD (n.d.b) 'Becoming a Participant in the DAC', available online: www.oecd.org/dac/dac-global-relations/Becoming%20a%20Parctipant%20in%20the%20DAC%20.pdf.

OECD (n.d.c) 'Countries, Territories and Organisations Adhering to the Paris Declaration and AAA', available online: www.oecd.org/dac/effectiveness/countriesterritoriesandorganisationsadheringtotheparisdeclarationandaaa.htm.

Olsa, J. (2003) 'The Czech Republic: an emerging party for ACP countries', *The Courier ACP-EU*, 198.

Olsen, G.R. (2001) 'European public opinion and aid to Africa: is there a link?', *The Journal of Modern African Studies*, 39(4): 645–674.

Olson M. (1971) *The Logic of Collective Action: Public Goods and the Theory of Groups*, Boston, MA: Harvard University Press.

Oprea, M. (2012) 'Development discourse in Romania: from socialism to EU membership', *Perspectives on European Politics and Society*, 13(1): 66–82.

Orbie, J. (2012) 'The EU as an actor in development: Just another donor, European norm maker, or eclipsed by superpower temptations?', in S. Grimm, D. Makhan, and S. Gänzle (eds) *The European Union and Global Development – An Enlightened Superpower in the Making?*, Basingstoke: Palgrave Macmillan, pp. 17–36.

Ost, D. (1993) 'The politics of interest in post-communist East Europe', *Theory and Society*, 22(4): 453–485.

Otter, M. (2003) 'Domestic public support for foreign aid: Does it matter?', *Third World Quarterly*, 24(1): 115–125.

Pagani, F. (2002) 'Peer review as a tool for co-operation and change. An analysis of an OECD working method', *African Security Review*, 11(4): 15–24.

Palubinskas, G. (2003) 'Democratization: The development of nongovernmental organizations (NGOs) in Central and Eastern Europe', *Public Administration & Management*, 8(3): 150–163.

Paragi, B. (2010) 'Hungarian development policy', in P. Hoebink (ed.) *European Development Cooperation – In Between the Local and the Global*, Amsterdam: Amsterdam University Press, pp. 195–222.

Parau, C. (2009) 'Impaling Dracula: how EU accession empowered civil society in Romania', *West European Politics*, 32(1): 119–141.

PASOS (2007) 'The Challenge of the EU Development Co-Operation Policy for New Member States', Report Prepared for EP Development Committee, EXPO/B/DEVE/2007/33 NOVEMBER PE 385.540 EN, available online: www.pasos.org/www-pasosmembers-org/publications/the-challenge-of-the-eu-development-co-operation-policy-for-new-member-states.

Paxton, P. and Knack, S. (2012) 'Individual and country-level factors affecting support for foreign aid', *International Political Science Review*, 33(2): 171–192.

Petrova, T. and Tarrow, S. (2007) 'Transactional and participatory activism in the emerging European polity: the puzzle of East-Central Europe', *Comparative Political Studies*, 40(1): 74–94.

Pleines, H. (2011) 'Weakness as precondition of smooth integration? Representation strategies of functional interest groups from new member states at the EU level', *Journal of European Integration*, 33(4): 507–521.

Polish Government (2012) 'Polish Foreign Policy Priorities 2012–2016', available online: www.msz.gov.pl/resource/d31571cf-d24f-4479-af09-c9a46cc85cf6:JCR.

Polish Ministry of Foreign Affairs (2003) 'Strategia polskiej współpracy na rzecz rozwoju', Warsaw: MSZ.

Pomorska, K. (2011) 'Poland: learning the Brussels game', in R. Wong and C. Hill (eds) *National and European Foreign Policies: Toward Europeanisation*, London: Routledge, pp. 167–188.

Pospieszna, P. (2010a) 'When recipients become donors: Polish democracy assistance in Belarus and Ukraine', *Problems of Post-Communism*, 57(4): 3–15.

Pospieszna, P. (2010b) 'New EU member states taking the lead in democracy aid: the Polish case', in K. Bachmann and E. Stadtmuller (eds) *The European Union's Neighborhood Challenge. Transborder cooperation, migration and Europeanization*, Wroclaw: Wroclaw University Press, pp. 65–89.

Pospieszna, P. (2014) *Democracy Assistance from the Third Wave: Polish Engagement in Belarus and Ukraine*, Pittsburg, PA: University of Pittsburg Press.

Pridham, G. (2008) 'Status quo bias or institutionalisation for reversibility? The EU's political conditionality, post-accession tendencies and democratic consolidation in Slovakia', *Europe-Asia Studies*, 60(3): 423–454.

Publish What You Fund (2013) 'Aid Transparency Index', available online: http://ati.pub lishwhatyoufund.org/wp-content/uploads/2013/10/2013-Aid-Transparency-Index.pdf.

Purcell, M., Wishart, I. and Bond, G. (2011) 'Busan – a new global divide on aid?', *Development Policy Blog*, Weblog 2 December, http://devpolicy.org/busan-%E2% 80%94-a-new-global-divide-on-aid/ (accessed 10 July 2014).

Putnam, R.D. (1988) 'Diplomacy domestic politics: the logic of two-level games', *International Organization*, 42(3): 427–460.

Radu, B. (2013) 'The Political Cultures of International Development: An Exploratory Study of Public Opinion in Central and Eastern Europe', Paper presented at UACES 43rd Annual Conference, Leeds, 2–4 September.

Radu, M. (1981) *Eastern Europe and the Third World: East Vs. South*, New York: Praeger.

Rajan, R. and Subramanian, A. (2008) 'Aid and growth: what does the cross-country evidence really show?', *The Review of Economics and Statistics*, 90(4): 643–665.

Rajan, R. and Subramanian, A. (2011) 'Aid, Dutch disease, and manufacturing growth', *Journal of Development Economics*, 94(1): 106–118.

Rehbichler, S. (2006) 'The unfinished eastward enlargement', *World Economy & Development In Brief*, 1(April–May), available online: www.word-economy-and-de velopment.org (accessed 30 May 2006).

Richelle, K. (2002) 'EU Enlargement and European Development Policy for a Changing World', EADI 10th Global Conference, Ljubljana, Slovenia, 19 September.

Riddell, R. (2007) *Does Foreign Aid Really Work?*, Oxford: Oxford University Press.

Rikmann, E. and Keedus, L. (2013) 'Civic sectors in transformation and beyond: pre-liminaries for a comparison of six Central and Eastern European societies', *VOLUN-TAS: International Journal of Voluntary and Nonprofit Organizations*, 24(1): 149–166.

Risse, T., Cowles, M.G. and Caporaso, J. (2001) 'Europeanization and domestic change: introduction', in M.G. Cowles, J. Caporaso and T. Risse (eds) *Transforming Europe: Europeanization and Domestic Change*, Ithaca, NY: Cornell University Press, pp. 1–20.

Rittberger, V. and Wagner, W. (2001) 'German foreign policy since unification – theories meet reality', in W. Rittberger (ed.) *Foreign Policy of the New Germany: Theories and Case Studies*, Manchester: Manchester University Press, pp. 299–325.

Rodrik, D. (2006) 'Goodbye Washington consensus, hello Washington confusion? A review of the world bank's economic growth in the 1990s: learning from a decade of reform', *Journal of Economic Literature*, 44(4): 973–987.

Rotberg, R. (2002) 'The new nature of nation-state failure', *The Washington Quarterly*, 25(3): 85–96.

Roth, S. (2007) 'Sisterhood and solidarity? Women's organizations in the expanded European Union', *Social Politics*, 14(4): 460–487.

Round, J.I. and Odedokun, M. (2004) 'Aid effort and its determinants', *International Review of Economics & Finance*, 13(3): 293–309.

Rowlands, D. (2012) 'Individual BRICS or a collective bloc? Convergence and divergence amongst "emerging donor" nations', *Cambridge Review of International Affairs*, 25(4): 629–649.

Ruckert, A. (2008) 'Making Neo-Gramscian sense of the DAC: towards an inclusive-neoliberal world development order', in S. McBride and R. Mahon (eds) *The OECD and Transnational Governance*, Vancouver: UBC Press, pp. 96–116.

Sachs, J. (2005) *The End of Poverty. Economic Possibilities for Our Time*, New York: Penguin.

Sagan, S.D. (1996) 'Why do states build nuclear weapons?: Three models in search of a bomb', *International Security*, 21(3): 54–86.

Schiltz, J.-L. and Bichler, M. (2009) 'Who's afraid of budget support? Perspectives on budget support', *ECDPM Discussion Paper* No. 88.

Schimmelfennig, F. and Sedelmeier, U. (2005) 'Introduction: conceptualizing the Europeanization of Central and Eastern Europe', in F. Schimmelfennig and U. Sedelmeier (eds) *The Europeanization of Central and Eastern Europe*, Ithaca, NY: Cornell University Press, pp. 1–28.

Schimmelfennig, F., Engert, S. and Knobel, H. (2006) *International Socialization in Europe European Organizations, Political Conditionality and Democratic Change*, Basingstoke: Palgrave Macmillan.

Schmidt, S. (2004) 'Eastward enlargement and EU development policy', *Osteuropa*, 54: 5–6.

Schraeder, P.J., Hook, S.W. and Taylor, B. (1998) 'Clarifying the foreign aid puzzle: a comparison of American, Japanese, French, and Swedish aid flows', *World Politics*, 50(2): 294–323.

Schrijver, N. (2009) 'The EU's common development cooperation policy', in M. Telò (ed.) *The European Union and Global Governance*, Oxford: Routledge, pp. 176–191.

Sedelmeier, U. (2011) 'Europeanisation in new member and candidate states', *Living Reviews in European Governance*, 6(1).

Sedelmeier, U. (2012) 'Is Europeanisation through conditionality sustainable? Lock-in of institutional change after EU accession', *West European Politics*, 35(1): 20–38.

Selmeczi, A. (2013) 'The Role of the Hungarian Civil Society in Development Assistance and Aid Effectiveness', CEU Centre for Policy Studies Policy Paper.

Simon, H. (1957) *Models of Man; Social and Rational*, Oxford: Wiley.

Skok, M. (2012) 'Slovenia and international development cooperation: who is interested in Slovenia's transition experience and who can benefit from it?', *Crossroads: The Macedonian Foreign Policy Journal*, III(2): 19–24.

Sládková, Z. (2011) 'Czech Republic and its Official Development Assistance', FoRS Briefing Paper 2/2011.

Sloat, A. (2005) 'The rebirth of civil society: the growth of women's NGOs in Central and Eastern Europe', *European Journal of Women's Studies*, 12(4): 437–452.

SLOGA (2011) 'Analiza slovenske uradne razvojne pomoči za leto', Ljubljana: SLOGA.

SlovakAid (2013a) http://issuu.com/slovakaid/docs/country_strategy_paper_kenya_2014-2/13?e=7658468/6338596.

SlovakAid (2013b) 'Official Development Assistance of the Slovak Republic, 2013', available online: www.slovakaid.sk/en/development-aid.

Slovak Government (2005) 'Zameranie Zahranicnej Politiky SR Na Rok 2005', available online: www.foreign.gov.sk/App/wcm/media.nsf/vw_ByID/ID_181727FE240 79C74C1257648004316B1_SK/$File/Zameranie_ZP_2005.pdf.

Slovak Government (2007a) 'Slovakia's Foreign Policy Orientation for 2007', available online: www.foreign.gov.sk/App/wcm/media.nsf/vw_ByID/ID_7BF86733773D5 A4CC125764800428721_SK/$File/preklad-AJ-Zameranie%2007.pdf.

Slovak Government (2007b) 'Act on Official Development Assistance of the Slovak Republic', Bratislava: MFA.

SMER (2012) 'Election Manifesto 2012', Bratislava: SMER.

Smith, K., Fordelone, T.Y. and Zimmerman, F. (2010) 'Beyond the DAC: The welcome role of other providers of development co-operation', DCD Issues Brief, May.

Smith, M.E. (2013) 'The European External Action Service and the security-development nexus: organizing for effectiveness or incoherence?', *Journal of European Public Policy*, 20(9): 1–17.

Smolar, A. (1996) 'Civil society after communism: from opposition to atomization', *Journal of Democracy*, 7(1): 24–38.

Špánik, J. (2012) 'Monitoring and Evaluation in Czech Development Cooperation', presentation at the conference 'Moving towards accession to the DAC', Bratislava, 3–4 October.

Starr, R. (1982) *Communist Regimes in Eastern Europe*, Stanford, CA: Hoover Press.

Ster, A. (2008) 'Opening Address at the Conference on the Challenges of EU-27 Development Policy', available online: www.eu2008.si/en/News_and_Documents/ Speeches_Interviews/February/0217GAERC_razvojna_konf_Ster.html (accessed 9 September 2014).

Stiglitz, J. E. (1998) 'More Instruments and Broader Goals: Moving Toward the Post-Washington Consensus', WIDER Annual Lecture 2.

Stokke, O. (ed.) (1989) *Western Middle Powers and Global Poverty – The Determinants of the Aid Policies of Canada, Denmark, the Netherlands, Norway and Sweden*, Uppsala: The Scandinavian Institute of African Studies.

Sumner, A. and Mallet, R. (2013) *The Future of Foreign Aid: Development Cooperation and the New Geography of Poverty*, Basingstoke: Palgrave Macmillan.

Szentes, T. (2005) 'Development in the history of economics', in K.S. Jomo and E.S. Reinert. (eds) *Origins of Development Economics: How Schools of Economic Thought Addressed Development*, London: Zed Books, pp. 146–158.

Szent-Iványi, B. (2012a) 'Aid allocation of the emerging Central and Eastern European donors', *Journal of International Relations And Development*, 15(1): 65–89.

Szent-Iványi, B. (2012b) 'Hungarian international development co-operation: context, stakeholders and performance', *Perspectives on European Politics and Society*, 13(1): 50–65.

Szent-Iványi, B. (2014) 'The EU's support for democratic governance in the Eastern neighbourhood: the role of new member state transition experience', *Europe-Asia Studies*, 66(7): 1102–1121.

Szent-Iványi, B. and Lightfoot, S. (forthcoming) 'Determinants of civil society influence. The case of international development and humanitarian NGOs in the Czech Republic and Hungary', *Comparative European Politics*.

Szent-Iványi, B. and Tétényi, A. (2008) 'Transition and foreign aid policies in the Visegrad countries: a path dependant approach', *Transition Studies Review*, 15: 573–587.

Szent-Iványi, B. and Tétényi, A. (2012) 'Assessing Existing Practices in Capacity Building and Experience Sharing for the Central European New Donors', final report of the mapping exercise commissioned by the World Bank Institute.

Szent-Iványi, B. and Tétényi, A. (2013) 'The East-Central European new donors: mapping capacity building and remaining challenges', *Journal of International Development*, 25(6): 819–831.

Szép, A. (2004) 'Oficiálna rozvojová pomoc Európskej únie a Slovensko', *Medzinárodné otázky*, 13(4): 3–22.

Tarrósy, I. and Morenth, P. (2013) 'Global opening for Hungary – new beginning for Hungarian Africa policy?', *African Studies Quarterly*, 14(1–2): 77–96.

Tarrósy, I. and Vörös, Z. (forthcoming) 'Hungary's global opening to an interpolar world', *Politeja*.

The Guardian (2014) 'Poland a challenge to EU 2030 climate goals, warns Ed Davey', 10 July, available online: www.theguardian.com/environment/2014/jul/10/poland-cha llenge-eu-2030-climate-goals-ed-davey (accessed 24 September 2014).

Therien, J.-P. and Noel, A. (2000) 'Political parties and foreign aid', *American Political Science Review*, 94(1): 151–162.

Thoolen, H. (2014) 'Radio Prague: interesting interview with People In Need Director Simon Panek', available online: http://thoolen.wordpress.com/2014/03/28/radio-pra gue-interesting-interview-with-people-in-need-director-simon-panek/.

Timofejevs Henriksson, P. (2013) *The Europeanisation of Foreign Aid Policy: Slovenia and Latvia 1998–2010*, Umea: Umea University Press.

Tingley, D. (2010) 'Donors and domestic politics: political influences on foreign aid effort', *The Quarterly Review of Economics and Finance*, 50: 40–49.

Topolánek, M. (2006) 'Projev premiéra Mirka Topolánka na výroční poradě vedoucích zastupitelských úřadů ČR v Černínském paláci dne 7. září 2006' ['Prime Minister Mirek Topolánek at the annual meeting of chiefs of diplomatic missions of the Czech Republic at the Czernin Palace on September 7, 2006'], available online: www.vlada.cz/scripts/detail.php?id=18863.

Transparency International (2012) 'Corruption Perceptions Index', available online: www.ey.com/Publication/vwLUAssets/2012_TI_CPI/$FILE/2012%20TI%20CPI.pdf.

Tulmets, E. (2014) *East Central European Foreign Policy Identity in Perspective: Back to Europe and the EU's Neighbourhood*, Basingstoke: Palgrave Macmillan.

Udvari, B. (2011) 'The role of the Aid for Trade in the European Union's development policy', Virtual proceedings, European Trade Study Group Thirteenth Conference, Copenhagen.

Ugar, M. (2013) 'Europeanization, EU conditionality, and governance quality: empirical evidence on Central and Eastern European countries', *International Studies Quarterly*, 57: 41–51.

UKAN (2011) 'Paris Declaration Monitoring Survey: What the Results Tell Us, and What They Don't', available online: www.dochas.ie/Shared/Files/4/Paris_Declara tion_Monitoring_Survey.pdf.

UNDP (2012) 'New Partnerships in Development Cooperation Initiative: Information Note', Bratislava: UNDP.

United Nations (2003) 'Financing for Development. Monterrey Consensus of the International Conference on Financing for Development', New York: United Nations Department of Economic and Social Affairs.

United Nations (2009) 'Doha Declaration on Financing for Development: Outcome document of the Follow-up International Conference on Financing for Development to

Review the Implementation of the Monterrey Consensus', New York: United Nations Department of Economic and Social Affairs.

UN Millennium Project (2005) 'Investing in Development. A Practical Plan to Achieve the Millennium Development Goals', New York: Millennium Project.

Vachudová, M.A. (2008) 'Tempered by the EU? Political parties and party systems before and after accession', *Journal of European Public Policy*, 15(6): 861–879.

Van Belle, D.A., Rioux, J.S. and Potter, D.M. (2004) *Media, Bureaucracies and Foreign Aid: A Comparative Analysis of the United States, the United Kingdom, Canada, France, and Japan*, New York: Palgrave Macmillan.

van der Veen, M. (2011) *Ideas, Interests, and Foreign Aid*, Cambridge: Cambridge University Press.

van Reisen, M. (2007) 'The enlarging European Union and the developing world', in A. Mold (ed.) *EU Development Policy in a Changing World: Challenges for the 21st Century*, Amsterdam: Amsterdam University Press, pp. 29–59.

van Renssen, S. (2014) 'EU deeply divided over 2030 climate and energy policy', *Energy Post*, March 5, available online: www.energypost.eu/eu-divided-2030-clima te-energy-policy/.

Vaughan, D. (2006) 'Simon Panek: a former student leader remembers the drama of November 1989', available online: www.radio.cz/en/section/one-on-one/simon-pa nek-a-former-student-leader-remembers-the-drama-of-november-1989.

Végh, Z. (2013) 'Lessons from Visegrad development Cooperation practices: Recommendations for Hungary', DEMNET.

Vencato, M.F. (2007) 'The Development Policy of the CEECs: the EU Political Rationale between the Fight Against Poverty and the Near Abroad', unpublished PhD Thesis, Leuven: Katholieke Universiteit.

Vittek, M. and Lightfoot, S. (2009) 'The Europeanization of Slovak development cooperation?', *Contemporary European Studies*, 1: 21–37.

Volgy, T., Fausett, E. and Rhamey, J. (2012) 'Is the Central European region a neighborhood?', in Z. Sabic and P. Drulek. (eds) *Regional and International Relations of Central Europe*, Basingstoke: Palgrave MacMillan.

Waisová, S. (2011) 'The Czech Republic and foreign development cooperation: from donor to recipient and back', in C. Ladislav and S. Waisová (eds) *Czechoslovakia and the Czech Republic in World Politics*, Lexington, MD: Maryland, pp. 87–105.

Wallace, C., Pichler, F. and Haerpfer, C. (2012) 'Is Eastern Europe different? Changing patterns of civil society in Europe and America 1995–2005', *East European Politics and Societies*, 26(3): 3–19.

Williamson, J. (1990) 'What Washington means by policy reform', in J. Williamson (ed.) *Latin American Adjustment: How Much Has Happened?*, Peterson Institute for International Economics, 7–41.

Woods, N. (2005) 'The shifting politics of foreign aid', *International Affairs*, 81(2): 393–409.

Woodward, R. (2009) *The Organisation for Economic Co-operation & Development*, London: Routledge.

Younas, J. (2008) 'Motivation for bilateral aid allocation: altruism or trade benefits', *European Journal of Political Economy*, 24(3): 661–674.

Zagranica Group (2011) 'Aid Watch Report Polish development cooperation 2010', Warsaw: Zagranica Group.

Zajączkowski, K. (2012) 'Poland in EU development policy', in A. Adamczyk (ed.) *Poland in the European Union: Adjustment and Modernisation. Lessons for Ukraine*, Warsaw-Lviv: pp. 157–176.

Zázvorkova, M. (2011) 'The Involvement of Development NGOs from Visegrad Countries in the Financial Instruments of the European Commission', Prague: FoRS.

Zemanová, S. (2013) 'When could new 'potent small states' emerge? A study of the recent metamorphosis of Czech human rights foreign policy', *Journal of International Relations and Development*, advance online publication.

Zolcerová, V. (2006) 'Rozvojová Pomoc Slovenskej Republiky po Vstupe do Európskej Únie a Ďalších Medzinárodných Štruktúr' ['Development Assistance of Slovak Republic after Accession the European Union and Other International Structures'], *Medzinárodné vzt'ahy*, 4(1): 45–56.

Zrinski, U. and Bučar, M. (forthcoming) 'Limited political support for development cooperation activities that focus on the Western Balkans and social services: case of Slovenia', in O. Horký-Hlucháň and S. Lightfoot (eds) *Development Cooperation of the 'New' EU Member States*, Basingstoke: Palgrave Macmillan.

Zürn, M. and Checkel, J. (2005) 'Getting socialized to build bridges: constructivism and rationalism, Europe and the nation-state', *International Organization*, 59(4): 1045–1079.

Index

For Product Safety Concerns and Information please contact our EU
representative GPSR@taylorandfrancis.com
Taylor & Francis Verlag GmbH, Kaufingerstraße 24, 80331 München, Germany